www.lifeanddeathbyintention.com

FIRST EDITION

Issued in print and electronic formats.

Hardcover: 978-1-967668-82-3

Paperback: 978-1-967668-83-0

Cover art and design by Christopher Brodie.
Copyright © 2025

WHEN DARKNESS COMES

LIFE & DEATH
BY
INTENTION

YOU ARE THE LIGHT

A true story

CHRISTOPHER BRODIE

Dedication

My children,

Of all the motivations that led to the creation of this book, my love and concern for you was the most powerful. I have loved you both so dearly from before you were born. Meeting your little selves was like meeting separated pieces of my own soul. My only desire as your father was to create the best life possible for you. Of all the ways I have fallen short, none compares with failing to prevent the loss of your mother. Even with all the beautiful life we have lived since, still, I will always be sorry for your loss, your missed life together, and for the pain.

You two are among my greatest inspirations and joys. Being your father has provided me with the invaluable opportunity to grow and come to know life more profoundly. I am so grateful that through all of the dark challenges, we have always had each other. I have no doubts about the wonderful lives you will live. Both of you, at your core, are joy and love. I felt it when you kicked in the womb, when I first saw your shining eyes, and I still see it in you every day. Life's most cunning deception is to try and remove this reality from our awareness and to have us believe the opposite. You have the closest example of when the experience of The Self goes terribly wrong.

If there is anything I know about your mother's death, it is that she did not want to leave you. She would have never wanted to cause you any pain. I never saw her love anything more deeply and completely than she did you two. You did nothing wrong and are as wonderful of kids as there have ever been for a mother. Her greatest desire is that you live a peaceful and full life, one she wasn't able to have.

I wrote this book to help the world, but it is also my sincerest effort to help you understand what happened, support your healing, and have more wisdom for living a beautiful life. Everyone deserves understanding, healing, and peace. So that love and light can be the story of all our lives.

Cindy,

The best of you is remembered. May your story save many.

For life.

Table of Contents

Disclaimer:

I am not a doctor nor a licensed therapist. The following content is for informational, educational, and inspirational purposes only and does not substitute professional medical advice or consultations with healthcare professionals.

Content Warning:

This book contains scenes of suicide, mature themes, and language that could be disturbing or inappropriate for younger readers.

PROLOGUE

PART ONE

THE GARAGE

IT'S A COOL AND BRIGHT FEBRUARY MORNING. A garage door begins to roll up on a small house. It appears someone may be heading off to work. Another routine day like countless others. Down the block, the elementary school playground bursts with fresh, exuberant life, an undulating sea of energy that ebbs and flows across the blacktop, surges over play structures, and soars high on the swings.

A little boy with bright brown eyes stands beside his friend outside a second-grade classroom, waiting for the bell to ring. He was lost in some unknown thoughts while he looked towards the playground. Then, his friend shivers, declaring, "I forgot my jacket today. It's so cold!" "Again?!" Responds the boy with the bright eyes. He looks down at his jacket fondly, pushing his hands deeper into the pockets. "My mom always remembers mine. She even warms it up in the dryer when it's extra cold outside." Suddenly, the bell rings out across the campus, and the disarray of hundreds of little bodies seems to magically organize into neat lines.

On the kindergarten playground, a lively little girl with brown hair and a zig-zag rainbow-patterned backpack eagerly takes her place in line outside the classroom. Behind her, another girl gently holds one of her long braids between two fingers, admiring its smooth texture and playful swing. "I like your braids," compliments the classmate. The lively girl turns around with a smile. "My mommy always likes to do braids in my hair."

Back at the open garage, a car passes by and continues down the street. In all directions, the sights and sounds of the neighborhood are ordinary and peacefully familiar. If, however, a morning walker happened to glance inside the open garage, they would observe a strange sight. Something completely out of place within the tranquility of the suburban neighborhood.

Inside, a man is kneeling beside a woman on the ground, lying there as if she were a lifeless doll. Up and down, up and down, he presses on her chest. Then he leans down, placing his mouth on hers, and breaths inside, her belly rising with the air. He breathes into her again, then returns to the rhythmic pumping. The total stillness and silence around them shift from serene to disturbing. Above them, a rope hangs loosely, its purpose unclear. Next to them, a dryer rests, its metal surface still warm to the touch. In the bathroom, a hairbrush rests on the counter, its bristles tangled with fine strands of brown hair.

Then, off in the distance, a high-pitched sound is heard, as the man continues pumping, up and down, up and down. The now unmistakable wail of a siren grows alarmingly louder and announces with piercing clarity that something on this quiet street has collapsed, out of the norm, out of order, and into chaos. He breathes into her mouth again, and then up and down, up and down. Still, nothing else moves in the garage except the man.

PART TWO

ALIVE!

Reading or hearing these words means that you're out there somewhere, blood pumping, lungs breathing, and life unfolding. Far beyond simply existing for survival, you are thinking and feeling deeply into life, with unique talents, gifts, and an essence all your own. You are truly something wonderful.

Swept along the immense spectrum of human emotion, you travel winding paths that climb up toward bliss and spiral down to despair. Love splashes vibrant colors across your world, flooding your heart with joy. Then, like delicate porcelain struck by a hammer, heartbreak and pain shoot fissures through every corner of your being. Leaving you grasping desperately, as pieces of yourself fall away. Sometimes, plunging to depths so bleak, you find yourself questioning whether it's even worth it.

The eternal struggle between darkness and light is inherent to all of our lives. We love to be in the light, but our pain has a potent way of blotting it out. If life is to prevail, there must be more light than darkness. We must feel more peace than torment. On the continuum of darkness and light on which we live, connection and self-love become obscured and risk being totally lost on the darkest end. It's a place where life's meaning can slip away, and existence becomes suffocating. Falling here may be an inevitable part of the journey, but it's not a place we can remain long. Down here, small shadows can grow monstrous. It's where the unthinkable can quietly take root and become embraced.

Relentless pain and desperation can have one looking towards death and see inviting arms stretched wide. There are traps in the darkness that are convincing and merciless. In some way or another, death has whispered to us all, only varying in its volume and allure. We all know death is out there. Inevitable with time, but also like a door we could just walk through if we wanted.

Humanity has been trying to understand the meaning of life and the nature of suffering since the dawn of time, offering explanations spanning from scientific to spiritual. These questions have led to all the confusion and division we know so well. Fortunately, there is one way of understanding existence that can unite us all—one that requires no belief or scientific theory. It can simply be observed in everything, by anyone, at any time. It is an understanding of chaos and order. These two timeless forces are intrinsic to everything. All possible "good" and "bad" experiences result as these two forces are endlessly manifest. The result for us is a life of struggle and pain, but also of wonder and bliss. Like a sky that changes from sunshine and light breezes into hurricanes and then back again. This is not inferring some kind of a fatalism in which we have no real choice or power but of the forces which will always be far beyond our control.

Although it becomes clear to us from a very young age that life will be both pleasant and unpleasant. Yet, we continue to feel deeply troubled by suffering. Yearning for a lasting sense of peace and joy, we crave positive experiences and recoil from the negative. However, moving through life with this high demand for happiness ends up resulting in a lot of frustration. Suffering is inherent to life. Being so desirous of happiness and intensely averse to all that doesn't feel good can make life exhausting and difficult to manage. In the worst cases, some are so emotionally crushed that their simple life process, the beating of their heart, and the movement of their breath become no longer tolerable. They want the life process to end because they can't even feel what life is anymore.

Death is where the human experience meets its end as far as anything we can perceive, and as such, represents, for our existence, ultimate chaos. Life is possibility, where we live within the endless dance of chaos and order — whether we're aware of it or not, or we like it or not. For a long time, I viewed positivity and negativity, creation and destruction, solely through the lens of a god and devil, sin and righteousness. In essence, as a cosmic drama of "good guys" and "bad guys." Some see it as fate, karma, or destiny.

Still, no matter what our beliefs may be, the reality of chaos and order manifests in everything. Existence is happening, and we are on the game board, so to speak. To succeed in any game, you must first understand the elements at play. Someone who believes they're playing Monopoly but is actually in Candyland is guaranteed a frustrating experience.

Understanding that life is a balance of chaos and order, and learning to flow with and adapt to these forces is essential. When we fail to accept this fundamental truth, emotions like bitterness, frustration, and disillusionment can become overwhelming. The woman on the floor of that garage lost herself in this very struggle. How we perceive ourselves and the world can make a life-or-death difference.

To conceptualize these forces, let's imagine a wide linear continuum. At one end is *total order,* and all the way to the other is *absolute chaos.* No matter what you are doing or where you find yourself, you are somewhere on this continuum, at times deep into chaos, but probably more regularly towards the orderly side of things. Sometimes, moving along it by your own will and decisions, and at other times, outside forces may suddenly shove you to some other point along the scale.

Most of us have the default belief that order represents the "good" side and chaos the "bad." We often believe that maintaining as much order as possible and having things unfold as we desire will lead to happiness. But the reality is that neither chaos nor order inherently brings good or bad outcomes, except at their extremes, where the effects are always harmful. If chaos were to take over, it would bring haphazard destruction. If order ruled unchallenged, we would be trapped by its oppressive limitations. But the extremes will come to assail us all one way or another, bringing darkness that has the potential to diminish forever, if not destroy, our lives. We can, however, overcome and even thrive despite this existential challenge. But to do this, we must be able to see things clearly, observing our experiences with awareness.

Let's begin by examining how the extremes can be harmful. First, we will use the creation of music as an example. At the chaotic extreme, we might hear a two-year-old banging indiscriminately on piano keys or randomly plucking guitar strings. On the opposite end, extreme order would result in a single note repeated endlessly, perfectly in tune and lacking any variation.

How about in the context of society? Extreme chaos would be the drug-addicted prostitute living on the streets. Extreme order, the child of controlling parents whose every action is decided for them, planned, and controlled. Both people are at opposite ends of the extremes, and therefore, both are assuredly experiencing deep suffering. No one would want to be either of these people or listen to either of these musical renditions. Extremes are always detrimental.

In the physical world, chaos and order can be clearly observed in everything. From the collision of an asteroid and the decaying of a flower to the steady rotation of the Earth and the complex structure of a beehive. Both forces interact to create and destroy. Understanding these forces within ourselves and our interactions, however, is a little more difficult. But they each play an important role in our lives. Order positively impacts us by creating stability, security, and structure. It is the stable foundation from which we can then imagine and experiment with possibilities. But with too much order, life becomes restrictive, repetitive, and depressing.

Far from being a purely "good" force, order can result in outright evil. At the societal level, it has brought unimaginable nightmares. In an effort to create a total order of their making, the Nazis established concentration camps, the Soviets created the gulags, and Pol Pot's Khmer Rouge imposed its killing fields. Under Mao Zedong alone, an estimated 65 million people perished as he pursued his vision of an ideal communist order. And just as each side of a coin is opposite yet never far apart, for the countless victims of these pursuits for total order, it was ultimately experienced as an abyss of chaos.

Whether at the individual, relational, or social level, pursuing too much order is a monumental error. The temptation to pursue more and more order will always be there because it brings an illusion of safety and comfort. But when unbalanced, the stability is only temporary and breeds stagnation in the individual, paralyzation in relationships, and oppression in society. When we find ourselves in too much order, our beings will naturally resist, as it is contrary to our nature. A human being is expanding experience. Something in us knows that we are always made for more. More experience, more knowledge, more discovery, more everything. This is why it's important to allow each other and ourselves as much expansion as possible.

Chaos, the oft-considered "bad" force, does indeed have negative impacts on us. It is risk, the unknown, and change. With too much chaos, we feel overwhelmed and lost. But on the other hand, all things are born or created out of some chaos. For a muscle to grow stronger, it must experience some destruction in the process. All living things take in resources from the outside and break them down to transform them into themselves. This principle also holds true with the non-physical, such as when old ideas fade and make way for new ones. Far from being simply a "bad" force, chaos represents the interesting, the curious, the motivating, and where discovery and growth occur.

It is a leap into chaos when the toddler releases that last finger from the coffee table, taking their first steps. When the young person moves far away from the security of their family to pursue their own life. To give yourself in a relationship with another human being, now that is embracing chaos and literally pressing your lips against it. Once again, chaos does not equate to bad. It is risk, vulnerability, and adventure, and it is necessary.

When a man is supposedly "suffering" a mid-life crisis, and doing new and unexpected things. This is likely a man who has been suffering from too much order for too long. His or her, because women go through this too, strange or "extreme" new behavior is simply their being, desperately trying to feel vibrant and alive again. When the walls have closed in too tightly, a step into chaos can be the experiential vehicle to take a journey, somewhere, anywhere. Toward anything that is not the stagnation and gloom of a continual, orderly, and repetitive life.

These forces also manifest in a simultaneous and complementary way, and not just in nature and individuals, but also in human society. Once your awareness opens to it, you will notice it everywhere. Take any dance club, for example. Observe the order of the carefully crafted building and the meticulously managed operations. Then notice the organized patterns of rhythms and melodies of the music. Why all this structure and order? Because it creates the space for the chaotic movement and play of the people who then fill it. The creative chaos literally dances on top of a stable foundation of order. This duality is important for the very functioning of our lives. With things like our principles and ethics creating a stabilized floor beneath us as we take each step into an unknown future.

Experiencing these forces as either positive or negative is subject to many variables, including our current perspective. Time has a way of reshaping how we feel about things in quite a dynamic and unpredictable way. Everything can shift in an instant. An experience that feels negative at the moment may later be recognized as a stepping stone towards something better, like when a painful breakup eventually leads to greater happiness with someone new. Or take the example of a military recruit suffering all the oppression of boot camp. Who then later looks back on it as an invaluable experience that taught perseverance, confidence, and discipline.

Chaos and order are also necessary for enabling us to experience life with perspective and appreciation. Take the old adages about how you can't know light if you don't know darkness, bitter to know sweet, and all the rest. This is existentially true. The differences are what create the contrast needed to know life at all, let alone to any profundity. You could legitimately say that the negativity we experience is the price that we pay for all we enjoy. Loneliness is a terrible feeling, but if we never knew what it was like to feel alone, we could never appreciate the joys of being with the people we love.

All the things we could categorize as good and bad are ingredients needed to create a life that has any meaning or any feeling at all. Even with good versus evil, this reality has been recognized. The theologian Thomas Aquinas said, *"Good derives its virtue from evil, just as it is that silent pause that gives sweetness to the chant."* Wonderful feelings like appreciation and gratitude only arise through contrast and comparison. It is our symbiotic relationship with both the positive and negative aspects of life that truly makes life feel alive. It is eye-opening to recognize how negativity plays a crucial role in partnering with us to shape the experiences we cherish.

Knowing this, why then should we hate or feel oppressed by that which is the co-creator of what we love? Let's be clear, though. Understanding the necessity of the negative doesn't mean we have to like it or make it lose all of its sting. Pain and suffering are brutal things. However, understanding this truth can alleviate some of the weight.

Where we go very wrong is when we are unconscious of or misunderstand the realities of these forces. Unwittingly becoming frustrated and feeling oppressed by them. Failing to embrace that chaos and order were always going to be a part of our lives. The solution to this existential challenge is to embrace life's joys while also accepting it's inevitable discomfort. Our greatest personal growth and many of our most fulfilling experiences are often associated with our most difficult experiences. Enduring, striving, overcoming, and achieving are rarely comfortable. In fact, they're often painful, with no guarantee of success. Yet, from these challenges emerge victories, celebrations, new insights, and a deeper understanding of ourselves and the world. Most importantly, it is in these depths that we learn the true meaning of compassion and love. Something about suffering also creates the greatest opportunities for our self-reflection, growth, and positive transformation.

Chaos and order are for you. Both are ingredients to the development of your best life and highest self, but it is a process. One that requires patience and adaptability. That woman on the floor of that garage lost herself when life became experienced as too much of a burden and an affliction. A complete loss of self is the clearest definition of suicide there could be. It is the ultimate expression of an inner collapse, and completely contrary to what life is designed to be.

PART THREE

"I"

In a universe out of our control, it is our ability to interpret and respond to life wherein our greatest power lies. And to do this well, we have to come to know this being within, this person we call "I." Who we are and how we manage this *self* is a central theme throughout this book. Because a beautiful life and a self-inflicted death are both possibilities that emerge from the *self*. And despite the mysteries, there are some things that can bring clarity to who we are and what is happening within us.

What we think about ourselves and the nature of the universe seems to be dictated by either modern science or a small handful of religions. For a long time, I felt frustrated by the contradictions and the things that didn't feel right. But now, I see that all of it has been a gift in my journey of self-discovery. By thoughtfully reflecting on the different ideas we encounter and juxtaposing them with our own experiences, we can learn a great deal.

Setting aside all the mysteries, it is clear that we are made up of three fully integrated parts. Our body, our consciousness, and the environment. Religion, spirituality, philosophy, and, most likely, each of us is most concerned with the consciousness part of this trinity. The life energy that knows that we know we are. We call it things like our spirit, soul, and energy. All of this is perfectly fine because we all understand what we're referring to.

This part of us is magical precisely because it lies beyond the reach of science, and religions will always disagree on it, as it can only be experienced and felt. It cannot be measured or contained in a bottle, nor can ideas, beliefs, or words fully capture its essence. A picture will never be painted that we can all see or agree on. It remains always a unique experience within each of us. A beautiful step in the life journey is accepting that there will be many things we don't know, and that both knowing and not knowing is inherent to life, and there is value in this.

Science, spirituality, and each of our personal experiences create a vibrant opportunity. The ultimate truth about existence seems to be a puzzle whose pieces are scattered and spread throughout our lives. It is our gift to move through life, finding pieces and doing what we will with them along the way. Maybe we will be able to put together a large section of life's puzzle or perhaps only some small ones. What else can we do besides take it all in and then do "the best we can" with life?

Fortunately, some critically important pieces of the puzzle have been assembled and reveal the fundamental aspects of our consciousness. Within us, there are three basic forces, or you could say, three distinct, yet coexisting versions of ourselves. While various philosophies may label them differently, their essence is nearly universal. For the sake of this discussion, we will refer to them as the Ego, the Shadow Self, and our Highest Self.

Throughout our lives, they exert a powerful influence, as each seems to be endlessly vying for dominance. Let's take a brief look at each, as we will be using these three terms throughout the book. Understanding these principal aspects of ourselves brings needed self-awareness critical for healing our wounds and progressing towards our highest selves and best life.

Our Highest Self is the truest version of ourselves. We all yearn to embody this *self* of love, truth, light, and life. Embodying this way of being lifts us and those around us to an existence where peace and happiness are the norm. In this state, we love, forgive, play, create, seek, and evolve. Compassion, patience, and gratitude lead our hearts. Curiosity, courage, and resiliency are boundless. Our highest self is all the ways we love to be and what we love to experience from others. You might call it the best version of ourselves or, if you prefer, our divine nature. It is who we are at our deepest core.

However, as we all sense within, our highest self does not exist without challenge or opposition. For every highest self, there must be a lowest self, or, as the psychologist Carl Jung described it, our Shadow Self. The shadow self is the dark force that brings destruction and suffering. Embodying the shadow, we lie, shame, disregard, abuse, hate, and despair. It causes the deterioration of our hearts, minds, and bodies. The shadow self is the darkness.

Finally, there is the Ego—the identity we construct for ourselves, neither inherently good nor bad. It begins its formation at a young age, driven by the need to fit in and survive in an uncertain world. Since it develops during our most impressionable and uninformed years, the ego is inherently flawed, often rooted in false perceptions about ourselves and the world around us.

The ego always seeks maximum mental and emotional stability, which is why it resists change so intensely and doesn't like to be wrong or be challenged. Its primary goal is self-preservation. The ego quickly forms conclusions and makes strong judgments about everything. It seeks validation and acceptance from external sources, making it highly sensitive to the actions of others. Beneath a veneer of confidence, the ego is often filled with limiting beliefs and self-doubt.

The ego endlessly searches for safety by attaching and identifying with things, ideas, and people. Unchecked, it would have you believe that you are what you possess, what you do, and what others think about you. Its fearful nature fosters a shallow and unhealthy connection with the world. An unchecked ego can result in emotional isolation, as it places its own preservation above everything else. No meaningful connection with others would be allowed if the ego had its way.

The ego can never be "killed," contrary to the popular saying. It is an abstraction, and as such, it is an extremely slippery customer. The only solution to the challenge of the ego is to recognize, understand, and manage it. The good news is that as you move further toward your highest self, the ego's influence becomes more and more diminished.

I understand that this way of understanding ourselves may seem oversimplified or not entirely align with your perspectives. Some may prefer to explain it in terms of religion, while others might choose the scientific language of neurology, and still others may turn to astrology, reincarnation, karma, or a variety of other frameworks. However, considering all of the many differences out there, we need some common ground with which to communicate. I hope that no matter what your background, you will see the parallels to these three fundamental parts of ourselves within your current belief system. Kind of like, if you call a spade by any other name, it's still a spade.

My intention is to approach these topics in a way that unites us. We all share the same fundamental struggle of overcoming darkness and finding peace. The nature of existence and the universe can be beautifully and simply understood through the existential truths that surround us. Consider the basic reality of chaos and order just discussed.

Whether you attribute it to a god or a mindlessly expanding universe, its impact on us is the same. Every human who has ever lived is shaped by this reality.

We all embark on the same journey with our highest self, endlessly seeking joy, love, and peace. But well-being isn't just experiencing peace and happiness in the absence of pain. Suffering will always be a part of it. Darkness may even prove to be a very large part, and that is OK, because we understand that we needed both. Uncertainty and discomfort aren't just part of the process; it is the process.

Through struggle and pain, meaning and purpose emerge, our capacity for knowing joy grows, much-needed wisdom is gained, and compassion blossoms. As you increasingly embody your higher self, darkness will become a smaller and smaller part of your life. Life can shift from feeling oppressive to becoming an enthralling adventure that fills you with wonder and vitality. Living with awareness and intention is the most powerful antidote to suffering and despair.

What is an intentional life? It means consciously seeking the life we want. Intention is a state of mind and continuous action with a commitment to achieving a certain desire or goal. Other words associated with intention are aspiration, purpose, meaning, objective, ideal, and dream. Ideals and dreams are wonderful things, but they are never attainable unless sought with conscious intention.

PART FOUR

LOSING SELF

IF WE TOOK A SURVEY AND RANKED THE WORST POSSIBLE HUMAN EXPERIENCES, suicide would be right there among the top. There are plenty of other seriously horrible things that we can experience in life, brutal, life-destroying ones. But all things not being equal, suicide would stand as one of the worst possible outcomes.

Suicide wreaks a terrible toll on the suicidal person, with dual devastation. The victim endures deep pain leading up to the point of suicide. In the end, they lose everything. The people close to them also suffer, as the struggles that lead to suicide bring a lot of negativity into relationships. When the suicide is actually completed, these loss survivors then become traumatized bearers of pain thrust upon them by the life they loved vanishing so completely.

What is this condition of the mind so anguished that embracing the terror of death becomes its preference? What transforms a hopeful and innately self-preserving human being into a despairing destroyer of the self? How can we save these lives, or maybe even our own, from this ending? What understanding and wisdom are there that can help us all with this issue? And perhaps, even more unexpectedly, what can it teach us about living and thriving? Growing in awareness about suicide is actually much more about life than it is about death.

This issue has already affected many of us and will continue to be a threat that can emerge within or around us. That much we can know and must accept. Because this issue is so common and deeply harmful, it makes sense to try and understand it as much as possible. It would be naive to believe we could save everyone, but that doesn't mean we shouldn't try. It is not an unstoppable force—it can be overcome with the right support and wisdom. Everyone is valuable and deserves to live life fully. But sometimes, the world makes us believe we are less than we truly are. That we and life are so miserable and hopeless that it is not worth living. This is the greatest lie we can come to believe. However, as with all lies, they can only take hold in the absence of truth.

The issues that most deeply afflict us have been part of human experience since time immemorial. The oldest known suicide note was written on papyrus in Egypt over 4,000 years ago. For tens of thousands of years, during the long hunter-gatherer era, our ancestors surely also struggled with the same desires for death as a solution to life's difficulties. Though in recent times our unwell state an-masse seems to be deteriorating at an ever-faster pace. Our current world may be much more advanced and convenient, but it has many elements that are extremely detrimental to our mental, physical, and emotional health.

Another reality of being human is that we have extremely fragile bodies. Death is not a long or difficult journey to take. Dying is no great feat requiring much imagination or effort. A small opening in us can drain us of life in seconds. A simple step from something, even just a couple of stories high, and it's likely all over. Relatively light pressure on our neck, a few gulps of some tiny pills, or a flick of a finger on a trigger, and poof, it's all gone. It's a cruel reality for those left with the lifetime tragedy of a loved one's suicide. What was done in a brief moment becomes an entire lifetime of complex grief.

Suicide is also a pervasive, human-specific issue, uniquely ours to wrestle with, as there is still no evidence of any other animal that willfully kills itself. All long-time misconceptions about any animals committing suicide have been debunked. Humans also suffer from a susceptibility to a plethora of mental health problems, exacerbating an already challenging existence. It is apparent that our profound sense of self-awareness and mental sophistication is a double-edged sword. On the one hand, this awareness has given us the ability to experience life in wonderful, expansive, and meaningful ways. We have an amazing memory and a fantastic imagination. These two gifts bring us incredible benefits, but also make us vulnerable to deep pain. Remember, chaos and order go hand in hand; everything has its opposite. Just as we have the potential to experience heights of bliss in which we would choose to live forever. So also, must exist our capacity to fall to depths so painful and hopeless that snuffing out our own existence becomes appealing. This journey downward is, however, an avoidable path. Nothing condemns nor fates us to it.

The following may sound obvious, but it bears stating because people regularly convince themselves otherwise. Suicide, being self-chosen and self-inflicted, means every single person has within them the freedom and ability to choose life and, on top of that, choose the experience of life they would like. While the outside world has a huge influence, every feeling you experience comes from within you. Your interpretation of events and reaction to them are also wholly yours to decide.

If you feel like darkness is gathering around you, and the heaviness is growing, it's time to change the paradigm of how you see yourself and the world. I invite you to join me in a simple mental exercise. Close your eyes and imagine yourself, let's say, sitting alone on a hill overlooking some beautiful landscape. Or even in the opposite setting, on a bus stop bench in a noisy city. Now, use all your senses to experience the sights, sounds, and smells. Now, imagine you are leaving your body, floating away several feet. Now observe yourself sitting there. What do you see? What is it that is sitting there? Who are you?

Are you the shape of your body or the style of clothes you're wearing? Are you your nationality, ethnicity, or profession? Are you your family? Are you your addiction? Are you the past abuses and traumas? Are you your ending relationship? Are you your religious expectations? Those suicidal thoughts, are those you? All of your mistakes and misdeeds, are these you? Take a long, curious look.

The one thing these all have in common is that they are just experiences. Experiences are just memories or moments happening right now—but they are not who you are. We naturally attach ourselves to things and believe they define us. We cling to what makes us feel special, valuable, and temporarily happy. And that would all be fine, except that the ego doesn't discriminate in its attachments. So, we also become attached and identify with all of the negative experiences as well. The ones that don't make us feel good at all. The ones that make us feel unsafe, lost, and worthless. This creates a chaotic cycle of attachment and loss, and would have us identifying with whatever darkness has happened to us.

The truth is that the negative things that so deceivingly destroy our well-being have nothing to do with who we really are. It's just that our whole lives, who we are, has been defined by outside forces. Great philosophers across the millennia have recognized that identification with things we are not, and our attachments, are often the source of our worst miseries.

So, what is it then we see sitting on that dingy bench with the lawyer's advertisement and the traffic blaring, or on that cool green grass overlooking that expansive view? Well, let's first reveal who you are by stripping away all of the layers one by one. Think about all the ways you see yourself—the roles you play in life. A father, a daughter, a nurse, an athlete, or part of any specific group. Even your age. Now, imagine letting all of those labels fade away.

Now, watch as your physical appearances dissolve one by one. Your hair, your clothes, and the color of your eyes. Then, your flesh and all the parts of your body. Watch it all slowly disappear. Now, let all the thoughts in your mind drift off into nothingness.

Now, look again and see. What is left? Just you, isn't it? The *you* that is beyond all the world's labels for you. The *you* beyond your body and thoughts. Beautifully unique yet connected with everything. Just as empty space and matter can only exist because of one another. Light only exists because of its counterpart, darkness, and so on. It is profoundly simple yet absolutely magical to realize that you and all that there is can only exist because of each other. That you are inextricably connected. Our feeling of separateness and our universal connection is the duality in which we have the privilege of existing. A most basic of realities so easily overlooked.

No? You think maybe not so much? Well, try and see if you could live for even one moment without all else around you. From the air you breathe to the ground you stand upon, and the things you eat. Then, observe how those things are connected to other greater things, like the ocean, the whole planet, and the atmosphere. Examining ever outward, you'll notice your connection continues, even millions of miles away, with the sun. Is life on Earth not solar-powered? You're solar-powered, that's for sure. The sun creates the needed temperatures for you to exist. Your very skin is a solar panel, using sunlight as a basic part of your biological functions. So even the distant sun is an intrinsic part of you.

You are not a visitor who arrived here from another place, or some stranger who is here alone and disconnected. The "you" that you are experiencing as so separate formed right out of the world. Despite the feeling of being so different, you are a part of all that is and of creation's continuous unfolding. Arguably, you are creation's most beautiful expression of itself. Not only are you supposed to be here, you *are* here and here is *you.* When conscious of this, it is very difficult to feel alone or lacking in meaning.

Several different philosophies try to convey this reality while incorporating their own nuances. Some, like Yoga and Taoism, seem to point the most directly at it. Jesus understood that he was one with the creator and tried to convey to the world that so were we. This reality of existence has been explained in many different ways over the millennia. But if you boil them all down, the simplicity is so profound that it can feel hard to accept. But what is, *is,* and stands on its own truth. It is clear for anyone to see who looks.

The fact that you and everything else exist within a universally shared space implies without any doubt that everything is a part, a vibration, spirit, energy, or whatever you'd like to call it, of the whole. It all has no other choice but to be. Can you exist without the universe? Can the universe exist without all of the parts, big and small, that make up its whole? No, and no. The truth of our full connection with everything transcends belief or religion, and it unifies us with all creation and, therefore, each other.

Your existence is creation itself. This is why there is truth when you hear talk of divinity. The one definition of divinity we can all agree on is that it is the source of creation, and its energy flows through everything. The same energy that moves solar systems and tiny atoms is the same energy that throbs within you. When you truly understand who you are, many of life's problems begin to feel small. The light, love, and creation that you are can be the greatest expression and experience of your life.

So, this profound duality, this beautiful connection with everything, and an awareness of our uniqueness within it, is where an existentially true understanding of who we are lies. This awareness is key to unlocking our soul. So that we can be the freest, most vibrant, and expanding we yearn to be. It is the opposite of being confused, oppressed, hopeless, and alone.

Still, in life's journey of discovery, there is never a final arrival to a destination of "the self." We are always growing and changing because learning never stops. Who you are today isn't who you'll be tomorrow, and is very different from who you'll be ten years from now. A joyful life embraces the journey and moves continually toward our highest self. This path is also the best way to prevent the worst from happening. Becoming completely separated from ourselves and experiencing a total collapse.

This complete collapse of *the self* is suicide, and it is the world's leading cause of violent death. According to the World Health Organization, about one million people die by suicide each year. The real number may be even higher since many cases go unreported. While we don't know the suicide rates throughout all of history, we do know that in recent decades, they have risen sharply.

In the United States, it increased 33% between 1999 and 2019. In 2019, when we observed the scene in that garage, there were 47,500 deaths attributed to suicide. In 2023, the number increased to 49,316. Globally, suicide rates have risen by 60% over the past 45 years. Today, it is one of the top three causes of death for people aged 15 to 44, and the numbers continue to rise among the young. For military and law enforcement, this problem is disproportionately more severe. These people are 54% more likely to die by suicide than those in other occupations.

The rate of increase is undeniable evidence that well-being for many of us is diminishing. There are dynamics of life experience that are clearly changing for the worse. If life were getting better for people, we would see suicide rates going down.

What's even more troubling is that suicide rates keep rising, even as awareness campaigns and prevention efforts have grown. Mental health services are more available than ever. There is significant community outreach at the national and local levels. Many occupational awareness programs and support services for mental health and suicide are available as well. Yet, in spite of all these efforts, the path we are on as a society is only increasing the rate at which we are killing ourselves.

The current methods and strategies are falling short of achieving significant positive change. But make no mistake; this is not to say that all prevention efforts have been in vain. In many cases, surely existing efforts have saved many lives, and every effort to help is valuable. But the truth remains that suicide rates are still rising, leaving more lives lost and more families and friends grieving.

The information, experiences, and insights in this book are my contribution to an issue that deserves our sincere attention. As one of humanity's most serious problems, it merits a united effort. Odds are, if it hasn't already, suicide is going to affect your personal world eventually. It is not an issue we can just turn a blind eye to, content to outsource it to "the professionals." The professionals are great, but they are a drop in the ocean. We are all here together. Support, healing, and thriving are going to happen right in the midst of your life. Right beside your friends, in your family, and most importantly, within yourself. This is where it all goes so wrong anyway, isn't it? Where it can end so badly, within ourselves and our relationships. So, this book is far from being just for the suicidal. It is for everyone.

The more you understand something, the more empowered you are within that issue. Truth and wisdom are key for real and lasting change. We can go through life by chance, hoping for a good outcome, or we can make a choice to take action and improve ourselves and the world around us. Important ideals, like lowering suicide rates or saving even one life, start with each of us. A life-and-death difference can and will be made by your awareness and actions.

The purpose of this book is to support you in navigating life's most pivotal struggles. It is to support you in your journey to develop and realize a more compassionate, capable, resilient, and thriving self. As a result, the tragedy that is relentless distress, despair, and suicide will have less and less impact on all of us. Lives can be saved and lived to their fullest. When we see the intrinsic value of others and cherish our own beings, the light inside us grows brighter than the darkness around us. In this state, not only do we thrive, but that same energy expands outward and touches the people around us. Love dispels the darkness like nothing else can.

PART FIVE

OUR STORY

Eight years before the morning in the garage.

"This is Zuko's tape!" Chris says as the camera pans from the little dog sitting at the bottom of the stairs, and over to Cindy lying on the couch. Her shirt's pulled up, leaving her bulging nine-month belly on full display. Cindy gently pats the large mound with a smile.

"This is your day," Chris says to the baby still inside. "Cindy is due in five days, but she is feeling some weird stuff right now, so we are not sure what may be going on, but hopefully, we are close. We can't wait to have you baby. Baby Zuko."

Chris's hand can be seen reaching out and caressing her belly. "I can't believe you're right in here right now. We've read to you and played music for you. Cindy talks to you all the time. We both love you very much."

Chris then turns the camera to face himself as he sits down next to Cindy and lies his head against her shoulder. "We wanted to record a little bit more before you are born." Then, turning the camera again towards her belly. "You can see yourself right there."

With the camera again facing them, Chris gives Cindy a gentle kiss on the cheek, and then both of them kiss the air in the direction of the camera. "The next time we're recording, we're going to be seeing you!" "Bye," they both say. Cindy gives a happy, playful wink to the camera. Then, panning down to the little dog, Chris says, "Chloe says, we'll see you soon!"

The next day, the camera is rolling again. Cindy is lying on her side in the hospital room, resting peacefully. She finally decided to get an epidural after going through contractions for more than 20 hours. The camera pans around the room, then out the window, until Chris turns it toward himself. "Our last moments waiting for you, Zuko."

The next scene opens to much more noise and commotion as the crying and just-born baby is placed on Cindy's chest and wiped with towels by the nurses. With a mix of excitement, love, and exhaustion, Cindy exclaims, "Oh my gosh! Oh my gosh!" Looking down at him and then towards Chris. Radiating joy and awe, she holds the baby delicately against her chest and says to him, "I love you, Zuko."

The MAN IN THE GARAGE WITH THE WOMAN ON THE FLOOR WAS ME. My children and I lost Cindy to the tragic thing we call suicide. We had been married for 16 years, and our kids were five and seven years old at the time. Her intentional death opened an endless void beneath us, into which our souls then plummeted.

As journaling about my experience evolved into writing a book, I had to figure out what that would look like. Was it going to be a dramatic autobiographical narrative? Maybe philosophical or purely informational? My heart told me that I needed to create a holistic resource regarding suicide that could help everyone impacted by this issue. And our personal story would be the thread that wove it all together.

Though this will be far from a biography of our life. Still, a basic introduction is in order since our experience is the focal point of reference throughout the book. Cindy and I lived this out together as the main characters in this real-life drama. If the most personal and painful parts of our lives are going to be exposed to the world, it seems proper that you get to know a little bit about who the people in the story are. Therefore, I will give a brief background glimpse into our life.

I was born in 1981 and grew up in Southern California with seven siblings. Though I do not identify with any religion, you could say I was raised in the Mormon church, although it wasn't typical in the sense that my dad had been excommunicated and my mother continually vacillated between different Christian sects. Still, in my younger years, we went to a Mormon church most Sundays, except for the two years we went next door to the Jehovah's Witnesses. By the time I was in high school, both my parents rarely attended church, and only a couple of us siblings, including myself, were still interested in Mormonism or anything religious, for that matter.

We were an isolated family with regard to extended family. Grandparents, uncles, and cousins were completely out of the picture. There were so many siblings that we hardly noticed. My early childhood was pretty typical for an American kid in the 80s and 90s, playing with the neighborhood kids, either in the street or in the forested canyon behind our house. The beach and the city pool were where I spent most of those summers.

It was cramped in our small three-bedroom house. But my resourceful father made more room by turning the garage into two bedrooms and later building two shed bedrooms in the backyard. Thank goodness, because we really needed the space. Luckily, the city inspectors never knew about all these heinous zoning law violations.

Dad was a computer programmer, and if he wasn't on his computer, he would be in the backyard digging or building something. He was a sweet-hearted man who avoided confrontation at all costs. A textbook "nice guy." Though his many personal life frustrations, commonly about money, would periodically have him blow his top, and he'd yell about things to himself. The general theme of these fits of rage seemed mainly to do with God not blessing him in ways he felt he needed and deserved, principally in a financial way.

I grew up conditioned with a scarcity mindset. Hand-me-down and secondhand store clothes, generic brand foods, and few toys. I didn't know the detailed reasons why. I just knew that money was a constant problem, and there was far too little of it, according to my parents. I witnessed it as a constant source of turmoil and suffering. However, we did, thankfully, always have our basic needs met. I make note of this because I empathetically recognize that for millions of people, basic needs are many times lacking. I know, comparatively, on a global scale, that I was and am highly fortunate in regard to quality of life.

My father loved his kids dearly, and we all felt it till the very end. He was the dad who, when he helped you with a school project, the results were clearly not the work of any school-age child. If he was going to be involved, it was going to be perfect. He once made a model of the solar system where all the planets actually moved in a rotation, using a complex system of wooden gears and rubber pulleys turned by a crank. He custom-made every piece (with, of course, the indispensable help of my 11-year-old brother, whose science project it supposedly was), and it was the size of a dining room table.

He was extremely intelligent, a Stanford mathematician, smart but socially awkward and aloof. Mom needed a romantic who could sweep her off her feet and give her lots of attention.

That's just not who my dad was. After a continually disharmonious relationship, my parents finally divorced when I was in the eighth grade. He also messed up pretty damn badly in the sexual behavior department, to say the least. And his greatest misdeed proved to be that precarious Jenga piece you pull out, and the whole family came crashing down.

After the divorce, home life became chronically tumultuous as drug abuse and general juvenile delinquency, one by one, became the way of life for many of my siblings. For some reason, I was born with a straight arrow stuck through my body, so I didn't find it hard to "be a good kid." I liked to do well in school and felt drawn to participating in church.

My dad really never talked to me about life. I cannot tell you a single piece of advice he gave me about anything. He never shared stories from his past to teach important lessons, like you often see older people do on TV, trying to help younger folks. Not my dad. No deep conversations at all. He and I were clearly very different when it came to how we wanted to communicate and connect with the world. Though interestingly, he did try to publish a couple of books. They were a collection of anagrams of scripture verses and old English poems. Anagramming is where you take a word or, in his case, whole sentences, and rearrange the same letters to write something else. It was a quirky hobby he had. I don't think he ever went further than printing a few copies, which he gave to family members.

I did learn a lot of things from him, though. There were the glaring, detrimental behaviors and mindsets that were lighthouse-size warnings on what not to do. But even without words, he was an example of many wonderful things that shaped me in positive ways—his commitment to providing for his children, kindness, affection, hard work, and generosity. The guy was hardworking and humble enough that while working for a major computer company. He then got a second job bagging groceries to receive the needed orthodontic insurance coverage and the extra money to pay for the braces several of his kids needed.

When I was in the process of buying our first little home, he insisted on supporting us in some way, even though he lived basically paycheck to paycheck. I will never forget opening the door to our apartment and finding him standing there. He handed me eight hundred dollars and told me how proud he was of me, wishing he could do more to help. I felt his heart for me on so many occasions that I know the love I exude now is, in large part, a reflection of his.

He never remarried. I think he was content just being there for his kids and providing for them. But in his final years, he gave romantic love one last chance. Around age 70, he stepped completely out of the routine he had followed for decades. He drove all the way from Oceanside, California, to rural Vermont to be with a woman he had met online. He was only there for about three years before failing health ended up having him come back home.

Though I missed not having him nearby during those last few years of his life. I'm so glad he gave himself permission to expand and experience something in life just for him. One last well-deserved personal adventure. He had a stroke not too long after coming home, which all but incapacitated him. He then lingered on, slowly deteriorating over the course of about seven months, not even able to talk or eat. I would talk to him as he lay there, but when he looked at me, I couldn't even tell if he understood anything I said or if he even knew who I was.

For what was to be his final couple of months, he seemed to be endlessly asleep. It was a long, one-sided goodbye. I poured out everything in my heart, but there was no response. He never got the chance to say the words I know he would have wanted to. Maybe he would have just reminded me of what he used to tell me when I was a child. That I was his "special little guy."

The last time I saw him alive, I somehow sensed it. After visiting him and leaving the room, I paused at the door and looked back at the scene. My barely existent father was lying asleep on a twin bed with my two sisters sitting on either side of him. Stuffing down sad emotions, I said, "I hope there is a life after this one because I want to see him again." Three days later, he was gone.

He died about a year and a half before Cindy's death. Before them, I had never lost anyone close to me. Losing my dad was my first experience with grief for the dead. My dad is indeed one of the reasons my heart hopes for there to be something of the afterlife we all idealize. He is missed dearly by his children, but lives on through the love and hugs I can still feel to this day. His hilarious laugh still makes me smile just thinking about it.

My mother was married once prior to my father. She married her first husband at twenty years old, was married to him for six years, and they had three children together. Yes, when you add the eight she had with my dad, that's eleven kids she birthed. It's evidence of the part of her that loved motherhood during pregnancy and the toddler years. She kept having kids to try to make those phases last forever. She openly admits that she didn't enjoy mothering as much after that.

She periodically worked as a Montessori teacher, which is in alignment with her love of small children. She was also a skilled seamstress and licensed hairdresser. She did not, however, consistently use any of these skills as an occupation. Dad was always the breadwinner. She is of that personality type who loves the process of buying and setting something up but never following through on the project or business, like that person who buys the home gym equipment only to leave it sitting to gather dust.

She didn't know how to cook and acknowledged the fact that she did not cook for us. Keeping milk, cereal, bread, peanut butter, jelly, and canned foods available satisfied her conscience with regard to providing for our nutritional needs. When she was young, she loved to sing and dance.

She was a highly critical person who wasn't able to experience anything without making note of something she thought was less than perfect. No matter what great news you had to share or things you were proud of. Along with a "That's nice," she couldn't help but criticize something about it. Unable to hold back her opinions and judgments, everyone seemed worthy of her condemnation. She was aware of this and admitted that her mother had been very critical of her. Thank you generational wounds!

After divorcing my dad, she remarried a retired Marine Corps major. Talk about a pendulum swing away from my soft and nerdy dad. While Dad stayed in our family home, Mom moved just across town. All of us kids were able to go back and forth, staying with whoever we wanted. I ended up moving between them about every six months. The "Major," however, didn't appreciate it when I moved over to their house. The first night I moved in, he took me on a walk and explained to me that my mom had promised him that no kids would live with them, and he especially didn't like boys. The "not welcome" message was clear. Obviously, no stepdad/stepson relationship was in the works there. Which I was fine with as I had my own father and a very full life.

I did actually have one other father figure in my life. I met Rex when I was 14 years old, right around the time my parents were splitting up. For some reason, he took me under his wing and included me in his family's life. Spending time with them made me feel valued and wanted, and gave me a sense of stability in the midst of the chaos at home. He was a fun-loving guy, and I'll never forget the advice Rex gave me, passed down from his father, about girls. "If you're ever kissing a girl and your pecker jumps up on you. Take it around the corner and beat it back down!"

I was fortunate to have many great friends growing up. One of them, Tim, has been my best friend since we were four years old. It is a true lifelong friendship. We did everything together growing up. Even going to the same church, all the same schools, and we lived just a couple blocks from each other. After high school, we finally had to part ways to serve our perspective church missionary assignments. We have been separated by distance ever since, but have never lost touch. He is one of the most solidly good-hearted people I have ever known. I'd do anything for that guy, and he would be there for me no matter what, and he, indeed, has always been there even in the darkest times.

As soon as I turned 15, I was happy to start working and earn my own money. Every day after school, I had the unique opportunity to work as a dental assistant. During high school summers, I worked at a Boy Scout camp up in the nearby mountains. I mostly taught aquatic-related merit badges like swimming, lifesaving, canoeing, and rowing. I believe this, combined with growing up at the beach, has instilled in me a love of the water that has never gone away.

Between school, work, church, friends, girls, and surfing, I wasn't really at home that much. My hobbies were drawing, participating in show choir, playing video games, breakdancing, and listening to music. Oh, and consuming Dr. Pepper and Taco Bell, delicious and detrimental amounts of them. Fun fact, I wasn't raised accustomed to drinking water. I don't remember drinking much water at all. Instead, it was milk, juice, and soda.

It seems I later paid the price for this at age 41 with a massive kidney stone. Which I don't recommend, by the way. As it moved through me, the stone felt less like a smooth creek pebble and more like a vicious alien with sharp claws. But don't worry too much about my health — I'm happy to say that around age thirty, fitness and nutrition became a priority.

So, after finishing high school, I went on my long-anticipated missionary adventure. I was sent to the Dominican Republic for two years. At nineteen years old, it represented the adventure of a lifetime. I quickly fell in love with everything about the country except the soaking wet heat and relentless mosquitoes. I became so attached that the night before returning home, I wept in mourning.

Living outside the U.S. in an impoverished country for so long opened my eyes to the world in so many ways. It gave me precious new perspectives on what matters most in life and forever deepened my sense of gratitude. There is still rarely a time when I take a hot shower or flush the toilet without savoring the luxuriousness of it.

While living in the Dominican Republic, I met a family with whom a strong connection was formed. In time, I became infatuated with the second youngest of the four children. The lively and beautiful 15-year-old Cindy. I know, I know, don't worry. I was only 19 at the time, and she was closer to 16, and nothing happened! Even though we both liked each other, we couldn't act on any of the romantic feelings. It is strictly prohibited to get involved with anyone while on a Mormon church mission. So, it was a very innocent and secret connection, only expressed by a few notes and passing glances. Her playful flirtation of choice was to catch me standing with my legs locked and, from behind, use her knee to make my knee buckle.

After living in her town for four months, I was transferred to a different part of the country. The last night before I left, in the dark beside her house, we shared our first hug. It was long, bittersweet, and completely forbidden. For the rest of my missionary service, I never saw or spoke to her, but continued to have feelings for her.

If she were still here, I'd have Cindy describe her own background story, but instead, my intimate knowledge of her life will have to suffice. She was born in a town called Sabana de la Mar in the Dominican Republic. This was a small and remote fishing town with a single paved road running through it. Like most others in the Caribbean, it was full of colorful buildings, boisterous people, sweltering humidity, mosquitoes, mopeds buzzing up and down the streets, and music blasting late into the night.

Her family lived at the edge of town in a small light blue house with white trim. Some walls were partially made of concrete block, but mostly of thin planks of palm tree wood. It had a rusty tin roof and wooden shutters. To be blunt, most people would have called it a shack. But despite the apparent poverty, it had an idyllic feel to it. There was a large backyard and no neighbors directly on either side, giving it the feel of a home in the countryside.

It was made comfortable and inviting by how it was all kept immaculately clean. The colorful hibiscus bushes were neatly trimmed, and the weeds and grasses were chopped short by machete. Every few days, the leaves were raked and burned. All done by her younger brother, who seemed to take endless pride in caring for the yard. With two parents and four children, there was always laundry to do. So, every day, clothes were drying outside on clotheslines and on the barbed wire fence. It was lush and green on all sides, with dozens of coconut, mango, and banana trees. The inside of the house was also meticulously maintained. When you're living in a tiny house with six people, keeping things organized and clean is a non-negotiable for making it livable.

Hers was a close-knit home. Her energetic and strong mother was the primary breadwinner, working hard as a maid for many years. She wore what we call here in America "the pants in the family." Her father could be described as a pushover "nice guy," a lot like my dad.

Her family was among the first converts when Mormon missionaries first arrived there in the early 1990s. Fun fact number two: Her family's tropical beach baptism was pictured in a Time Magazine article on the Mormon church. The night I met Cindy's family, her father proudly pulled out a laminated copy of the page they were pictured on. It was her father's most prized possession. His five seconds of international fame.

I was instantly taken aback because I had put the very same picture up on my wall years earlier. It was part of a larger display of Mormon religious zeal expressed on my bedroom wall. What were the chances I'd end up meeting this same family in this remote corner of the world? I found myself falling for Cindy while also being a young person deep in belief about God, miracles, and the like. It was hard not to take this coincidence as a bit of a sign.

In that magazine picture, Cindy was a little eight-year-old girl with bronze skin and light-colored curly hair. Far from the norm in the Dominican Republic, her hair had a blondish copper color when she was young. This rare light-colored hair of hers earned her the nickname given to her by her aunt. "Goli" was supposedly inspired by a little doll with blonde curly hair, which I can only assume was Goldilocks.

She grew up in an environment of extreme scarcity and virtually no privacy. Her home was only about the size of a two-car garage. The dirt-floored bedroom had two full-size beds, which somehow slept mom, dad, one brother, and three sisters. In the backyard was a shower stall slapped together from discarded corrugated roofing sheets. A shower entailed pouring water over your head from a 50-gallon metal drum. Way towards the back of the yard was an outhouse, also made from those old roofing sheets.

Food consisted mainly of rice, root vegetables, and plantains, accompanied by small amounts of meat. But because of the poverty, Cindy told me that many times throughout her childhood, she went to bed hungry. Water was fed to the house by a single plastic pipe, producing water for a brief period once a day. Hence, the large metal drum to store it for later use. On many days, no water flowed at all, and it was a regular chore to carry water from the river about a mile away. For entertainment, they had a little stereo and a small old TV with six fuzzy channels. Electricity was only available for several hours per day. But sometimes, black outs lasted for days and even weeks.

All of the family especially loved Cindy. She was an intelligent, funny, and active girl who did well in school and loved playing volleyball. She was the parents' clear favorite and, as such, always got her way. Even though they lived in poverty, she was spoiled in the sense that she knew everyone would do their best to appease her. With her strong will and short temper, this favored status was detrimental to her development, as she learned nothing of healthy conflict resolution. Apologizing or compromising were completely foreign concepts to her.

Her negative emotions were particularly intense, and this was evident from a very young age. Her father recounted how, when she was a small child, when upset, she would clench her fists and tense her whole body, straining up onto her tip toes as she cried. He described it as being so extreme that it was almost funny. Cindy recounted to me that when she was around twelve years old, she got a new pair of sneakers. Second hand of course, but new for her. As she walked down her street, a neighbor girl said, "Those don't look good on you." Cindy immediately pounced on the girl, knocking her to the ground, and began to choke her. She thought it was funny how she had to be pulled off by onlookers and proudly shared this story as an anecdote illustrating how she would not tolerate taking any insults from anyone. Sure, the other girl was acting mean, but Cindy's reaction was extreme and violent, to say the least.

I later came to understand that from a very young age, Cindy suffered from all the standard symptoms of borderline personality disorder (BPD), such as an unstable self-identity, impulsivity, self-destructive behavior, self-harm (self-hitting in her case), suicidal ideation, extreme fear of abandonment, severe mood swings, intense anger, and persistent feelings of emptiness.

People with BPD often have very unstable relationships, which isn't surprising due to their inner struggles. Our relationship was definitely a roller coaster with extreme ups and downs. It may have helped us a lot if we had learned about BPD earlier in our relationship instead of after she passed away. Mentioning Cindy's negative characteristics does not bring me any joy. Cindy was also amazing in many ways. I feel compassion for both of us for the ways we struggled. We were both doing our best with the little wisdom we had. I wish she could send a book back from beyond, telling all in her own words, but I am left to try and tell it on my own.

After returning home from my church mission, why did I go back and marry her? Well, besides the raw attraction I felt, I assumed that because she grew up poor and in a more traditional culture, she would be more appreciative, feminine, humble, and embody a more traditional female role. I saw nothing resembling a healthy relationship with my parents, so it makes sense I would try something that seemed radically different. Also, marrying this girl from a small village in a far-off land was an exciting fantasy.

I was also operating within a religious culture where young marriage was expected. I also needed to marry a "good Mormon girl," which she was at the time. I also suffered a lot of self-shame for impure thoughts and masturbation. So, at 22, still a virgin and not able to have sex outside of marriage, hormonally, I was at the proverbial breaking point.

Finally, if I am totally honest with myself about the deepest reasons for wanting to marry so young and quickly, is that I was so anxious to create for myself the family that I never had. The one where mom and dad love each other, and home is a place of peace and safety. I was desperate to find what I thought would make me feel wanted, worthy, and valued.

So, I saved up some money and flew back to finally see her a year later, staying with her family for a month. This was the extent of our dating phase. By the end of that month, after lots of making out and the resulting bluish-aching nights, we were engaged. A few months later, I returned, and we got married, starting our life together in a one-room little "casita" I paid to have built in the backyard of her family's home.

My closeness with her whole family continued for all the years of our marriage, and we traveled there every year, sometimes staying for several weeks at a time. We even had her parents come and stay with us in the U.S. on a couple of occasions. I prioritized keeping her as close to her family as possible. It was always apparent how much she missed them. During the first several years of our marriage, I poured all of our extra funds into building them a decent house with all the modern amenities they never dreamed they would have. They never asked for what we gave them, but it just felt natural to love them in that way.

So, after navigating through the required immigration process, Cindy came home with me to Southern California for the very first time. Before this, the girl had never spent a night away from home, let alone traveled very far from her small town. Cindy was 18 years old and didn't speak any English. We really didn't know each other very well. Just two young people, suddenly thrown into the intensity of marriage and the challenge of building a life together. Like many other young couples, we were in way over our heads. Neither of us had a developed sense of self, nor the relational skills and experience needed to create a healthy relationship together. Just blind faith and false expectations. As will be revealed more and more, I was totally wrong in what I thought our relationship would be.

Although I was much more open to talking about our issues, both our communication and conflict resolution skills were woefully inadequate for building a healthy, intimate relationship. But we loved each other and tried our best, nonetheless. Cindy suffered greatly from the separation from her family and what could also be described as "culture shock." I think she would have preferred to live in her home country, and for several years, I actually thought about living there, hoping it might make her happier.

It turns out, according to basic psychology, if some of our more detrimental childhood conditionings aren't rectified. We will often attract someone who will rub up against and trigger our deepest wounds. Someone who will help us recreate the dysfunctional relationship environment we were used to in childhood. Usually, someone who is very much like our parents. It quickly became apparent that Cindy's negative traits were, indeed, very similar to my mother's. Emotionally chaotic, depressed, short-tempered, impulsively violent, and unaffectionate, among others. I settled right into the nice guy, people-pleaser role. Trying to do whatever I thought it would take to make her happy, win her approval, and be loved. Unfortunately, it was after Cindy died that I learned more about these childhood wounds and all the ways we can be horribly conditioned in our younger years. But gaining this awareness was a big part of really changing my life for the better.

Some of my earliest memories are of my mother regularly crying in her bedroom and wailing with all dreadfulness, "Please, God, take me; I wish I were dead!" I, along with some of the other siblings, would always go in and try to console her. As a young child, that behavior felt terrible and scary. It lasted for so many years that even when I was fifteen, I remember my youngest brother crying and complaining how his "tummy hurt" during these episodes.

A mother who does not have a man to emotionally connect with often ends up creating a very unhealthy relationship with her children. Making them feel like they are responsible for her emotional needs, which often causes them to take on roles that are not appropriate for a child. This and then broader societal and some religious conditionings created in me the "white knight syndrome" or "rescuer" role with women. This meant that I was only lovable and valuable if I could serve and protect a woman who needed saving. I learned from very early on that my needs were not a priority.

Cindy fit the bill perfectly for me to continue the pattern I experienced in childhood. Who could possibly need saving more than a young girl living in a dirt-floored, tin-roofed shack in a very poor country? A girl who, within our first month of marriage, banged her head against a concrete wall in frustration during a disagreement with me, my first indication of her deep lack of inner stability.

Though we had many good times, there was enough discord and frustration that, on several occasions, I would feel hopeless enough to want to end the marriage. She was unwilling to cooperate with seeking support for our relationship, and conflicts between us never got resolved. There was only sweeping things under the rug and days of the silent treatment. When the mutual unhappiness seemed overwhelming, I would suggest that we separate and that she could go back home. Me getting serious about ending the relationship was always the catalyst for her suicidal episodes.

From the earliest days of our marriage, it became a recurring theme. There was also a disposition toward self-violence that manifested itself in various ways, including fits of frustrated rage where she would strike her own face with open palms. Over the years, I patched several holes in doors and walls created by her fists. I couldn't count using all my fingers and toes how many times I felt fearful enough to remove all the kitchen knives and any bottles of medicine from the house.

There was a trip to the emergency room because of an attempted overdose of over-the-counter pain pills. There were attempts in my presence to jump out of moving cars and second-story windows, which my interventions of grabbing onto her would apparently stop. She once called me by phone and asked if I would be "capable of retrieving my dead body" as the sound of a train on the nearby tracks rumbled in the background.

Still long before we had children, a particularly frightening episode occurred during a very difficult evening of arguing. I came out of the bathroom to find her with my handgun to her head, highly agitated, breathing heavily, and pacing back and forth. I did and said whatever I could think of to try and calm the situation and keep her from pulling that trigger.

Miraculously, she put the gun down. It turns out that it wasn't anything I said that night that stopped her. Years later, when I asked her about it, she told me that she hadn't heard anything I said. She said the only thing that kept her from pulling the trigger was thinking about how much her mother would suffer if she had done it. I had no idea that she knew the code to my little safe. But after that razor's edge of a close call, I made sure the code was impossible for her to figure out.

The last serious suicidal episode she survived was when she threatened to kill herself with a kitchen knife. My response was to take the knife from her, toss it across the room, and then run outside to defuse the situation. I called the police, and she ended up being forcibly admitted to a mental health facility for two weeks. The time she spent in the facility seemed to be a turning point in her life. Although she decided not to continue taking the medications they gave her or continue with therapy, her well-being, social life, and our relationship all improved greatly after that experience. It must have served, at the very least, as a serious wake-up call.

So, after two years of marked improvement and eight years of marriage, I finally felt comfortable having children with her. The next few years with our two young ones were the happiest of our time together. Pregnancy and taking care of children brought out the best in her. She was an attentive, caring, and affectionate mother. When I say those two kids never even had a diaper rash, I'm serious. I couldn't have asked for more, and I'll always be thankful for the immense love she gave them during those critical early years. I suppose children alleviated much of her loneliness.

The American dream seemed to be materializing for us as I started my career in federal law enforcement, bought our first home, and had our little boy and girl. From the outside, we would have appeared to have it all, but this was not the case. Fast forward several more years, and eventually, her unresolved inner instability and the deep lacking in our relationship eventually manifested itself in an earth-shattering way. I had been completely in the dark when it was suddenly revealed that she had been in a secret romantic and sexual relationship for a prolonged period of time. An already painful revelation aggravated even further because the man was a mentor and close friend of mine, and also the husband of one of her closest friends.

This revelation dropped a bomb on my world. My view of our relationship, who she was, and our future together was shattered in an instant. Although we had our share of struggles, there was one thing I highly valued between us. For me, it was the bond we shared through our sexual relationship and exclusivity. We were both virgins when we married, and that special connection with her meant a lot to me. I had never imagined that she would have been capable of an affair.

It also didn't take long to discover that their relationship wasn't just some lustful fling. It was a full-on supposed love affair, and they had planned to be together. Her lover had promised a future with her. For Cindy, he now represented a critical lifeline as she had never worked, lived alone, or taken care of herself. She lived wholly dependent on me, literally along for the ride.

She must have known that such a tremendous betrayal would be intolerable for me after how difficult our marriage already was. Therefore, she placed all her fragile eggs in his basket. It turned out that he was lying about being with her in the end, no big surprise there. He broke it off with Cindy and chose to stay with his wife and family when she decided to forgive him.

I had already felt a lot of unhappiness with her for a long time. This horribly disrespectful treatment of me was the straw that broke my back. I told her we were going to end the marriage. Cindy didn't do anything to try and change my mind either. Never did she sincerely apologize or express anything to try and make amends.

Losing both her relationship with him and our marriage must have rocked her to the core. I don't think she ever imagined things not going the way she wanted. Her whole life taught her that she would always get what she wanted. Her parents drew no boundaries for her. Then, sixteen years in a relationship with me cemented her belief that she could do anything with no consequence. That she would always win and certainly never be abandoned.

It must have been the ultimate mind job for her when two men whom she believed she had all power over were actually done with her, and at the same time, no less. She lost control over both of us, and I don't think that was something she could handle. I learned later on that being a so-called "control freak" is not an uncommon trait for many people who kill themselves. For people like Cindy, a loss of control is almost intolerable. This self-created chaos ignited the emotional fire that ultimately consumed her ability to stay alive.

One week after I found out about her affair, I woke up to find her in our garage, hanging in the dark. It was gruesome and shocking to see her there, but with no hesitation, I did what I could to save her life. In what seemed like one movement, I hit the button to open the garage door, untied her, got 911 on speakerphone, and began performing CPR. There was no doubt as to the grim reality unfolding, as Cindy's body was completely lifeless. Her eyes opened and rolled halfway back. There was no need to spend time checking for a pulse.

As I communicated the situation to the 911 operator and gave our address, my previous training kicked in. I went about pumping her chest deeply, using the beat of the Bee Gees' song "Stayin' Alive" to pace the chest compressions. I made sure my elbows were locked, and my shoulders were above my hands so I could use my whole upper body as I pumped. After about six seconds, I tilted her head back and gave her two breaths. Looking back, I realized how much prior training helps you handle stressful situations. A healthy amount of shock must also go a long way to help one stay calm and clear-minded during the initial moments when all hell has broken loose.

Within minutes, I heard the hopeful sound of a siren growing closer and closer. A female sheriff's deputy arrived, ran up the driveway, into the garage, and pushed me back so she could take over CPR. Once the deputy took over her care and I was no longer occupied mentally and physically, the dam of emotions was freed to burst within. The initial numbing shock disappeared, and the true horrifying gravity of what was happening shot throughout my body. My whole being, spiritual and physical, was instantly flooded with all the darkness that could possibly assail a person.

You know, the oft-repeated moment in movies when a character's loved one is murdered right in front of them, and the movie goes into slow motion, and all sounds are muffled. Then the witness's face melts into an expression of tragic horror, collapsing to the ground, overcome with anguish. Well, I learned that's pretty much how it goes. It is experiential overload, and the suffering is monstrous. At that moment, chaos of the worst kind had come to my personal world. My heart immediately felt the weight of my children's entire lives, now to be lived without their mom. It was unfathomable sadness.

Then, the sound of more sirens in the distance. I ran out to the middle of the road, in an effort to guide paramedics more quickly to our house. I knew they had more lifesaving capabilities, and I wanted them there as fast as possible. I must have looked somewhat crazy in the middle of the road as I frantically waved my arms, motioning toward our house.

I then called my brother John. When he answered, all I could say with a cry was, "She hung herself, John!" He and I are very close, and he was well aware of her troubled history. It was also no secret that we were in a time of relationship breakdown because of the affair. Therefore, he was probably not entirely surprised to hear what would normally be a totally shocking statement. His immediate response wasn't to question or express any disbelief. He just said, "I am on my way down."

A few minutes later, while I was crying on the grass in the front yard, I was told "they got her heart going" and were taking her to the hospital. In addition to CPR, the paramedics had successfully used a defibrillator to restart her heart. Suddenly, there was hope. Maybe I had reached her in time, and she was going to be OK. Even though this attempt was more serious than ever, now I had hope that I had once again been able to protect her from her suicidality.

Even though it had been ten years since she made any threat or attempt, suddenly, here we were. Her terrible affliction had roared back with malevolent force. With her now still alive, things felt eerily familiar. Could it possibly be that this was just another suicidal episode in our lifelong drama? Just the same story continuing on? More suicide threats and attempts, but no one actually dying? I certainly hoped so.

Now, this dismal drama was to move to the hospital. As I was about to get into my friend Kevin's truck, I looked up. Noticing the sky, I said to him and mostly myself. "Look at the sky. It's so beautiful. How can it be so beautiful right now?" The bright blue sky with picture-perfect white clouds made me feel even more sad. It felt like an insult or careless disregard from the universe. At that moment, it just didn't make sense. The darkness that had fallen upon us seemed so all-encompassing that it should've been reflected in the sky. It should've been a gloomy gray, at the very least. More appropriate still would have been a torrential storm with stabbing lightning and roaring thunder.

On the way to the hospital, I called her family overseas. Her older brother answered, and I told him to get his mom and be prepared to support her. Not having a well-thought-out plan ahead of time, the first thing I said to her was, "She hung herself." Before I could continue on and explain that she was still alive, I heard the phone drop while her mother began to let out the saddest wails. Again, the news's impact was immediate, with no disbelief or questioning.

As her mother's cries continued in the background, her brother picked up the phone and asked what was going on. I explained what happened and that she was still alive, but in an unknown condition. The following night, I purchased plane tickets for her mother, and she was quickly at the hospital next to her daughter. Cindy's father recently had a mild stroke and wasn't in a condition to travel.

Upon arriving at the hospital, I was taken to a private waiting room while Cindy was still being stabilized in the emergency room. Some of my family were already there waiting. It also didn't take long for the leadership of the station where I worked to arrive and show their support. I don't remember saying much in that room. With no clear idea of what Cindy's condition was, what could anyone really say? I'm sure everyone, like me, was just hoping and praying that she'd be okay.

At this point, our children were still in school, completely unaware of what was happening. I thought about them a lot while sitting in that waiting room. Suddenly, I had to figure out how to care for them through this new nightmare. I started worrying about how I would talk to them about suicide, and possibly her death. Just the day before, my biggest concern had been how to talk to them about divorce. A heavy topic that now felt relatively mild. For now, arranging for them to be picked up from school and taken to a friend's house was the only immediate need. I would go to them later and have to tell them something since Mom was definitely not coming home anytime soon.

After about an hour, word came that she was stabilized on life support and now in the intensive care unit. I could finally go up and see her. We all went up to the fourth floor, and then I continued on alone to her room. When I first walked in and saw her there, I felt a calming sense of relief. The worst-case nightmare, which had seemed almost certain just hours before, was somehow avoided. She had been dead when I woke up that morning. I saw, felt, tasted, and heard death. And then, there she was, lying on the bed, miraculously alive. I was literally looking at life and order, snapped from the jaws of chaos and death.

Any relief I felt was short-lived and quickly replaced by overwhelming sadness. Anyone who walked into that room would know her condition was grave, given the amount of medical equipment all around, attached to and going into her. The most obvious being the ventilator tubing going into her mouth. There were also tubes going into her between her legs, to circulate fluid to cool her body down as part of the process to help prevent further brain damage. Then there were the more standard things like the IV going into her left wrist and the wires for all the sticky pads monitoring her vital signs.

My heart crumbled into lifeless, defeated pieces. This was the girl I had loved since she was 15, now lying there, on full life support after a completed act of self-murder. The ultimate casualty of this whole damnable mess. Nothing she did that hurt me mattered. It was just Cindy—my children's mother, the girl I had seen smile and laugh countless times. A human soul, full of value, love, and endless potential. Yet now, so broken, she had ended up in that most pitiful and tragic state.

Having a front-row seat to the destruction of a person's life is not something I would wish upon anyone. It's impossible not to be struck down by its darkness. I felt overwhelming empathy for all she must have been going through. If I knew her like I think I do, her feelings of shame, anger, loss, frustration, and sadness must have reached volcanic levels of intensity.

I placed my hands on her bare arm. She felt warm, just like any other of the countless times I had felt before. There was her chest, calmly moving up and down as if she was simply sleeping. It was so wonderful, amazing, and dreadful, all at the same time, because her future was still totally uncertain. But when there is even a glimmer of hope that your loved one may be alright; that's what you hold onto. So, I chose to believe that once again, even though this was her most frightening and dangerous act yet, she was still meant to live on. That I had found her in time, and she would make a full recovery.

I had been in many moments with her after suicidal episodes. This was a part of our life. But we had always made it through. Life always went on. This time was just more serious because the crisis leading up to this was so much more severe. It is amazing how life can teach you what really matters. The affair had been all-encompassing in my mind, but from the moment I found her in the garage, it lost all of its torturous impact. None of that mattered at all anymore. I felt only worry, compassion, empathy, love, and regret. Lots of regret.

I lied down and held onto her. It was life-restoring mercy to be able to hold her, to feel close physically and, more importantly, emotionally. The previous week had been the worst week of our lives as the disclosure of the affair wrought its havoc. And just a couple of hours earlier, I thought she was gone forever. Lying down with my arm around her was where

I would spend the majority of the following five days. I only got up to eat, use the bathroom, and go home to our kids at night.

A couple of hours later, it was time to go and talk with my kids. For parents who have children and lose a spouse to suicide, what to tell or not tell them presents a huge dilemma. There is no clear consensus on the best way to go about it. And there are different factors to consider, such as a child's age and maturity. After a lot of thought and some internet research, I decided that I would be postponing full disclosure of what happened. First of all, Cindy wasn't dead. Secondly, knowing my children and their young ages of five and seven, my heart told me that it was in their best interest not to know about any suicidal aspects for a long time.

I arrived at the house where they had been taken after school and found them happily playing with their friends. Brisa had been indulging in her friends' extensive stuffed animal and doll collection. I took a picture of her there in that room. She and her friend smiled ear to ear. I wanted to capture an image of her one last time before her peace and innocence would forever change. I kept my sadness and tears bottled up. Zuko had been playing video games with his friend. I snapped a picture of him as well, lamenting all that was about to change for him.

To talk privately, I sat with them in the back seat of my friend's truck. I told them that Mom was in the hospital because I found her on the ground, and she wasn't breathing, so I performed CPR. I told them how the paramedics got her heart beating again and took her to the hospital. I explained that we did not know if she was going to be okay or not. They obviously became very worried but remained calm.

During the next few days, while I was at the hospital, family and friends stayed at our house to care for the kids. Friends from our community brought dinner every night. The ICU waiting room was always filled to capacity with friends and family. With all they brought for us to eat, there was no need for cafeteria food. The love and support for Cindy, our children, and me was nothing less than immense. There is no doubt about the positive impact it all had. I couldn't begin to name all of the people. So, I will just say, this world is filled with beautiful ones, and in those darkest of days, their love and light helped keep me from sinking.

The next day, my family brought the kids to the hospital after school. I then took them in to see Cindy for the first time. I can't imagine what that must have been like for them. Zuko approached carefully and placed his hand on her arm and said, "Hi, mama. I love you", leaning in a little, assuming that she would have a hard time hearing him. Little Brisa was very uneasy about the whole situation and stayed clinging onto me, too afraid to get close to Cindy. It must have been overwhelming for her to see her mom like that, causing her little nervous system to go into freeze mode. When it was time to go, Zuko kissed her on the cheek and said goodbye, that he hoped she would get better and that he loved her.

After a day and a half of waiting and hoping, the official diagnosis came, and I was brought into a small conference room. The body language and faces of the doctors said it all before anyone even opened their mouth. I knew that good news was not what was about to be discussed. As they described the extent of damage to her brain, using such words as "universal," my hopes evaporated and were replaced by a sinking, dark feeling in my head, chest, and stomach. As a heavy and disorienting atmosphere enveloped my perceptions, the whole space seemed to take on a hazy, dream-like state. Even with all reason and logic, moments so dire and hopeless are difficult to process. It's so much.

Still holding onto a shred of hope, not wanting to accept a finality, I asked them to show me the brain scan images. If I was now to be the one who had to make the "hard decisions" for her, I needed to see for myself how her brain looked compared to a healthy one. They had already prepared the images. I'm sure they had this same loathsome meeting many times before with other families of brain injury patients.

They showed me the images on a large screen, pointing out the signs of how the irreparably damaged brain tissue on Cindy's scan compared to a healthy image. The difference was unmistakable. So, then it hit me fully that she wasn't going to be OK, that she wasn't ever going to wake up. The heavy feelings grew so intense that it was hard to think clearly. Something even more draining than sadness fell over me, and it felt as if the air itself was pressing down. Impossible to find words to either agree or disagree, my eyes wandered around the room before settling into the kind of stare one does when lost in thought.

The doctors continued on to explain that all indications were that she was in a full vegetative state and that was the best she could ever hope for. They told me things like, "Think about what Cindy would want," and "What kind of life would she have?"

The roller coaster of emotions had taken me from horror and despair upon the first discovery of her body, then to hope and thankfulness that she might be OK. But now, for the second time, I was losing her forever. My two children weren't getting their mom back. Even within my malaise of emotional overload, I still was able to understand that there was no "decision" to be made. The decision was made by her a day and a half earlier. Though she appeared to be just lying there sleeping in the hospital bed, it was just an illusion created by modern medical technology and pharmaceuticals. There was nothing of life left for her. The truth was, she had been gone since the morning in the garage.

Now that she was on life support, she unwittingly put me in a position to have to partner with her in choosing her death.

I will tell you. This is not a nice position to put someone in. What a stark lesson on how relationships and marriage bond two people together in profound ways. Even in the throes of death and beyond, there is enmeshment. Having to be the one to let go of her hand as she dangled over death was one of the most uniquely terrible parts of my life. As in the garage, her life was again slipping through my fingers, and again Hell was breaking loose within a still and silent room. I felt her drifting down into oblivion, and I was right next to her. With nothing to grab onto, we were like two dead leaves wafting down the shaft of a deep well.

Even though the efforts to save her life ended up being in vain, and hopes lifted only to be dashed. I'm still so grateful that modern medicine gave me the chance to spend a few more days with her. It gave me, and everyone who loved her, time to say goodbye. I talked to her a lot in that room. I spent the days holding onto Cindy and the nights holding onto the kids. As if maybe if I didn't let go of any of them, it wouldn't all fall apart.

The kids were also able to experience a more holistic journey of their mother's death. I feel that seeing her in a hospital bed a few times was a gentler and more logical ending for them, rather than if she had just virtually disappeared that morning after dropping them off at school. Every night, I went home late in the evening to be with the kids. And every night as we lie in bed, the last thing my son would ask hopefully was, "Is Momma getting better?" "No, Zuko, Mama's not doing very good." I told him as compassionately as I could. I couldn't tell them that she was going to die, but I didn't want to give them false hope either. The pain I felt in addition to what I felt for the kids, set me adrift on an ocean of dark and oppressive feelings I could never have imagined before.

At the hospital, I was asked if I would authorize the donation of Cindy's organs. I agreed to this, and it ended up dictating the time we had left with her. So, a few days later, once the organ transplant recipients arrived and were ready in nearby surgery rooms. The time came for life support to be removed. A few hours earlier, I brought the kids in to see her for the last time. They didn't know it was their final goodbye, but how could I have told them what was about to happen? Brisa, still feeling uneasy, stayed on my lap. Zuko was standing on the other side of the bed, watching her with deep concern. My sister Desiree was there, and without us knowing, she snapped a picture, capturing the scene. I guess goodbye photos can take many sad forms.

By that time, Cindy's tongue was involuntarily protruding out to one side of her mouth. And both sides of her neck had dark bruising from the strangulation trauma. So, I placed a small hand towel over that part of Cindy's mouth and neck to prevent the kids from being disturbed by the sight. She also required medication to keep her body relaxed. You knew when the medication was beginning to wear off, as her eyelids would begin to spasm, along with her left hand. I once overheard her mother talking to her family on the phone, where she described this in a quite raw and graphic way. She said that it was like when an animal is hit by a car, and as it lies there dying, it continues to twitch. In Cindy's case, this was due to the extreme damage to her brain, therefore causing her nervous system to misfire, basically like a computer glitch. When this started to happen, you wanted it to stop as fast as possible. Even for adults, the sight was highly unsettling. In addition to the fact that she hadn't woken up, it was one more piece of undeniable evidence that her body was beyond any point of return.

Shortly before the life support was removed, the nurse gave me a basic description of what to expect since I would be staying with her. They told me that once the machine that was breathing for her was removed, a few minutes later her breathing would stop, and then shortly thereafter, so would her heart. Cindy's body simply didn't know how to breathe on its own anymore. Her body would die in the same way the process had begun in the garage, by asphyxiation.

The nurses came in and administered medicine to prevent any pain. Cindy's mom softly placed her hand on Cindy's forehead and gazed at her daughter's face for the last time. She kissed her cheek and then left the room. She couldn't bear to be there for the end. Then they pulled the tube out from her mouth while I sat beside her, holding onto her left arm with both my hands.

When you are in the presence of death, when your loved one's last breaths and final heartbeats are drifting away, it is a surreal time and space. It's one of those things that can't be described. The transition from life to death, when those moments are anticipated, known, and perceived in their entirety. There is a numbing heaviness in the air. It's an extraordinary experience of severe and total presence. All you can do is hold on.

The nurses were right. Cindy seemed to be trying to breathe, but it was weak and sounded strange. I placed my phone on her stomach, playing choir hymns "Nearer my God to Thee" and "Abide with Me." Partly to hide the sounds of the dying breaths, and I guess my Christian roots were also grasping for whatever could bring comfort in these heartbreaking moments. I held onto her. I couldn't accompany her to her ultimate destination, but I'd be beside her for as far as I could go.

She was my wife and the mother of my children. I had spent 16 years living with her every day. I felt deeply responsible for her life. Even through all the ups and downs, and even seemingly unforgivable betrayal, my love for her never went away. I guess no matter what, I was still going to care for her so much, and be able to see the struggling child deep inside her. At the end, she had nothing but my empathy and compassion. I not only witnessed how her journey obliterated her sense of self. I also had the most intimate view when it cost her life itself. That final night, lying on that bed, was nothing but an innocent girl. She was a happy and sweet girl who wanted to live, but in the end, she couldn't withstand what life can do to us all, have us lose ourselves. Those who die by suicide, well, there remains no question to the degree which they became lost.

About seven minutes after life support was removed, Cindy's breathing stopped. Then, that notorious flat-line beep sang its terrible single note. The nurses immediately came in, documented the time of death, disconnected the remaining monitors, and then rolled her out of the room. Rushing her to surgery in order to give parts of her young, healthy body to other people in need. And so, at 1:30 a.m. on Valentine's Day, I found myself sitting against the wall alone in the now-empty hospital room. She was forever gone this time. That big empty space in the middle of the room where she had been appearing to sleep for the past few days was a harbinger of the hole she was going to leave in my family's life.

Death always leaves a literal emptiness in its wake. Death by suicide adds to the standard feelings of loss and grief, feelings of rejection, and abandonment. The normal grieving process is aggravated and given another level of intensity because anger, guilt, frustration, confusion, and horror all pile on. Because it wasn't old age, an accident, or disease, there is that most maddening of thoughts. That this didn't have to happen.

But it did happen, and there I was, in the ending scene. It was the end of her life, and also the end of our relationship. To say that we failed would be a gross understatement. Surely, we both wanted peace and happiness, but we lacked the wisdom and ability to overcome our challenges. Yes, we had lots of great times together, but we also struggled mightily with each other. What we built over the years was a precarious structure of disconnection, growing resentments, and complacency, all behind the façade of a long, stable marriage. The whole thing was just waiting for the right push or strong wind to blow.

When that perfect storm did arrive, and the pendulum swung toward chaos, it was breathtaking in its speed and ferocity. When Cindy suddenly found herself facing both the abrupt end of her love affair and her long marriage to me. All at once, the house of cards came crashing down on top of us. And because her suicidality still lurked within, it was less like a house of cards and more of brick, steel, and glass. The merciless collapse crushed her with barely a pause, all the way down to the grave. And due to being so intimately intertwined with her, I was not to be spared. The disaster raced outward like an avalanche, smothering me and inflicting severe wounds on everyone who was important to her.

Arriving home from the hospital, I lay down next to Zuko and embraced him as he slept. After a few minutes of holding onto him, I did the same with Brisa. She was sound asleep as well, looking just like an angel, and oblivious to the fact that her mom had just passed away. I held her close and looked at her face for a long time. This was Cindy's little creation, even looking so much like her. I realized I would always see Cindy through the children, and embracing my daughter felt like holding Cindy in some way. Lying there with them was the most comforting place I could be, knowing that a lifetime of grief was waiting for us the next day. Holding onto them felt like holding onto something good, something hopeful, something that wouldn't die. At this point, after everything—the affair, suicide, the intensive care unit, and her last breaths, I was completely exhausted. I finally fell asleep for the first full night in two weeks.

When the sun rose the next day, it was time to talk to my children. Though I would be delaying disclosure regarding the truth of how she died, there was no avoiding the reality that she was now gone. In preparation, I requested that all my family be present to support them. While everyone waited in the living room, I called Zuko into the bedroom. I sat my little boy down and did the impossible task of telling him that his mom was gone. After I sent him out and into the arms of my family, I then brought in my little girl and proceeded to break her heart as well.

I had wrestled within my mind and researched for several days leading up to telling them, trying to figure out the best way I could break it to them. I even wrote down some notes to review before talking to them. My principal intention was for them to feel comforted, loved, supported, and safe. But still, when the moment came, and that word dagger of "Mommy died Zuko" was plunged in. Well, you have never seen a child's face melt into pure anguish like one who's just been told their mother is dead. Very few images are burned into my mind, like the breaking of their faces that morning. If any part of Cindy's act was to punish me, the lashings were swift and wholly effective.

The next week was a surreal one: picking out a casket, buying a burial plot, and organizing pictures for a memorial slideshow. At the same time, my thoughts and feelings became more complicated. While she was in the hospital, the pain from the affair had vanished, as I was only worried about her, but once she was gone, it all came rushing back. So, on top of my grief, I also felt deep anger — both for the affair and for killing herself.

On the day of her funeral, it overflowed with people who loved her and will always feel the loss of her, forever wishing she didn't go. Brave little Zuko stood up in front of everyone, wearing the small black tie we hastily bought at Walmart on the way there. He spoke so sweetly and simply, expressing the gratitude and love he felt for his mom.

When it was my turn to speak, I was so overcome with grief and pain that I could barely get my voice above a whisper, struggling to say each word without beginning to cry. Without preparing any remarks, as I wasn't sure I was going to speak at all, the first words out of my mouth were, "I feel like my soul is in a storm," and the worst of it was indeed an onslaught of emotions and life-changing forces. Though the anger had returned, on that day, my heart effortlessly chose to see only her goodness, and my words were of a loving husband who lost his wife and the mother of his children.

She was unique, valuable, and loved by many people. I loved her. She was quick to smile and laugh, brightening any room she entered. She was a wonderful mother who cared deeply for our two children. I choose the comfort of believing that her love for them is somehow able to continue on in ways that could never be known or understood. After nothing else remains, at least love can endure, right? Even if it's just the love that was imparted into their heart from hers. She was just 34 years old.

PART SIX

LIFE AFTER DEATH

Cindy's death caused an emotional earthquake that changed everything for me and the kids. I loved Cindy so much, for so long, that when our 20-year bond was severed, it tore me asunder. I came to know depths of human experience I had not even fathomed prior. As I changed on the inside, my whole life on the outside changed, too. I sold my house and moved to another town where my family could help me with the kids. I received a work transfer, and my kids entered new schools. Suddenly, I found myself single after being married for so long. It was as if someone had hit the reset button on my life.

It was indeed a new beginning, but it felt nothing like a fresh start, as there were many months of severe emotional suffering still to come. The mental images of the affair and suicide wouldn't leave me alone. It felt like my peace of mind had been stolen for good, and I wondered if I'd ever feel normal again. For months, sleeping was nearly impossible. My hands always had a slight tremble, and a bitter taste lingered in the back of my throat. The sickly feeling in my stomach became just a part of life. Every terrible feeling, from rage and hate to despair and guilt, took turns continually cycling through my body.

My situation made me feel like an alien in a world filled with "normal" people. Many times, I would feel an overwhelming desire just to lie face down on the ground, right where I was, and melt into nothingness. As if the ground could just swallow me up, take away the torment, and let me rest. The trauma was profound and exhausting.

This experience makes me now wonder. The feelings I had were so intensely horrible, and yet still, I was not suicidal. So, what then must have been her feelings that made death not only an option to consider but the only option? I'm grateful I've never experienced that degree of darkness or hopelessness. However, a few years later, a divorce did end up triggering the most severe struggle of my inner life. An experience that gave me a new level of empathy for the suicidal. I came to understand, as never before, the allure of what death seems to promise: relief. Simply stopping the suffering that seems to be all that life has become. When emotional pain is severe enough, we can all become lost in it.

What a heartbreaking tragedy it is for all of those who suffer from this affliction. Make no mistake, it is an affliction, a scourge of the mind and soul. No person would choose to have suicidal ideation be part of their lives. No one would write a story about their life which ends with them killing themself. For those of us who know and love those who suffer this plight, it is a distressing and overwhelming experience. What more worry and stress could there be within a relationship than having the other person's sudden death be so constant a threat? When the danger is outside, at least you can run away, hide, or lock the door. When the enemy resides within, there is little respite from fear.

The whole experience was a nightmare, and that's from me, the one who survived. Cindy never got to wake up from it.

There was no future for her where things could get better. A time when she could look back and say, "Wow, I'm so glad that's over, and I'm so grateful for where I am now." After experiencing all the suffering that preceded and then followed Cindy's suicide. I became passionate about helping as many people as possible avoid such a fate. My desire to understand her, what happened, heal myself, and support my children all led me to dive deep into this issue. My journey was fueled by an insatiable desire to learn and grow in the most important parts of life.

Life is too short and valuable to be allowed to languish in an unresolved state. No matter what happens in this uncertain life, we all deserve to be happy and live fully. After chaos and destruction, there's always a chance for renewal and growth. As long as there is life, there is possibility. There is always goodness to be found and hope to hold on to.

A crucial part of my healing journey was seeking knowledge about all things most consequential for my well-being. It was obvious that things went terribly wrong for me and Cindy. So, I read, listened to podcasts, and watched videos of experts on topics such as suicide, psychology, childhood trauma, health, relationships, affairs, breakups, philosophy, masculinity, and femininity. Combined with my personal experience, the learning gifted me so much clarity with regard to all I was going through and how Cindy and I ended up as we did.

It is easy to see the shortcomings in others. But if I was ever to be able to forgive myself and regain peace, I would also need to recognize my own negative impact in the relationship. She and I both played a part in creating our situation. We were both operating under belief systems about ourselves and relationships that did not serve us well. Looking back, it's clear that we made many mistakes along the way, many of which are all too common for a lot of people.

A huge initial mistake was how I chose to move forward with dating her, much less marry her, after discovering she had very serious emotional issues. Thinking that I was mature enough, coupled with my "white-knight syndrome," I foolishly took on the responsibility of her well-being as her husband. I did not find out about her suicidality, however, until shortly after we were married.

I, at age 22, and she, 18, were both beyond unwise to get married, being so young and also so completely inexperienced with relationships. I was her very first boyfriend, and I just had a few girlfriends as a teenager. Never anything resembling a serious long-term relationship.

I also wasn't embodying a healthy masculine energy within the relationship. I did not lead with the enduring and confident masculine energy she needed. I had been taught to believe that if I just did everything I was "supposed to," became her "everything," and always put her needs first, I would receive love, affection, and appreciation in return. However, being her doormat did not inspire respect, loyalty, or attraction from her. So, when, despite all my best efforts, she was regularly unhappy and detached, I became resentful, complained, and would withdraw.

Many of us men live in great incongruency with who we really are. Healthily masculine in our lives outside the home, but feminized in a very unhealthy way within relationships. You know, the whole "she is my better half," "happy wife, happy life," and "she wears the pants in the house" unhealthy, weak, submissive husband dynamic. This ends up being to everyone's detriment. Women report being happier when they have a solid, healthy masculine partner they can respect, admire, trust, and desire. Due to his inner strength, stability, competence, and sense of purpose, she is enabled to feel at her best with him.

Compounding our problems, Cindy mostly expressed a more masculine energy. She did not embody the life-giving feminine traits of flow, compassion, nurturing, supportiveness, and sensuality, which I needed from her. Many women today are living out of harmony with their feminine natures, which also negatively affects their relationships and personal well-being. Modern life has resulted in many conditions that lead women to embody many masculine traits within their relationships. The demands of work and feminized men, to name just a couple of reasons.

Both of us equally contributed to a negative feedback loop that was not uplifting for either of us. It was like we were the same poles of a magnet, pushing each other away. Instead of mutually supporting and uplifting each other's core beings, we spiraled ever downward into disharmony and frustration. This underlying problem contributed significantly to our downfall. Obviously not the only reason, but a significant one. No matter how much people want to imagine the world differently, the laws of sexual dynamics are unavoidable.

Cindy also had an irrational and extreme possessiveness and jealousy. I lived constantly walking on eggshells so as not to offend this jealousy. It was humiliating, and I resented it deeply. It crippled her ability to assimilate and integrate after moving here from a foreign country, as she chose to see every other woman as a threat. Learning about borderline personality disorder and how one of its universal traits is a deep fear of abandonment made me realize where the jealousy and need for control came from. In her final years, she did find a sense of community at her gym, which helped with her loneliness. But it turned out to be a double-edged sword; it gave her social connection, but it's also where she got involved in the affair.

Cindy's engagement in an affair was, in hindsight, not surprising, nor would it have been if it had been me. Our relationship had so much discord, and something had to change. An affair is not the healthiest way to bring about change, but it's still something. Sometimes, anything is better than feeling stuck and hopeless. But when we act without wisdom and outside of integrity, the change is almost always going to be a more painful experience than it has to be. And it likely won't give us the result we are really looking for.

Setting aside any moral or social judgments about her affair. At some fundamental level, she wanted to extend beyond the boundaries of the normal order of her life. People crave change and expansion, and for good reasons. How one goes about making changes and living out an expanding life is where we make our most important judgement calls. When someone engages in an affair, they are often looking more for a new sense of self than they are an abandonment of their existing partner or a particular sexual experience with the new person. She was not at peace with herself. The affair was her way of being someone different from who she was, and an opportunity to find whatever feelings she was searching for. Unfortunately for Cindy, how she chose to experience something new ended up resulting in a change that was too extreme and too painful for her to handle.

Although I couldn't have known it in the beginning, the catastrophe that was my wife's death also became the catalyst for me to look inward as never before. When your sense of the world falls apart, it makes you question everything, even who you are. When she died, a lot of who I was went with her. So much of who we are is a complex combination of information, beliefs, conditionings, habits, and ideas that were virtually programmed into us as we developed from birth. Much positive and helpful, but along with it came varying degrees of awful things. This is inevitable, and usually, no one does this to us with an insidious agenda to make us into a person we are not happy being. It is just the nature of life.

All of us have problems unique to our journey, but we all share the same foundational struggles. Finding ourselves, overcoming difficulty, and healing our hearts and minds. In other words, living more in alignment with our highest self. Eckhart Toll's words speak wisdom we all would do well internalizing. *"You can use a challenge to awaken you, or you can allow it to pull you into even deeper sleep."* Life, a great life at least, *is* the journey of waking up. Going from total helplessness and ignorance at birth into a confused, and damaged young person, and progressively becoming more truly you. Present, aware, and consciously creating the life you want.

To the depressed, suicidal, and all those who are suffering:

The greatest aim of this book is to help you wake from the nightmare, the shadow over your being, and the lies you have come to believe about yourself and about life. If this is you, you know exactly what I'm talking about. All that oppressive and draining weight you feel. This misery isn't going to be your life, and it's definitely not going to be your undoing. Your journey will be of one who travelled the darkest roads and felt the emptiness of death before it even arrived. Your story will be about someone who went through all of this and still kept going. You'll wake up from the lies, rise from the darkness, and experience sweet feelings of life that few others could know. If you make *life* your intention, this will be you.

Now, let's cut right into the depth of this matter and go far beyond any dry, clinical talk or superficial anecdotes. Let's journey into the black hole that is self-inflicted death. Then let's emerge out from the darkness and into life.

SECTION ONE

UNDERSTANDING SUICIDE

CHAPTER ONE

WHAT IS THIS?

*"To understand suicide is one of the absolutely fundamental
and puzzling challenges of the human condition."*

-Maris, 1981

The BIGGEST SECRET TO UNDERSTANDING SUICIDE IS
THAT THERE IS NEVER ARRIVING AT A FULL UNDERSTANDING.
To understand even a small piece of someone who is still alive
is an elusive thing. How much more impossible than to
understand someone who is gone? Even understanding
ourselves is a never-ending journey. This is just one of the
difficult truths about suicide that we must accept. Attaining full
clarity, whether it's about those who are continually depressed,
suicidal, or those who have already passed, can never be
achieved. Arriving at an acceptance of things as they are is
ultimately an inextricable part of dealing with any issue.

With that said, still, an enormous amount of understanding
can be had. And in the case of an issue as highly impactful as
suicidality. Every shred of understanding and wisdom is
extremely helpful to all. Whether you are suffering suicidality,
care about someone who is, or have lost someone. Personally,
dealing with suicidality in any way heaps an enormous weight

upon your back. It's bone and soul-buckling stress and pressure. With any little piece of understanding gained, some amount of this weight can fall away.

I felt this relief in real time as I explored and sought understanding. There were other major keys to liberation as well, such as the simple passage of time and acts of self-care. But as a loss survivor, understanding suicide itself made a huge difference for me. For those who are suffering suicidal thoughts and urges, understanding sheds light on what is happening within them and what the impacts on others are.

Suicide, as it is discussed in this book, is defined as the willful ending of one's own life. For those with severe mental illness, the term "willful" becomes somewhat problematic. How much do their mental struggles affect their ability to truly *decide* to take their own life? While I'm not professionally qualified to diagnose someone's mental state, I believe common sense suggests that people with extremely severe mental health issues aren't fully capable of making a "willful" decision to end their lives. Their self-inflicted deaths, of course, are officially still classified as suicides. But for the sake of more clarity, perhaps the suicides of those with debilitating mental illness could be designated as a distinct class.

The other class of suicide, which is the kind this book more specifically applies to, but not exclusively, are those suicides in which the victims live the majority of their lives mentally normal, capable, and stable. Even those diagnosed as bipolar, depressed, borderline personality, anti-social, and the like fall into this second category, being those who are much more clearly capable of rational decision-making. Yes, these people have emotional struggles, but they are capable of controlling themselves and successfully navigating their mental and emotional issues. The vast majority of these people are far from insane, delusional, schizophrenic, or any other of the much more severe conditions. They live lives full of all the normal things people do. They attend school, socialize, pursue hobbies, maintain careers, get married, have children, retire, and so on. We work with them, sit next to them in church, and laugh together at parties.

Suicide for those who are by far normal functioning people can more appropriately be classified as "willful." When these people carry out their suicides, it is commonly in reaction to difficult life events. Some type of crisis event or multiple events combine with underlying suicidal risk factors and result in a catastrophic downward spiral. In other words, as long as life is happening in an acceptable enough way for them, a plunge into suicide is not a threat. It is significant traumas and life difficulties that trigger their loss of self. Some of these are the ones people talk about in the aftermath, saying, "I had no idea." It is these people that this book is most going to help, and "these people" can really be any of us.

Optimistically, the phrase you hear most associated with this topic is "suicide prevention." Preventing or eliminating all suicides is a lofty and noble goal. In fact, the term "suicide prevention" is used so much that it creates a perception that it is an issue with a specific cure waiting to be discovered or that it is a problem we could ultimately eradicate. Unfortunately, this idea would be akin to believing there could also be some type of perfect solution to end, once and for all, alcoholism, anger, murder, depression, or any other undesirable issue.

There are many ways to help and support someone who is suicidal, but this issue, like other struggles, is a common part of being human. Suicide and similar challenges aren't going away. The only thing we can do is get better at loving and supporting ourselves and others who are suffering, lifting each other to a better place.

From time immemorial, across every culture and place, self-killing has been with us. Suicide has been studied, analyzed, and thought deeply about for a very long time. Surely, even long before writing was invented to record their thoughts, people were pondering this horrible thing that took their loved ones away, never to return. The ancient Greeks have philosophized about it from the days of Plato, and it continued into the so-called Age of Enlightenment with the likes of Sigmund Freud, and the questions continue to this day. What has always been a scourge to the human experience and a philosophical puzzle about life and death has become, as we now see it, an urgent public health issue.

We humans are problem solvers. It's what we do best, and it's how we've created a world of such comfort, convenience, and almost magical technology. For us, letting human beings kill themselves is not an acceptable state of affairs. What more terrible, consequential, and urgent problem could there possibly be than our loved ones' lives ending at their own hands? Apart from some debates in regard to the terminally ill, this problem isn't divisive like many of the big political issues. It's a problem we all see as worth coming together about.

And as such, the fields of study that seek to understand and attempt to contribute to remedying this issue make up no small list. Among them are philosophers, cultural historians, anthropologists, sociologists, psychologists, spiritualists of all types, evolutionists, and, more recently, neurobiologists and geneticists. All have used their unique expertise in the search for answers and solutions.

Religious, cultural, and political interest in suicide has also been intense throughout human history, with much variation in how suicide has been thought about and handled. Suicide has been classified as a grave sin in many religions. For example, in Christian culture, people who died by suicide were once denied burial in cemeteries. Instead, they were buried at a crossroads with a stake driven through their heart. And as if that wasn't enough, they were also condemned to eternal hellfire. How comforting is that for the families?! On the opposite end of the spectrum, there have been other cultures that have viewed certain suicides in a positive, even honorable light, such as in the Japanese samurai culture.

In terms of the law, in the not-too-distant past, suicide was a criminal offense, and those who survived attempts were imprisoned and fined. Can you imagine if this were the case today? Your son or daughter wakes up in the hospital after a suicide attempt and is then questioned by a police investigator in preparation for criminal charges! Understandably, humanity in general has seen suicide as a serious problem with many negative connotations. Usually considered taboo, wrong, shameful, and selfish.

Thankfully, as time and knowledge have progressed, we have come to understand so much more about ourselves regarding suicide. Superstition, fear, and ignorance no longer dominate the issue. Advancements in biology and psychology have unlocked many mysteries about human behavior. We understand more about the relevant social and relational dynamics at play and the effects experienced by suicide-loss survivors. We know that it can occur as the ending of long-term emotional deterioration or more spontaneously and impulsively. It affects all, sparing no specific group of people. It's as if the seed is there inside all of us.

Although the outcome is the same, the path toward and the way people take their own lives can be very different. From the outside, it might seem like it was coming for a long time or something completely unexpected. Even if there's a clear catalyst, suicide is still always a mix of psychological, biological, and social factors. None of us is so simple. Though we would all want to believe this issue can be remedied once and for all. It will be with us for as long as humans exist, with all our complex minds, bodies, and emotions in a world of chaos and order. Accepting that suicide is a ubiquitous part of human experience is not a comfortable thing to accept. But really healing and accepting the loss of someone we love will be supported by knowing, really internalizing, and accepting that this kind of thing happens; it just does.

The scope of suicides' impact is immense. Beyond the tens of thousands that do kill themselves every year. Millions more struggle with significant suicidal ideation and attempts. In addition to the 44,834 people who died by suicide in 2020, a study that year by the Substance Abuse and Mental Health Services Administration revealed that in the U.S.:

Adults

- 12.2 million had serious thoughts of suicide.
- 3.2 million made plans to kill themselves.
- 1.2 million attempted suicide. In 2023, attempts rose to 1.5 million.

Youths Age 12 to 17

- 3 million had serious thoughts of suicide.
- 1.3 million made a suicide plan.
- 629,000 attempted suicide. In 2023, youth suicide attempts rose to 856,000.

As these statistics show, completed suicides are just the tip of the iceberg when it comes to the magnitude of the suffering out there. In 2018, there were 312,000 emergency department visits for self-harm injuries.

The person who commits suicide is, in the end, a tragic victim. A victim of their own hand, but undeniably, also due to some inherited biology and surely countless impacts from their environment, possibly going all the way back to the womb. Some of us will personally confront suicidal desires. Some of us will be the ones left behind to mourn the tragedy and pick up the pieces.

Even though ending suicide once and for all would be impossible. It does not mean, however, that we will ever give up on our efforts to prevent this tragedy at every opportunity. A difference can be made, and there is much to be hopeful about. People can receive life-saving behavioral health care support, and there are effective ways to get through times of severe suicidal crisis.

Most importantly, we all can develop and enjoy a personal experience of well-being such that suicide ceases to have anything to do with our lives. It's a matter of learning and then practicing what empowers one to live a thriving life. We will start to see suicide rates drop as more people learn to build lives of true well-being. If the rates go down, it means thousands of people will live who might not have otherwise. Each of those lives is incredibly valuable and miraculous. Saving even one life is beyond priceless and beautiful. I feel euphoric just imagining the countless moments of life they would be able to go on to experience. The love and goodness they will be able to continue to exchange with the world. All of which would have disappeared if they had died.

CHAPTER TWO

WHY?

THE BIGGEST QUESTION LOVED ONES HAVE IS, WHY? Our minds desperately want to make sense of any act as extreme and destructive as suicide. However, we have all had to consider the meaning of our existence and question whether life is worth living. But these doubts rarely linger for long. For those who are not suicidal, the idea of someone actually following through with the act is difficult to understand. The continuance of our lives is usually a fundamental priority, if not the absolute highest. So, how can this become so completely reversed for someone?

Suicide is never so simple as to be able to point to one single issue being the cause. It is always a combination of various underlying risk factors and then the right, or better stated, *wrong* event that combines to wreak havoc on the victim's heart, mind, and body. If not immediately known, with time, many of these contributing factors may be revealed if you are willing to look. The most prominent risk factors will be talked about in Chapter 3. Gaining any helpful wisdom about suicide starts with understanding these risk factors.

As we search to understand some of the *whys* for suicide, we acknowledge again that suicide is an exceptionally complex issue. There will always remain unanswered questions. Still, what we can make sense of, what can be understood, is invaluable information. Any bits of clarity we can gather are like precious jewels for the soul. An at-risk person comes to understand themselves better and what is happening within them. For those offering support to someone in crisis or helping loved one's cope with loss, greater understanding fosters awareness, hope, healing, and a sense of peace. Conversely, a lack of understanding fuels confusion, frustration, anger, guilt, and fear.

Of the many factors that contribute to suicidality, it is apparent that the genesis of this inclination towards death is that a certain belief system takes root in the person at some point. A belief that killing oneself is a desirable response to suffering. That dying is an acceptable solution to escape from pain. When, where, how, and why this belief system became adopted by any given person would be unique to them. Nonetheless, the glaring distinction between people who kill themselves and those who do not is an adoption of this self-destructive belief system. For the overwhelming majority of us, suicidal thoughts are transient and never evolve into anything serious. For the suicidal, thoughts of killing themselves become more persistent.

Rarely does a suicide happen seemingly out of nowhere. There will usually be some observable reason or motivation for the act. When a suicide involves a severe mental health issue, there is usually less guilt and less agonizing over *why*, as it is easier to accept that mental illness eliminated or at least drastically reduced the person's capacity to think and act rationally. However, it's important to clarify, so as to prevent unnecessary concern, that even the vast majority of people living with depression or other mental health challenges do not ultimately die by suicide. It is just that among suicides, they have the overwhelmingly highest representation.

It is important to understand that personality disorders are not always what the mainstream makes them out to be. What we often call a mental health disorder is, many times, simply a person whose body and mind are in a state of chaos due to negative impacts from outside themselves and detrimental belief systems within them. They may have unhealed past trauma or be experiencing ongoing trauma. The result is being stuck in a loop of fight or flight, and the ensuing mental and physical stress. The world in which we live can do an incredibly effective job of wreaking havoc on our hearts, minds, and bodies, something we will discuss in more detail a little later.

Countless people are not really doomed to live forever with a "personality disorder" or depression, along with endless dependence on medication. Many people experiencing mental and emotional distress are fully capable of healing and living at their best. In the final section, we will explore some of the most effective strategies for achieving this.

I would also adamantly argue that the normally mentally healthy person who commits suicide ultimately reached a significantly disturbed mental and emotional state. In the end, they 100% suffered from a mental health crisis and breakdown. Suicide could be fairly described as the most tragic and destructive mental health condition one can experience. This truth is very important and helpful for suicide-loss survivors. To know that the victim did not have a sound, healthy mind at the time of suicide and, in reality, reached a horrifically afflicted state. A state that we have never experienced and never will unless we fall victim in the same way.

Let's make clear early on that anyone with a mental health problem should be receiving professional care, whether suicidal or not. If you know someone who needs care but isn't receiving it, your top priority should be helping them access the support they need. Studies estimate that 80-90% of individuals who seek treatment for depression experience successful outcomes.

As soon as I knew there were serious mental health issues affecting Cindy, I should have been more encouraging, persistent, and persuasive in seeing that she received professional help. Obviously, I deeply regret that she did not receive the help she surely could have benefited from. No outcome can be guaranteed, but professional care should be the foundation.

There are several predominant risk factors for suicide, which we will explore in the following chapter. The most dangerous is when depression is combined with substance abuse. These two problems often seem to go hand in hand. When someone struggles with one, the other often follows closely behind. Those suffering from depression may turn to drugs or alcohol in a desperate search for relief, while substance abuse frequently leads to depression as addiction takes a toll on their life and well-being. Depression and substance abuse make a vicious partnership that only knows how to travel in one direction, downwards.

Suicides are hard to top when it comes to tragic life events. But, in the case of a "murder-suicide", the nightmare is surely taken to another level. This is when someone's personal "why" for death combines with hate, blame, and contempt for others. The most common occurrences are when, before killing himself, a man kills a female partner because of jealousy or because she has left or is threatening to leave the relationship. We all hear about murder-suicides of the more notorious kind.

Those involving mass killings followed by the perpetrator's suicide. Approximately 40 per cent of mass shooters commit suicide.

Consensual murder-suicide also occurs within groups. History is sprinkled with this type of event within religious groups and so-called cults. In 1978, 909 people lost their lives in the tragic Jonestown Massacre. The group, known as the People's Temple, died in a mass murder-suicide orchestrated by their leader. Among the victims, one-third were children.

Murder-suicides also occur among desperate people who see it as a preferable alternative to an impending threat, such as when capture, torture, enslavement, or murder appear imminent. Such as when a family or even a population chooses to kill their children and then themselves to avoid what is believed to be a worse outcome.

Recognizing the reality of murder-suicides is important in any discussion about suicide. At the very least, its victims should not be overlooked. While it can offer insights into potential "whys" in some cases, suicides involving murder are a more rare and distinct phenomenon, making up only a small percentage. Therefore, we will not delve deeply into this topic. I will, however, express my deepest sympathy for those who have suffered the impact of something so extraordinarily heinous and heart-rending.

There is evidence that genetics plays a role in suicide, though very little in this field of study is conclusive. Childhood trauma and traumatic experiences are known to raise a person's risk. There are, of course, social and cultural influences. There is even a contagion effect for suicide at the familial and societal levels. Well-documented "clusters" of suicides have occurred all over the world. As humans, we learn virtually all of our behaviors through observation and imitation, and it is no different when it comes to suicidal behavior.

Cindy recounted to me once that when she was very young, around seven years old, she saw firsthand two deceased suicide victims she knew in her neighborhood while the bodies were still unmoved. One was a young boy hanging from a tree, and later, a man who hung himself in a bathroom. Clearly, these are experiences no young, impressionable child should ever witness. Seeing such events undoubtedly had a deep impact on her developing mind, making suicide feel unexpectedly real and tangible. Her young brain must have received the message, "This is something people do when they are upset." "This is a way of dealing with hard, uncomfortable feelings and experiences."

No matter who we are or where we grow up, we will all be exposed to suicide in some way. We will hear about it or see it portrayed on TV. But when it's up close and personal. That surely has a different level of impact. That is traumatic and, therefore, affects the mind deeply. In the same way children shouldn't be exposed to sexual matters at an underdeveloped age; suicide is also an issue far beyond the maturity level of a child. Regarding the darkness of suicide, a child would be well served to remain innocent until a more developed age.

Several days after Cindy died, her mother recounted to me that when Cindy was around nine years old, about two years after she had witnessed the two suicides. That one night, after a heated argument with her brother over dinner, she stormed out to the backyard. A few minutes later, her mother went outside to check on her and found Cindy tying a rope to a tree branch, preparing to hang herself. Was this a case of contagion? It's clear that what she witnessed at such a young age must have had some effect of normalizing the act in her mind.

So, what is it exactly that people are trying to accomplish by suicide? According to suicide notes, the two main reasons given for suicide are an escape from mental and emotional pain and from what is perceived as an unbearable situation. At its core, despite all possible explanations, it ultimately comes down to an experience of pain.

Among the various fields of study that have sought to uncover the deepest "why" behind the connection between pain and suicide in humans. The most insightful understanding comes from evolutionary psychology and biology. It's simple yet profoundly enlightening. Chapter 33 will cover this paradigm-shifting wisdom in detail. So, hold that thought.

Understanding our relationship with pain is one of the most important ways we can overcome suicide. Instead of reacting unconsciously to pain and hurting our lives more, we can respond to our pain with awareness and instead use it as a catalyst for positive change.

I, too, felt this strong need to understand why Cindy killed herself. I ultimately reached a point where I felt I had a good grasp of what happened. However, in the end, they are still only my personal conclusions and, therefore, may contain inaccuracies and missing pieces. If only the dead could speak, as they say. However, in one sense, the suicidal dead do have a voice. All those who have been fortunate enough to survive lethal attempts are truly messengers from the other side of suicide. People who fully committed to taking that leap, but somehow survived, are the closest thing we have to speaking to a dead suicide victim. They confirm the same thing revealed in the notes. It comes down to pain and hopelessness.

In Cindy's case, I looked at everything possible, putting as many pieces together as I could. Interestingly, at the time of her death, I had been assigned to an investigative task force for the previous two years. Skills I put to good use in order to find out everything I could. I conducted a thorough personal investigation. Much was indeed left behind to discover and analyze. But first and foremost, I had my experience of 16 years of marriage to her. This, of course, entailed being privy to all her past suicidal behavior and her general lack of healthy emotional regulation. I got important information from her mother regarding the earliest instances of suicidal behavior that happened long before I knew her. A few days before Cindy took her life, I swallowed my pride for a few minutes and spoke by phone with her ex-lover to learn the details of their relationship. I also had conversations with her closest friends and others she interacted with in her final days.

With some creativity and persistent effort, I obtained the password to her phone without her knowing, the very night before her suicide. At the time, I was motivated by the need to understand the affair. But after her suicide, the contents took on a new level of importance. The messages on her phone gave deeper insight into her affair and the pain it ultimately caused her. I saw her raw thoughts and emotions, which I otherwise would not have known.

Because of all these efforts, I was able to get quite a clear picture of the final days leading up to the end. I took everything I knew about Cindy and then looked at it through the prism of what I had learned about suicide from the experts. The following is my basic summation of the "whys" for Cindy's suicide:

1. The clearest and most dire issue was that she had **suffered from suicidal ideation** from a young age. It was something that took hold within her and never left.

2. For as long as I knew her, she exhibited all the symptoms of **borderline personality disorder**, which are all significant risk factors for suicide, particularly for women. For people with traits of BPD, episodes of suicidal crisis are highly linked to relationship problems.

Cindy fit this pattern perfectly. When the fallout from the affair happened, it took only one week for her to spiral down into suicide.

3. She experienced a self-inflicted **major life crisis and trauma**. The simultaneous end of her love affair and our long marriage. This was a nuclear emergency-level crisis for her and her lifetime struggle with suicidality.

4. I later learned of one other significant event, which was clearly adding to her suffering at the end. A few months prior, Cindy had become pregnant. Not knowing who the father was, combined with not wanting to conceive, she chose to have an abortion. The tremendous guilt and shame she felt for this was expressed by two social media posts just days before she took her life. One post pictured a tiny baby cradled in two hands, and what she wrote spoke of a baby as the greatest victim in the affair. A day later, another post stated, "I already know I am going to hell, but I'm not going alone because I'm taking (lover's name) with me."

It's no secret that an abortion can be an extremely traumatic event for the mother. Very often resulting in all the symptoms of post-traumatic stress disorder. Studies show higher rates of psychiatric hospitalization during the four years following an abortion. Teenagers, divorced and separated women with a history of more than one abortion, are at even greater risk of significant psychiatric problems. Pointing right to the issue at hand are studies showing that approximately 60 percent of women who experience negative psychological effects post-abortion report suicidal ideation, with 28 percent actually making an attempt.

No matter what your personal stance on abortion may be, there is no debating the detrimental effects it can have on a woman. In Cindy's case, it represents one more piece of the puzzle. Was it the sole reason or even the most significant? No, clearly, her final breakdown was due to the ending relationships. But fires take multiple pieces of kindling to ignite, and buildings take multiple explosions to be demolished.

5. She **lacked the self-worth** and **emotional maturity** necessary for resiliency during difficult times.

6. Many of her actions and words in the final week were indicative of intense **anger**. Anger is understood to be a secondary emotion. This means that there are deeper emotions underlying the anger. For Cindy, I believe that **sadness**, **shame**, and **fear** fueled her anger. Unable or unwilling to confront and address these emotions, she suppressed them beneath a layer of rage. For a few days, all this negative energy was focused on her ex-lover. She posted various dark messages on her social media, referring to him cryptically and outright. Her post talking about going to hell, but that she was going to take her ex-lover with her, made morbidly clear just how dark her rage was becoming.

After her passing, I discovered a small kitchen knife in her purse — something she had never carried before. I truly believe that, had she thought she could succeed, she would have used it to harm him. But he was a very strong man with S.W.A.T. team training, and she must have known she would not have been able to get the better of him with only a small knife. Thankfully, my guns were locked away. I had decided long before that she was never going to be able to have access to those, no matter how many years passed without suicidal issues. So, consumed by her intense frustration and anger, I think she did what she thought she could do to hurt him and took herself out instead. I have no doubt that revenge and punishing him played some factor in what she did.

7. I believe she mostly wanted to **punish herself** while simultaneously **ending all of her intense pain**. When the affair was revealed, she must have felt utterly ashamed and humiliated. Prior to disclosure, she had maintained a reputation as an honorable and faithful wife and mother. She was the apple of her family's eye and must have known they would be devastated over the affair and imminent divorce.

8. She got **extreme tunnel vision** due to all her inner chaos and pain. It seems clear that she lost all hope for a decent future. She had little patience for any situation in life that was uncomfortable for her or out of her control. The pain of this experience became intolerable for her. I believe she reached a state of mind where suicide was the only solution she was able to see.

9. She had **hardly slept** for the past several days and was **abusing THC edibles**. As I dealt with Cindy's personal belongings a few weeks after her death, I discovered the edibles hidden in the bottom of her gym bag. It turns out there were other big secrets besides just the affair. For an already emotionally disturbed person, anything that further impairs their rational and clear mind is very often a deadly additional ingredient to a stew of pain and distress already at the boiling point.

10. She felt she was **a burden**. I know she hated how she regularly felt. And she must have also been aware of

how her behavior so regularly resulted in problems and conflict over the many years, with the impending divorce being chief among them. She likely convinced herself that she was such a problem that others would be better off if she were gone.

11. Many other **prominent underlying risk factors for suicide** were present as well, such as **isolation** at the end, an **impulsive and violent nature,** she **did not seek mental health care support,** had an **obsessive need for control,** and she had several **previous attempts.**

During the week of her worst life crisis, with her body drowning in stress hormones, and her soul tormented with abandonment and self-hate. She eventually released all this sickening energy in the unhealthiest way she knew how, through violence against herself. It's devoid of any humor when I say that she could literally be the poster child for having had virtually all suicidal risk factors lined up against her.

While escaping emotional and mental pain is the common thread linking all suicides, there are always other unique reasons behind each one. Understanding these will help those struggling with suicidality gain clearer insight into their experiences, enabling them to address the root issues more effectively. Answers to "why" are highly important for loss survivors in their healing journey, and the next chapter is going to provide even more. Reading this book means that you are taking action to move in the direction of understanding. The more you have, the better you will feel.

As you continue your search, remember that some things will always remain unknown. At some point, when you find yourself completely exhausted in the effort, allow yourself to lay the issue down. In a very real sense, leaving the dead to rest while you get busy living again.

CHAPTER THREE

RISK FACTORS

As WE EXPLORE THE MOST COMMON RISK FACTORS FOR SUICIDE, it is important to understand that most suicides occur with those who have severe depression and substance abuse disorders. However, conditions such as bipolar disorder, anxiety, trauma-related disorders, and other personality disorders (borderline and antisocial) also raise a person's risk for suicide significantly. Individuals with mood disorders, for instance, are about 25 times more likely to die by suicide compared to the general population. These suicides still often involve multiple underlying risk factors and typically occur in the context of a crisis event.

Other Risk Factors

- Previous suicide attempt
- Impulsive nature/behavior
- Aggressive/violent behavior
- History associated with abuse or trauma
- Family history of suicide
- Social isolation

- Overwhelming feelings of hopelessness
- Obsessive need for control
- Recent discharge from a psychiatric facility
- Drug and Alcohol Abuse

Drug abuse and alcoholism are particularly detrimental for a person who suffers from suicidal ideation. They inevitably add to one's problems while also decreasing inhibition. Inflicting a devastating one-two punch. In other words, the complications brought on by addiction lead to increased emotional pain. While reduced inhibition diminishes their ability to make thoughtful decisions. There's no doubt that mind-altering substances have often played a crucial role in whether someone followed through on suicidal thoughts or not. People do all kinds of things while intoxicated that they otherwise wouldn't do sober. In the US, alcohol use is indicated as a factor in a quarter of all suicides.

Common Catalysts

- Major physical illness (chronic physical pain)
- Grave relationship issue (divorce, breakup, affair, death in family, etc.)
- Serious job or financial problems
- Personal loss of significance
- Serious legal issue
- Loss of sense of belonging
- Seeing oneself as a burden or failure
- Overwhelming guilt, shame, anger, or humiliation

Additional Detrimental Factors

- Access to highly lethal means (guns, prescription drugs, illegal drugs, etc.)
- Lack of health care support
- Sleep deprivation
- Influence from other suicides
- Cultural belief honoring suicide
- Factors that impede seeking support, such as shame, reputation, career ramifications, and ego.

This list of risk factors and catalysts is by no means all-encompassing, as suicidal behavior can have complex underlying causes. These are simply understood to be some of the most prevalent. To make this information more useful, think about it this way. When someone with any degree of suicidality and has any number of these risk factors, who then experiences a triggering event, it's time to stay vigilant. This is a time to take proactive steps in suicide prevention and to prioritize overall well-being.

What are the feelings that accompany suicidal thoughts? It's shame, humiliation, angst, guilt, despair, rejection, loneliness, anger, self-deprecation, and burdensomeness. All of these feelings cause psychological pain, which then results in physical pain. People who have survived serious attempts often report that it wasn't about wanting to die; it was really about escaping emotional pain so extreme and seemingly unresolvable that death became the only answer they could see.

If we look even deeper, all of their suffering is indicative of a problem with being itself. With the person's experience of the *self*. Regardless of the individual circumstances, the person who dies by suicide ultimately lost their sense of self-worth and no longer valued their existence. This crushing loss of self-worth and complete devaluation of life is the difference between those who experience devastating difficulties and still choose life and those who do not. Even someone who commits suicide for the reason of putting an end to their physical pain still ultimately made the decision that their life wasn't valuable enough to continue, despite the pain. This holds true even for someone who takes their life with the intention of providing financial benefit to their family. Financial concerns became more important than their own life. Even when people commit suicide because they truly believe that others will be better off with them gone. Still, the underlying issue in every case is that the suicide victim lost grasp of their own value.

A person who chooses suicide comes to believe that life is not worth the struggle. Their sense of self-worth and resilience runs out. The challenges of life came to define their experience and how they saw themselves. What happened or didn't happen, what they had or didn't have defined whether their life experience was good or bad, worthwhile or not, rather than being defined by who they truly were. We are all vulnerable to falling into this pattern of thinking. To be led by the world instead of our own beings. And this world has an infinite number of ways to assail us everywhere it matters most.

Societal conditioning leads us to operate under the following detrimental belief system. It's known as the "do, have, be" psychological schema. If I do X, I will have Y, then I will be Z. Don't worry, this isn't algebra; that's all the letter equations were going to do, I promise. Let's look at a couple of examples of what this looks like: "If I *go* to college, I will *have* a good job, and then I will *be* happy." Or. "When I *fall* in love and get married, I will *have* the life I want, and I will *be* fulfilled." The fatal flaw with this type of thinking is that it ties your well-being to what you do or have and as opposed to who you simply are.

This disempowering formulaic thinking works in regard to negative experiences as well. Example: "I *lost* my job, now I *have* no income, and I *am* ashamed." Or "If my wife *leaves* me, I will *have* no family, and I will *be* miserable." Or "My life *is not* how I wanted it to be; I *have* lost hope; I *am* a failure."

This core psychological operating system is highly detrimental because it allows things that are naturally chaotic, out of our control, and very often negative to determine our well-being. A belief system that would truly serve us is one that shifts the order to "be, do, have." "I *am* worthy and happy. I will *do* everything I can to *create* the life I desire." With this perspective, personal well-being and self-worth form the foundation. What you *do* or what you *have* never eclipse who you are.

While it is important to understand the various risk factors and catalysts. We need to see the bigger picture and understand the deeper issues with a suicidal individual. This enables one to be better able to address the root causes. Being impacted by hard life circumstances to the point that a person chooses death over life is the result of their own being and their own existence coming second to what they do, have, or experience. Becoming a mentally and emotionally healthy person is attained and maintained by choosing mindsets and value systems about yourself and the world that serve you well. Ways of seeing ourselves and events that enable us to be at peace and even thrive despite any situation. This will be the focus of the book's final section.

Suicide is always a symptom and a response. Suicide is not a monster that emerges on its own. It is, in essence, death from an unresolved, unstable, and chaotic sense of self. A person who is thriving and knows who they are is not swayed, let alone destroyed, by the challenges we encounter in life.

Therapy is also an important part of suicide prevention, which we will talk about in Chapter 28. Psychiatric drugs, including placebos, result in a majority of people showing marked improvement, no matter which one they are given. Beyond the placebo effect, this is also because any support gives some sense of hope and helps someone feel like they are worth saving.

Social taboos against suicide also have a significant statistical impact on lower suicide rates. As inherently social beings, human behavior is highly influenced by social pressures. We would all benefit from fostering a society that eliminates the stigma from seeking help for mental and emotional health challenges. At the same time, it is crucial to take a firm stand against suicide. In other words, the suicidal person is compassionately acknowledged and supported, but the act of suicide is abhorred and seen as the horrible act of murder that it actually is. No one should die in this way. The way we treat ourselves and others is intricately connected to social norms and culture. As long as society breeds self-loathing, inauthenticity, loneliness, hopelessness, and violence, suicide will continue to be one of its staple products.

CHAPTER FOUR

NOT ME!

WE ARE ALL SUICIDE SURVIVORS TO SOME DEGREE. No, not someone else's, but of our own. Yes, I am saying that we all have some level of suicidality within us. For some, it may be quite apparent, and for others, it may be hidden within deeper recesses of the shadow self. Some may see this as a controversial statement, and I understand why. However, there is truth and importance in it. It ultimately comes down to degrees. I am striving to be brave enough to confront this reality myself. Acknowledging our own potential for suicide, along with all the darker aspects of ourselves, is an essential part of emotional growth.

We are full of positivity and light, but as we now know, the universal principle of chaos and order implies that with this light, there must also be darkness inside of us. If you are capable of all great and wonderful things, you are also equally capable of the most terrible and savage. And not just in the broad platitudinal way with a shrugging off statement like, "Sure, everyone can be capable of anything." This is not what I am talking about. I'm saying that the destructive darkness is much closer than we are comfortable admitting.

Earlier, we talked about our Shadow. The denied, repressed, and often unconscious side of ourselves. "Unconscious" means that it is a very real part of us, but is far away from our awareness. Progressing towards living in awareness and with intention is one of the most life-enriching messages I intend to impart with this book. Therefore, as part of this awakening, our shadow self must be addressed. If you had to count with one hand, the most powerful psychological keys to understanding the self, this reality of the shadow would be one of them.

We all have innate impulses, desires, and feelings that would have a negative impact and are deemed socially unacceptable. We all experience raw emotions such as anger, envy, greed, and contempt. Powerful sexual instincts and desires can sometimes manifest in harmful ways. There is also a drive for power and control. We each have a dark side. Often, we unconsciously deny our shadow because it doesn't align with the ideal image we have of ourselves. It's unsettling and frightening, and even its impulses can make us feel ashamed or guilty. This denial of our shadow only serves to give it more power because it remains more in our unconscious, where it will be less controlled.

The most emotionally strong and wise are people who are willing to accept that this shadow self is a part of their whole self. They recognize it and face it with clarity so that it can then be consciously managed. Those who deny the existence of their dark side ignore it to their detriment. Anything denied, ignored, or repressed finds a way to be made known one way or another.

One of the most common ways our denied shadow makes itself manifest is through projection. This is when we assign to others what we don't want to face in ourselves. Understanding this helped me make sense of Cindy's years of jealousy and controlling behavior. She had curiosities and desires toward other people that she wasn't willing to confront, so she projected these feelings onto me. In other words, she placed on me what she was unwilling to acknowledge in herself. This created turmoil in our relationship and destroyed the possibility of trust and true intimacy. A much healthier relationship would recognize the universality and varying degrees of these sexual desires. Being honest and understanding with each other. Then, with care and consideration, continue to create a relationship that is as harmonious as possible together.

Being strongly judgmental of other people's flaws is a sure sign of an unresolved shadow. If other people's behavior severely disrupts our personal emotions, we may want to look at ourselves and ask, "What is this person's behavior teaching me about myself? Why does it make me feel so angry?" "Is there any part of their behavior that is a reflection of me?"

Identifying constantly as the victim is another way we avoid looking at our shadow. Because being the victim means we don't have to look at our own faults, negative behaviors, or where we contributed to a problem. Owning and taking responsibility is painful and hard. It requires admitting that there is work we need to do on ourselves too. We all experience legitimate victimization during our lives, of course. But be watchful of yourself or anyone else whose whole story and identity is that of a continual victim.

Recognizing our own shadow can be hard to do. A way to fast-track the discovery of your own shadow is to get feedback from a few people who know you well. They need to be willing to be totally honest with you. Ask them to tell you about their experience of you. In what ways are you negatively impactful? Some parts of you, however, may be so hidden that only you could see them. We journey in two simultaneous directions in life, the outward and inward. True reconciliation with our shadow ultimately happens within.

Speaking to the problem of being unconscious of our shadow, Jung wrote, *"Everyone carries a shadow, and the less it is embodied in the individual's conscious life, the blacker and denser it is. If an inferiority is conscious, one always has a chance to correct it... But if it is repressed and isolated from consciousness, it never gets corrected and is liable to burst forth suddenly in a moment of unawareness. At all counts, it forms an unconscious snag, thwarting our most well-meant intentions."*

Suicidality is one of the darkest shadows we have, right up there with the capacity to even murder others. The light and darkness within each of us fluctuate. Life is a very unequal experience, and the answer to why some people have shadows that are more powerful than others is due to many factors. Our early development and life experiences undeniably shape us, but there is also a unique nature and essence inherent to each of us. On top of this, each person interprets and responds to their experiences and emotions in their own way. What is true for all of us, however, is the need to confront and take full responsibility for our shadow. Those who do not will be unconsciously led by their darker aspects, and it will hurt their life profoundly. Understanding this concept can bring more understanding for those who are in serious emotional pain and those who did not survive their suffering. Suicide is a sober reminder of the inherent vulnerability of being human and the importance of being proactive in continually pursuing well-being.

"But wait!" you still may say. "I have never attempted nor seriously considered suicide." Granted, that is probably true for most of us. You just say that you never "seriously" considered or attempted it, but you can't deny that it has crossed your mind at some point. Even if only for a brief moment, during a time of deep frustration or depression, we've all had a fleeting, morbid thought or visualization.

How many times when things have been at their worst, have you said to yourself, "I hate this fucking life" or "I can't take much more of this"? As I said, we are all suicide survivors. Just because you didn't go so far as slitting your wrists or taking a bottle of whatever pills doesn't mean your sad, brief ponderings of death as an answer for your suffering were nothing. Countless others were not so fortunate as to have thoughts that stopped there. They didn't survive those thoughts, but you and I have. We have lived past what starts as an idea, then grows into an impulse, and becomes the final decision for so many unfortunate people.

"But suicide, just crossing my mind, just like killing someone, crossing the mind, doesn't mean anything. I would never kill myself, and I would definitely never murder anyone", you may say. I'm not sure you can be completely certain of either of those. History has repeatedly shown that humans, regardless of who they are, are capable of unspeakable actions. If you had asked any German man in the months leading up to World War II if he could ever commit mass murder of innocent men, women, and children, he would have sincerely said "no"—just as sincerely as you or I would today. And look at how things turned out. History and any nightly news report flaunts how that dark side can become a powerful, very real monster.

Every victim of suicide is a person just like you and me. Dark thoughts that, for many of us, are non-serious and fleeting have spiraled down into tragic actions for others. We may think we are immune, but who knows? Consider the possibility that a combination of enough dire life circumstances and a disruption in the chemical functioning of your brain due to severe stress, sleep deprivation, and possibly alcohol and narcotics could inspire more potent thoughts of death's seducing promise of an end to pain. Some people are afflicted with suicidal thoughts for many years. But many people who commit suicide spend the vast majority of their lives without thinking about nor ever seriously considering it.

I personally have never been what we would call suicidal, but I have had strong enough feelings of anger, deep emotional pain, and hopelessness at various points that I could fathom how the siren's call could get louder and louder. Life is hard for everyone. It is fortunate that self-preservation and resiliency overwhelmingly win out over despair and self-destruction.

Death, as an inherent part of life, means that we all have a unique relationship with it. At some point, we all face the sobering realization that we will die. How and when it will happen remains unknown, but the certainty of it is undeniable. To live with this realization and not let it drive one mad with worry or become depressed into nihilism requires us to settle into a certain level of comfort with our contradictory natures as creatures of both life and death.

We all manifest an acceptance of our mortality in different ways. Some fully embrace and even yearn for it. Whose beliefs about afterlives not only dull the fear or dread of death but create an allure to it. With "Heaven" being wholly linked to the grave, death becomes quite a desirable thing, actually. I can't help but wonder how much more acceptable and appealing death, even by suicide, is for many people because they expect a continued existence after death. Being raised in and still living in a mostly Christian society. I have heard many people I know express statements of yearning to "go home" or "meet their savior." It is very clear that their idea of heaven after death is a place so wonderful that it will be an infinite improvement compared to this life.

Accepting death's inevitability, combined with the expectation of continued existence after, I believe, can create a morbidly facilitating atmosphere for those who do the least well with life's suffering. This dynamic may not overtly manifest itself, with suicidal people citing this as an important part of their reasoning. These core conditionings and belief systems also operate at the subconscious level. An acceptance of death as the gateway to something better is a song that plays subtly in the background for many. Many of us have been conditioned for years, if not decades, to believe in a life after death that is a literal paradise. The effect this has on our self-preserving behaviors would make for an enlightening study.

Now I understand that most theologies, including Christianity, teach that suicide is a sin and therefore strictly prohibited. For those who are predisposed to be especially fearful of this, it surely can be a protective factor against suicide. But from what I observe in current times, churches give an overwhelming impression of a God with a generously forgiving nature. That a belief in Jesus saves virtually all who simply believe, no matter what behavior follows after. It seems likely that the suicidal believer would choose to assume they would ultimately be forgiven their prohibited act against themselves. Even if this wasn't a conscious rationalization at the time of suicide, it's a legitimate question to ask: How does a belief in an idealized life after death reduce the imperative to preserve one's current existence?

What do I think about this aspect of life and death? The best description out there for my view of a creator and afterlife would be agnostic, as I don't claim to know the unknown. I still find myself hopeful for some continuation of existence or experience after death. Hoping for a "heaven" does feel very nice when losing a loved one or facing our own end. However, instead of mentally wrestling with what may or may not happen after death, I find peace in accepting that I don't know. Acknowledging the possibility that my existence may eventually end with death inspires me to embrace and extend my life to its fullest. This life, right here and right now, is what I can know and experience.

Observing current humanity reveals that vast numbers of people are actually living with a certain level of active suicidality. Knowledge about health and well-being is becoming quite universal. While we may not know every fine detail, the key factors that impact our health are widely understood. Most of us are aware of what foods and drinks are healthy or unhealthy. We know our bodies need regular exercise. We understand that stress is harmful, and that plastics, chemicals, and additives in many products are detrimental to us. Yet, look at the way we regularly put things into our bodies that we know are damaging and how we neglect the fitness our body needs. The way we lose hours of critical sleep pursuing entertainment. Using personal hygiene and household products that are poisoning us. Do we wear a helmet on a motorcycle or a seatbelt in a car?

When we consciously choose or act with reckless disregard for our health, it is undeniably representative of a certain level of suicidality. We all live with a level of acceptance for our choices that are harmful or outright killing us in slow motion. Habits like heavy smoking and drinking come to mind. Is this partly because we know we will be dead someday, anyway? Perhaps. I have personally known people who, because of significant unhappiness, are not in the least concerned about living in a way that is hastening their demise.

I don't claim to be taking perfect care of myself either. There are times I make decisions that I clearly know are not conducive to longevity. However, for many years now, I have endeavored to live at extremely high levels of health, precisely because I do idealize an extraordinarily long and healthy life. Still far from perfect, there are times I indulge in harmful foods for reasons of pleasure and convenience. Sometimes, I sacrifice optimum sleep for fun and entertainment. The point is, to some degree, we all act with some or even total disregard for our health and longevity. Choosing what is optimal and avoiding what is not entails a lifetime of learning, effort, and commitment. Is it realistic to live in a padded organic house, only breathe clean mountain air, exercise our bodies just right, and ingest only ideal foods? Not really. But we all have to choose where we will be on the spectrum of how well we take care of ourselves.

Enlightening Statistics About Suicide

- Methods of Suicide 2023 (approximate):
  - Firearms 55%
  - Hanging, strangulation, suffocation 24%
  - Remaining percentage: Jumping, drowning, cutting, vehicular, and others.
- Approximately three-quarters of suicides occur at home.
- Spring to summer is when most suicides occur. Winter has the lowest number.
- The majority of completed suicides have no previous attempts.
- Nine out of ten people who survive a suicide attempt will not go on to die by suicide. This means that only 5% to 11% of attempters go on to commit suicide. This is

still a much higher rate than the .01% suicide death rate for the general population.

- Children younger than 12 years old experience comparatively low rates of suicide. With rates rising dramatically in adolescence. For example, in 2012, the U.S. had about 40,000 suicides, and only 311 were aged 5-14. That equals 0.7 per cent of suicides for that year.

- Men commit suicide at much higher rates than women. 2022 U.S. total suicides by gender: Males 49,449, Females 10,194. This pattern is consistent year after year. There are about four male suicides for each female suicide, representing about 80%. It is the fourth leading cause of death for men under 65. Men are at heightened risk after divorce. When in divorce proceedings involving children, the father is eight times more likely to commit suicide than the mother. Men tend to use more lethal means and are less likely to seek mental health care.

- Anti-social personality disorder is much more common in men. This disorder's symptoms include a lack of regard for others, high aggression, and low capacity for remorse or empathy. This disorder logically raises a person's risk of suicide because it results in more severe and regular life problems, such as relationship and familial conflict and failure, employment struggles, and even criminality.

- Women suffer much higher rates of depression than men and also attempt suicide at higher rates. There are approximately three female attempts for each male attempt. Borderline Personality Disorder is also much more prevalent in females than males, with three-quarters of sufferers attempting suicide at some point.

- In the U.S., whites commit suicide at significantly higher rates than non-whites. In 2023, whites made up 42,259 of the 49, 316 suicides.
- The age group that commits suicide at the highest rate are those between 45-54 years old.
- Suicide rates as a percentage of the population are highest in rural areas.
- Children who lose a parent to suicide are at three times the risk of suicide than those who have not.
- Suicide is not hereditary. Risk factors can be inheritable, such as temperament and personality traits.
- Only 1 in 4 people leave a suicide note or message.
- Each year in the U.S., an estimated 295,000 people become suicide-loss survivors, with, on average, six people being severely impacted by each suicide.

SECTION TWO

SURVIVING SUICIDAL CRISIS

CHAPTER FIVE

AT THE PRECIPICE

Among those experiencing suicidal feelings, the INTENSITY WILL VARY GREATLY. The stronger the feelings of wanting to end life are, so does the level of crisis. One could think of it as a meter gauge between life and death. When the needle is in the green, life is experienced in peace and joy. With hopelessness and misery, the needle falls into the red. The middle of the scale represents a neutral state, neither particularly happy nor depressed. True well-being can be described as consistently residing on the optimal end of the spectrum. Where dark and deathly feelings are not part of our experience.

Of course, living this way would be best for all of us and an especially ideal existence for those who have ever shown a risk of suicide. But right now, for many people, just staying alive is a struggle. And we need ourselves and our loved ones alive so that a higher experience of life can even be a possibility. Therefore, this section is for the time when the needle is dropping into the red. When the light of existence has almost gone out. When the black hole of death is opening up, swallowing everything that is good and hopeful about life. In the fight against self-inflicted death, every battle is high-stakes, and none can be lost.

From the many accounts I have read about people's feelings as they reach the point of taking their own lives a common theme emerges. An emptiness and pain so deep that it seems like nothing can make it stop except death. This section is about facing those darkest moments and still holding on. We will explore how to win this battle, which may be a one-time event or something encountered repeatedly.

One of the most frustrating and sad realizations for loss survivors is knowing that a temporary time of intense struggle was converted into a permanent loss. It is an ending that doesn't have to be your or your loved one's story. Still, we must recognize the fact that there ultimately could be no stopping a suicidal person who is wholly determined to kill themselves. Not being able to control anyone except ourselves is a basic truth we must accept.

That being said, let's face "crisis time" head-on. This specific time period is when a person is at the highest risk of carrying out their suicide. Let's analyze what this looks like and what can be done to make it through alive. Because if an individual can make it through their suicidal crisis or even survive a lethal attempt, statistics show that they have a high probability of never going on to die by suicide.

Every person and situation is different, but there are two main types of people at high risk for suicide. The first are those who have been struggling with deep emotional or physical pain for a long time and exhibit multiple suicidal risk factors. Eventually, they reach a breaking point, like someone who has been severely depressed for years. The other is an otherwise contented person with some of the principal underlying risk factors who then encounters a serious trauma or life crisis.

The most effective prevention against suicide on a population scale would be if family, relationships, society, and culture cultivated and nurtured the well-being of the individual. A world where people feel connected, valued, and free to be their true selves—where physical, mental, and spiritual health come first. Sadly, this isn't the reality for most. Instead, many experience disconnection, regular emotional pain, and poor health. Society and culture, by nature, seem to be oppressive to the individual, leaving most people struggling to mentally and emotionally cope. Still, many groups of people are trying to help.

The Suicide & Crisis Lifeline is available 24/7 and provides confidential and free support for anyone in need. Simply dial 988. If confidentiality is very important to you, please know that you don't have to disclose who you are or where you are to receive support.

The following is what you can expect when making a call to the 988 Lifeline. First, you'll hear a message offering various service options. After you choose one, you'll hear some hold music while you are connected to the appropriate counselor. Either Spanish-language, LGBTQI+ services, or your local 988 Lifeline contact center. For veterans, it will ring until a counselor answers your call.

You will be connected with a counselor as soon as possible, who will introduce themselves. They will then ask if you are in any immediate danger. Then, "Your skilled counselor will ask if you are safe. After they ask about your safety, they will be calm and comforting, listen to you, and provide support. They may also share helpful resources."

The Veterans Crisis Line, also available for service members and their loved ones, is accessible 24/7 by dialing 988 and pressing 1, or by texting any message to 838255. The Veterans Crisis Line is also confidential. "When you contact the

Veterans Crisis Line, you decide how much information to share. If you'd like support from a local VA suicide prevention coordinator, the responder may ask for your name and some personal information to help set up a meeting."

The Suicide & Crisis line is also a resource for those who know someone who may be at risk of suicide. These individuals can also contact 988 for support or visit the website at 988lifeline.org. The website is full of helpful information and resources for those at risk of suicide, attempt survivors, and loss-survivors.

The Trevor Project is a national organization specifically providing crisis and suicide intervention support for LGBTQ young people ages 13-24. They have 24/7 phone service at 1-866-488-7386, or you can chat with a counselor on their website at thetrevorproject.org. The contact information for these important resources is also located at the end of this book.

SAVE – Suicide Awareness Voices of Education at www.save.org is another great resource for anyone affected by this issue.

Because trust and familiarity are so important to us, resources such as these may not feel comfortable for many people. More ideally, a person in a suicidal crisis would have one or even several people with whom there is a close relationship who could effectively provide support in a time of need. If help from others is available, it's important to reach out and use it. Even though love and care from others can make the difference in a suicidal crisis, it may not always be available. Therefore, above all, we should be learning how to save ourselves, to be our own biggest supporter, advocate, and hero.

The first step to having any success in suicide prevention is gaining a general understanding of suicide itself. We need to understand what's going on inside us when we feel suicidal, how we can help ourselves, and how we can be there for others. If you or someone you know has suicidal thoughts and desires, seek more information about the issue. Your worst enemy, apart from that draw towards death, is ignorance and unawareness about the phenomena. When facing something as consequential and horrific as suicide, one should be dedicated to becoming an expert or close to it. Gaining an understanding of risk factors, warning signs, effective support strategies, resources for getting help, and the effects on loss survivors.

Preparing yourself for how you will confront the problem if and when it occurs is also critical. If you're going to help a friend or family member, what's your plan? How will you react, and what will you say? Remember, when it comes to suicide, there's little room for mistakes. This is as high-pressure as it gets; it's either death or life by intention. One of these will be chosen.

The suicidal act represents the culminating moment of many factors. No matter how the person arrives at the suicidal crisis, it is important to understand that the mental and emotional state of the victim is going to be such that logic, reasoning, and healthy perspectives may not be dominating their reality. Many suicides occur during a very short time period. One study looked at how long people spent thinking about suicide before acting. It found that 24% of people made their decision in less than 5 minutes, another 24% took between 5 and 19 minutes, 23% took 20 minutes to an hour, 16% took 2 to 8 hours, and 13% took a day or more.

This survey was of people whose attempts were so lethal that they resulted in severe injuries. Therefore, this study can be illustrative of those who actually completed their suicides. Several other studies also reveal how suicide is so often an extremely impulsive act. A survey of 306 Chinese patients who had been hospitalized following a suicide attempt found that 35% had contemplated suicide for less than 10 minutes and 54% for less than two hours. It's important to note that just as severe suicidal risk can rise suddenly, it can also subside just as fast.

CHAPTER SIX

WARNING SIGNS

The following are some of the most common warning signs you may notice in yourself or observe in others.

- **Thinking** about killing or hurting yourself.
- **Talking** about wanting to die, expressing severe guilt or shame, being a burden to others, making a plan, or researching ways to die.
- **Feeling** empty, hopeless, trapped, having no reason to live, extremely sad, more anxious, agitated, full of rage, or unbearable emotional or physical pain.
- **Changing behavior** such as withdrawing from friends, saying goodbyes, giving away important items, making a will, taking dangerous risks, displaying extreme mood swings, eating or sleeping more or less, or using drugs or alcohol more often.

Being aware of these warning signs can be helpful, but many of us also know or have heard of people who committed suicide with seemingly no warning. Or, sometimes, the warning signs are so subtle that they go unnoticed. Ideally, someone at risk will have close family or friends who know them well and can spot these signs. They should be prepared to provide assistance or seek additional support if needed. A person is only going to get help if they ask for it or if someone recognizes the warning signs and steps in.

In contrast to these warning signs, which can clearly indicate a danger of suicide. Sometimes, there's a tricky situation called the "calm before the storm." This is when someone who is at risk of suicide seems calm and normal in the moments or hours before carrying out the act. It can deceive those trying to help, because even a person struggling with mental illness might seem fine, even though they are on the verge of suicide. There are two main reasons why this occurs. One is that they may be purposefully deceiving those around them in an effort to prevent any intervention. The other is that the person may legitimately be feeling at ease because they have truly decided to kill themselves. Resulting in feelings of relief as they anticipate that it will all be over soon.

CHAPTER SEVEN

CRISIS TIME

Knowing A PROBLEM EXISTS IS THE FIRST STEP TO RESOLVING IT. Fortunately, most people who attempt or commit suicide clearly express their desire to die before acting. Even people who don't talk about it usually still show warning signs. If you think someone might be suicidal, ask them directly if they're having thoughts of suicide. If they share their feelings with you, you have a chance to help them during a critical time of need. There is no perfect script of what to say or not say. There are, however, general principles that should be followed.

Do's

- Express empathy and acknowledge the person's feelings. Assure them that you are glad they opened up to you about it.
- Give them an opportunity to be heard by asking questions and listening.
- Reassure them that you want to support them and that many other professional resources are available for them as well.

- Offer to connect them with professional support. Make the call right there with them if they are willing.
- Ask them how they would best be supported by you.
- Make sure to acknowledge the seriousness of having suicidal thoughts and feelings.
- Express all your love and positive feelings for them.
- Affirm how valuable their life is to you.

Don'ts

- Minimize or dismiss their feelings in any way.
- Tell them that they shouldn't feel how they do.
- Judge or criticize the person's feelings.

Having the at-risk person feel comfortable talking to you should be the goal. The intention is for them to feel like they were seen and heard, and that you are available and want to partner with them in getting through their struggle. If the person seems to be in a state where you feel they should not be alone, stay with them until help arrives. If appropriate, let their family know what's happening. If you think they're in immediate danger, call 911.

CHAPTER EIGHT

MAKE A PLAN

Planning AHEAD COULD SAVE YOUR LIFE OR THE LIFE OF YOUR LOVED ONE. Once it is known that you or someone you care about has the potential for suicide, a plan should be created for any crisis that may arise. If timely and effective support is provided during a critical moment, the individual may overcome what could have been their most difficult time. The periods of heightened risk of suicide are just temporary phases; they come and go and do not last forever.

Making it through a real suicidal crisis can serve as a catalyst for positive change. It provides a profound opportunity to rethink and reevaluate one's life. Experiencing being on the brink of killing oneself and surviving will, at the very least, change the way a person looks at things. It can trigger a serious awakening. Virtually all the survivors of lethal attempts report regret for their attempt and are thankful to have survived.

Developing proactive measures for preventing one's own suicide may sound strange, but it is possible and one of the most important things that can be done. But the plan needs to be made in advance, when the person is calm and clear-headed. Taking proactive steps for prevention is also a positive experience for the person at risk, as it serves as a strong reminder of the value of their life and that they are worth fighting for.

Ideally, if you are suffering from suicidal ideation, you are receiving care from a mental health professional. If you are not, this is your top priority. Professional help is invaluable, and you deserve every support possible. They can help you with the following:

- Recognizing the warning signs of a suicidal crisis.
- What you can do personally to manage yourself during a crisis.
- What you can practice for coping, and where you can go for relief or distraction from suicidal thoughts.
- Ways to reduce access to lethal means.
- Deciding who among your friends and family would be the best support.
- What professional and public resources to contact if needed.

Apart from professional resources, it is recommended to choose someone close, such as a friend or family member, as your principal support person. For a youth at risk, this person should ideally be a responsible and caring adult. If there is no adult they can trust for this type of support, then they should rely on a friend who has other adults they can enlist for help.

Have a clear conversation with this person about what exactly you are feeling and going through. Being honest will give you a better chance to heal and help others understand how to support you. Ask if they are willing to be there for you during a suicidal crisis. If you've chosen the right person, they will feel honored by your trust and more than willing to help.

This person should ideally have as close a relationship with you as possible, such as your spouse, parent, older son or daughter, grandparent, or close friend. Close physical proximity is also extremely helpful, meaning they live with you or are very close by. You can have more than one critical support person, but you must have at least one. Talk to this person about what kind of support you need. You are essentially planning to save your life. It might feel a bit uncomfortable, but what else could be more important?

Carefully consider all possible options. The suggestions I will present here are not all-inclusive. They are recommendations that could be helpful. As stated already, you should consult with any available health care professionals, in addition to trusted family and friends. Develop a plan that is tailored to your specific needs and unique situation. Decide on a simple and clear way to communicate to your support person when it's time to put the plan into action. It can be a single code word, or you can just clearly state that it's time. This may seem simple, but decide on this ahead of time, nonetheless. It will help you if and when the moment comes.

The support person should also be keenly aware of the at-risk person's important life events. In other words, they are close enough and paying enough attention that they will likely see the crisis coming without even being told. If a significant negative life circumstance occurs, such as a divorce or serious loss, they can be proactive in providing support before it's even asked for.

Of all possible supportive measures, one that should be very highly considered is having available some type of sedative for treating acute anxiety and stress. Many people who take their own lives do so in a highly distressed state, making an impulsive decision. When a person is at the highest levels of emotional distress, whether angry, sad, frustrated, etc., they are not going to be able to make sound decisions, especially when suicidal ideation is a factor. Therefore, part of any plan should be to get some type of calming medication administered. The cortisol, adrenaline, and norepinephrine spilling into the body need a tourniquet. This emotional "bleeding-out" must be addressed. If you feel this could be helpful to your situation, the at-risk person should seek a prescription sedative and then have their support person hold onto the medication for them. Obviously, we want to avoid the risk of suicide by any overdose. If the medication is not obtained in advance, the person can be taken to a doctor who can provide the needed emergency pharmacological intervention. No matter who you are, there is no shame in getting this type of support.

Essential Elements for a Plan

1. **Emergency Help:**

   Depending on the severity, be decisive about when it's time to call 911, go to an emergency room or a mental health care facility. Phone numbers for important resources should be prominently visible and easily accessible.

2. **Staying Physically Close:**

   Make every attempt to stay physically close to the potential victim. Most suicides occur when someone is alone.

3. **Limit Access to Lethal Means:**

   Limiting lethal means should be done immediately, ideally by someone other than the at-risk individual. Guns are among the most lethal and, as such, should not be accessible to someone who is at high risk of suicide.

Other common items used for suicide can also be restricted, such as knives, ropes, and medicines. Although this isn't the most effective solution because common items like these are not hard to find. Also, a determined person could do things such as break a glass and use it for self-cutting or use a belt for strangulation.

Still, methods like strangulation, cutting, and poisoning can be less lethal than firearms, as they at least provide an opportunity for the person to change their mind as pain is felt and instincts to live may also arise. These methods can also afford enough time for someone to change their mind, stop and decide to seek help. Or, because death is not instantaneous, there is an opportunity for them to be discovered and helped before the situation becomes fatal.

4. **Emergency Calming Medications:**

   Prescribed and available to be provided by the support person or medical personnel when needed.

5. **Employ Your Pre-Planned Support Strategies for Well-Being:**

   These are the proactive steps you will take to reverse the deterioration of your mind, heart, and body. All of the following are easily accessible and highly effective.

   a. **Connect With Family and Friends:**

      Possibly one of the most important things you can do when in a suicidal crisis. Spend time with the people you love and who love you.

   b. **Get to An Uplifting Environment:**

      Go to a place that will be the most conducive to improving your emotional state. Changing your surroundings can significantly change how you feel. Nature is a great environment where fresh air, beautiful sights, and wide-open views lift the mood.

c. **Do Activities that Distract from the Pain:**

Have some kind of positive experience. This could be going on a trip, enjoying the outdoors, listening to uplifting or peaceful music, or doing something you love. What can help you heal some of the pain and hopelessness? Whatever the answer is, seek these experiences.

d. **Connect With Your Body:**

When the mind is being overpowered by negativity, and the stress hormones are raging. The most powerful way to stop that emotional freefall is not to fight against it within your own mind. Mind against mind can be a difficult and losing battle when thoughts and emotions are at their worst.

One of the best ways to shift yourself into a more positive state is by engaging your body. Physical activity triggers the release of "happiness chemicals" like oxytocin, dopamine, endorphins, and serotonin. These natural, self-produced chemicals are your best medicine and can be lifesaving during a suicidal crisis. To provide yourself with healthy doses of these happiness chemicals: exercise, dance, shake your whole body, cry, hug, get sun on your skin, laugh, do an act of service or kindness, meditate, socialize, breathe deeply and slowly, get a massage or self-massage, take a cold shower, have a warm bath or sauna.

Whether experiencing "normal" stress, anxiety, or a severe suicidal crisis. These physical activities are the guaranteed fastest way to calm your nervous system and your troubled heart and mind. Do them! I know when we are depressed or upset, we tend to shut down and we don't feel like doing anything. This is exactly why we are planning in advance and why you are going to have someone to help you. Get your mind prepared and determine now that you will do several of these activities when you are feeling at your worst. These will be like your shield when you are about to be struck by a killer blow. Doing these types of things is important for all of us and should be a regular part of all our routines for self-care.

6. Avoid the Trap of "All or Nothing," "Black and White," Thinking

Your life can feel really horrible right now, and it can also be full of reasons to be grateful. You can be responsible for much of your suffering and also deserve compassion and forgiveness. Things can feel hopeless, and yet there are still infinite reasons to be hopeful. Do not allow your mind to think in terms of "never, forever, or always."

7. Find Gratitude

Even recognizing the simplest thing that you feel grateful for can be like finding a piece of driftwood as you struggle to stay above water. Grab onto all the gratitude that you can. I also suggest writing down a list of the things you most love about your life, and keeping it posted in a prominent location for easy review when you're feeling especially down.

8. **Healing Sleep:**

Sleep is a critical need for the suicidal person, but as we all know, it's often difficult during times of emotional crisis. A sleep-deprived state compounds an already volatile situation by further deteriorating mental capacity. Reducing decision-making ability and causing extreme mood swings. If sleep is lacking for long enough, it exacerbates depression and can result in mania, hallucinations, paranoia, and increased impulsivity. These are all very bad things for a person at risk of suicide. You must do everything you can to create the best possibility for restful sleep. One solid night of deep sleep can do wonders.

Effective Ways to Prepare for Quality Sleep

- Engage in some type of strenuous physical activity during the day.
- Don't eat anything within three hours of sleep.
- Avoid alcohol or caffeine several hours before bed.
- Dependence on sleep aids should be avoided. However, in a time of heightened suicidal crisis, a sleep aid may be helpful. Melatonin can be supplemented quite safely.
- Dim all lights an hour prior to bedtime.
- Take a shower preceding sleep.

- Create the optimal space that works best for you. For example, I like the room to be as dark as possible, with some type of low-volume white noise.
- No device use or screen time during the hour prior to sleep.
- Read something uplifting or listen to calming music.
- Get a massage or self-massage.
- Listen to a guided meditation for sleep.
- Slow and deepen your breathing.
- Let go of the pressure on yourself to fall asleep. Instead, focus on relaxing your body and mind. Move your attention to every part of your body and consciously relax each area. From your feet to your heart, all the way up to the muscles on your face. Let yourself relax so deeply that you feel yourself melting through the bed.
- Think about what you are grateful for.
- Speak or think positive affirmations about yourself.

Doing *all* of these pre-sleep activities may not be realistic or even possible on any given night, but the more you can do, the better. Lack of sleep has a very high correlation with suicide, which makes sense. Being sleep-deprived affects us very negatively, primarily with how our brain functions. We've all felt the negative effects of just one night lacking in quality sleep.

After formulating your plan, it is helpful to then "wargame" possible scenarios together. Wargaming means that you create hypothetical suicidal crisis situations and then think and talk them through thoroughly. Walk through the action steps that will be taken. As you do this, you can discover potential problems ahead of time and make improvements to the plan. This results in being more prepared and confident if and when a real crisis occurs.

Someone experiencing suicidality can experience several instances of suicidal crisis, make multiple threats or make various attempts. When this occurs, the "crying wolf" element may come into play. This could, unfortunately, result in the support person and others underestimating the danger of a future suicidal crisis. If you are supporting someone who has repeatedly expressed suicidal thoughts or made several threats, you are in a difficult position, and I sincerely empathize. I have been there too. This situation requires deep patience and love. As there is no room for error, every threat must be taken seriously.

CHAPTER NINE

SLOW DOWN

If YOU FIND YOURSELF IN A SUICIDAL CRISIS, please do yourself at least this one favor and *slow down*. The impulsivity associated with suicide is frustratingly tragic. If you are feeling strong urges to act on suicidal desires, try to remind yourself that this intensity of feelings will pass. Please give yourself the precious gift of time. A severe suicidal crisis usually lasts minutes, hours, or sometimes days, but it will pass if you let it. Even if you feel devastated and hopeless right now, remember that it is impossible to know how you will feel in the future. Hard times are referred to as "hard *times*" for good reason. When in the midst of a struggle, it feels the worst, but you can overcome anything with patience and focused intention.

When you're feeling your lowest, try not to let your thoughts become trapped in a cycle of negativity. Your future holds possibilities, and there is hope. Allow yourself to imagine a future where you are happy and living the life you truly want. Yes, right now, feeling at your worst, all that afflicts you is indeed terrible, and you deserve to acknowledge those feelings. Now, at the same time, allow yourself to come back to gratitude for all the things in your life that are good and positive.

If you're able to open your awareness and if you are willing to take an honest look. Many of the things you want and value in life may already be present. Shift your focus to what you can appreciate and feel good about. This can help free you from the grip of hopelessness, which distorts your perspective and weighs you down. Recognize yourself as a growing, valuable, and capable person deserving of peace and joy. This is the truth. Death as a solution is the ultimate lie. Don't allow yourself to be deceived.

If you were able to take a step back from yourself and look objectively at the situation, you would see suicide's deceptive trap. You'd see that suicidal urges have arisen because of overwhelming feelings of emotional pain due to specific aspects of your life experience. You have been hurt, disappointed, lost a relationship, been offended, shamed, feel overwhelming guilt, been abandoned, neglected, or any other number of hard experiences. They may be sourced wholly from someone else, or you could also bear some responsibility.

Ultimately, multiple factors have combined to lower your life experience to a degree where you have lost enough and feel unvalued enough that your life now seems unbearable. This pain is combining with a sense of hopelessness, creating an illusion that these terrible circumstances and feelings are your whole life, that they are you, and that you are doomed to suffer endlessly.

To survive a suicidal crisis, one must overcome this mental trap that pain can so effectively set. You are not wrong for feeling negative emotions now or at any time throughout your life. Life was always going to bring challenges and difficulties. However, it's important to recognize that you are fully capable of overcoming them, learning from them, and growing stronger. Every experience has the potential to contribute to your growth. If struggles have led you toward thoughts of suicide, it means you have been ensnared by this trap. All the pain has you believing lies about yourself and your life. I can't wait until we get to the book's final section together, so we can go deeper into how to overcome this.

For now, I will share a beautiful truth that can be a potent tool for you during any hard time, suicidal crisis, or otherwise. When you feel painful emotions arise and persist within you. When your heart is aching, when your soul feels so heavy that you feel physically sick and weak. Instead of being sucked further into the pain and deeper into despair. You can remind yourself of the truth of what is happening.

Place your hands on your chest against your heart and tell yourself sincerely: "It's OK to feel." "What I'm feeling is my heart actively healing my wounds and pain. This is just the process happening in real-time. It feels terrible right now, but I trust in the infinite healing power of my heart." Then, while continuing to hold your heart, breathe slowly and deeply. Take all that pain, all those negative emotions that are coursing through your mind and body. Now, invite it all into the infinite depths of your heart. Visualize all that pain being dissolved by the healing power of your beautiful heart. Remind yourself: "This will pass. I am healing. Love is in me and all around me. I am love."

If positive self-talk and visualizations are something you have never done, then I'm honored to welcome you to a new and healthier evolution of your relationship with yourself. Practicing self-love and care should become a way of life for all of us. One powerful method is positive self-talk. When other people encourage and lift us up, it is wonderful. We should surround ourselves with these kinds of people. If others can have a positive impact on us with their words, then doesn't it make sense that we, who know our own selves infinitely better, we who feel within our own body, could have an even more powerful impact?

Give it a sincere try and see for yourself. In some way or another, we have all engaged in both negative and positive self-talk. We have just done it with a low level of awareness. For example, if we make a mistake, we might say, "Awe, you idiot." When we're about to do something difficult, we might tell ourselves, "Alright, you got this!" Although this kind of thinking occurs naturally, we can learn to control it and utilize it to our advantage.

Intentionally avoiding negative self-talk and proactively practicing uplifting self-talk will change anyone's life for the better. Everything begins in the mind, which then becomes more powerful when spoken, and then actions take it to a whole other level. Progressively take control of your mind and your words, one thought and one statement at a time. Doing this will do wonders in moving your life into alignment with your higher self and what you really want.

CHAPTER TEN

THE "BETTER OFF WITHOUT ME" LIE

L ET'S ADDRESS ONE OF THE BIGGER LIES MANY SUICIDAL PEOPLE CONVINCE THEMSELVES OF. Believing that those whom they care about will be better off if they are gone. This detrimental belief enables a person to slip deeper into suicide's trap.

Analysis of suicide notes reveals that suicides strongly motivated by revenge or the intent to hurt someone else represent a minority of cases. A much larger portion of people who commit suicide believe that their permanent departure will be a net positive for the people around them.

If you are having thoughts like "They will be better off without me," as part of your justification for suicide, consider the following. There are likely some real reasons behind these thoughts, which is why they can be so dangerous. None of us is perfect, and we all have an impact on others, both good and bad. It may be true that you have contributed to some problems for others, even egregious ones. But thinking that others will be better off with you killing yourself is an enabling excuse that supports your mind's desire to use death as an escape.

In regard to the highest possible good of others, thoughts like this aren't just far from reality; they actually result in the opposite. Whoever told you that death was the best option in order to reduce or eliminate our negative impacts on others? Think about it for a few moments, death, self-murder, suddenly disappearing forever from your loved one's lives. From people who may truly need and depend on you. Can you honestly argue that your dead body is going to have a good impact in the short and long term on the people you love and care about? On people who love and care about you? Couldn't there be a different way of seeing things that is more life-uplifting for everyone? Aren't there other courses of action that would actually make yours and others' lives better?

Having thoughts that others may be better off without you means you have recognized that there are ways you are having a negative impact. At least you are not ignorant that there are some problems. But, instead of traumatically leaving your loved one's lives forever, consider adopting a belief system that prioritizes life and love. Instead of making things far worse, you could ask yourself, "What can I do to improve myself or my circumstances so that I become more and more of a force for good?

Overcoming problems and progressing towards higher levels of living is what life is all about. Intentionally dying does not factor into this equation at all. If you're considering ending your life because you think it might help others, then you've either been misled or are deceiving yourself. Taking your own life was never the answer. It's simply not true and believing this only makes a tragic decision feel easier to justify. If suicide becomes the chosen course of action in the midst of any troubled situation, it only makes bad situations infinitely worse. If indeed you feel some action on your part will improve the lives around you, know that it is never suicide and death. Only actions towards positivity improve the lives around you and, of course, your own. This is the only way. No one is "better off" if you're gone.

I know that Cindy told herself that the people she cared about were better off without her. She did indeed cause tremendous pain and problems with some of her actions. She betrayed her best friend by having an affair with her husband. She also neglected and cheated on her children's father, leading to an impending divorce and a broken family. Her family, who had always admired her, would feel great shame because of her actions. They were also going to lose decades of valuable economic support that had flowed in their direction because of their daughter's marriage to me.

She betrayed me, who had tried to love and care for her for so many years. And these were just the most prominent negative impacts on others at the time of her suicidal crisis. She undoubtedly heaped on top of herself whatever other long-term shortcomings she may have had. Her periodic habit of self-hitting was clear evidence that she regularly experienced herself as a problem.

She must have known that a divorce was going to change her life drastically, that things were going to become much more difficult and uncomfortable for at least a time. I don't think she felt confident in taking care of herself, since she had never been required to do so. Knowing Cindy well, thoughts of "They are all better off without me" and "I am better off dead" were loud in her mind. But as stated above, this was a great lie.

Permanently leaving may seem like a fast and easy fix for the negative impact we've had. However, the true solution is taking responsibility for ourselves. Which means changing harmful behaviors and making healing a top priority. The answer is to strive for something better. If you genuinely want the people you care about, including yourself, to be better off, then stay and focus on becoming the best version of yourself. Cindy staying and loving herself and others better, especially our children, would have been way "better off" for everyone. Death did the opposite. Death injected severe pain into everyone's lives around her and cast an endless shadow over us.

We all have to recognize the shadow within us, this lesser self that has a negative impact on ourselves and others. It makes itself known when we are selfish, wrathful, lazy, deceitful, ungrateful, prideful, envious, gluttonous, violent, manipulative, controlling, neglectful, irresponsible, and unremorseful. The list goes on, but you get the idea. These behaviors are extremely damaging to ourselves and our relationships. Anyone who says they don't exhibit any or even most of these in some ways is seriously lacking in self-awareness.

You are not worthless or evil because of all your imperfections, great and small. Bettering ourselves and the world around us is intrinsic to living life. Every day, we can strive to improve. The most inspiring stories are often those of people who have overcome the greatest challenges. Those who endured the darkest of times and still chose the light.

Your story is unique and amazing. It is one that's still in the making, just as everyone else's. Those who have tasted the darkest depths are also those who most intensely savor all of life's sweetness and beauty. This can be your future—the brighter one beyond any suicidal crisis.

CHAPTER ELEVEN

THE SUN OR THE GRAVE

Death is not the solution for what you are FEELING. It does not end any of the suffering. This is an interdependent life. Much of the pain you feel is shaped by what others have done or failed to do. In the same way, your intentional death would bring untold levels of suffering to all those you care about. Far from ending pain, suicide actually does the opposite by transferring and expanding it.

And what will become of you? Well, there is only one thing we can be sure of. You will be thrown into the ultimate chaos of what death means. All concepts about what happens after death are unknowable. What if death as an ending is just an illusion? Maybe you believe it leads to oblivion, heaven, hell, or even reincarnation. But what if it brings something entirely different, something beyond anything we've ever imagined? The truth is, you can't know for certain whether it holds anything good or bad.

Choosing to plunge yourself into such a thorough mystery in hopes of something better or an end to your suffering is quite a monumental gamble. If a better situation is what you truly desire, then the probability of achieving it is infinitely higher by pursuing it here in life.

The Intensity of emotions reaches a fever pitch during a suicidal crisis. It is beyond dangerous. It should go without saying that few times are as pivotal in a person's life journey. It requires all our higher selves to be present and powerful so that the lies and darkness are kept at bay.

Unfortunately, I failed to be effectively supportive when Cindy faced her greatest moment of risk, and she had no one else to fill that needed role. Alone in her struggle, she was overwhelmed by the moment. I had concerns and tried to support her, but it wasn't nearly enough. Looking back, with the understanding I have now, I can clearly see all the indications that she was in a severe suicidal crisis. I also now know that she had an overwhelming number of underlying risk factors exhibited regularly for years.

I knew she was in a terrible emotional state, but this was to be expected given the circumstances at the time, with the affair and marriage ending all at once. It is only logical that as negative factors add up, it raises the risk that a person will make the proverbial or literal jump. The more severe the life crisis, the more underlying risk factors, and the more current aggravating forces, the more dangerous the situation. If all of these factors could be known with a given suicide, it would likely shed light on why some suicidal crises are worse than others or why someone went through with it when they did.

Given Cindy's history of suicidal threats in years past, I expected that they might surface again during this time. I had already decided I wouldn't let them manipulate me anymore. My past experiences with her had conditioned me to believe she was just "crying wolf", that it wasn't serious, just another tactic for control. I convinced myself that dismissing it, not giving it weight, was the best way to diffuse the situation. And because she never actually followed through in the past, how much less willing would she be now that she had two beautiful young children whom she adored? The kids and several other factors had me convinced that she may threaten, but surely wouldn't actually kill herself.

Still wanting to take precautions, a few days before she mentioned anything about dying, I called her from work. I reminded her that if she ever felt like hurting herself or someone else, there were resources available through my employer and the suicide hotline. I told her there were people she could reach out to. But without hesitation, she dismissed the idea, insisting she didn't need any help.

Two days before she committed suicide, we had another brief phone conversation. She called me to present possible things for her to do now that I was going to divorce her. One was going to another state for a while, where she had a friend offer her a job. I told her that wasn't okay, she needed to stay, help with the kids, and cooperate with the divorce process. Then she said she could just go back to the Dominican Republic and let me keep the kids. I didn't believe she was serious about this. I told her she'd miss them too much, that she wouldn't actually go through with it. Then, just as calmly as she had mentioned the first two options, she said, "What if I were dead?" I immediately responded by flatly saying, "You're not going to do that, so let's just talk about reality." I was ready for the threat, and sure enough, there it appeared. She didn't say anything more about it after that.

Talk about guilt and regret. She was my wife, my partner, my friend for many years, and the mother of my two little children. Failing to show up as my best self, to be there for her in the way she needed, is a pain that lingers in my soul and always will. That's the damnable part of regret, though, right? And with suicide, there is no going back, and there are no second chances. It is frustrating to have learned critical knowledge about suicide long after it would have been of use to help her. However, I learned to forgive myself because I was simply responding with the limited understanding I had at the time. I did what I thought was best during a time of ultimate emotional crisis for both of us.

If we had both pursued individual and relational growth, as well as intentionally planned for any suicidal crisis, it's very possible she would be alive today. And the crisis of our relationship ending might not have resulted in the end of her life. Or maybe it would have. Life is unpredictable, and outcomes are never certain. Some of what I learned from the terrible ending with Cindy can be summed up by the following. Be proactive, learn, and grow. Aim for higher states of well-being, always. Confront problems that need resolving, especially when it's difficult. If you don't intentionally take care of yourself and your relationships, they may unintentionally fall apart.

We must also acknowledge that, ultimately, people are free to do as they choose. We cannot make other people's lives happen the way we want. As suicide shows, even holding onto our own lives can be a real struggle. The risk of self-killing will always be there as long as the following things exist. An ability to feel pain, a desire to escape from pain, and a conceptualization of death as relief and an end to the suffering. Still, all of us who love and care for those with this plight will do all we can to help.

As you move forward with all of these tools for dealing with a suicidal crisis. Remember that up to 70% of suicides are extremely impulsive events, with many people going from the point of thinking about killing themselves to committing the act within just a matter of minutes. It can and does happen very fast. Remember that suicides are almost always precipitated by life-crisis events like break-ups, severe relationship conflict, and other painful losses.

The most effective way to support someone would be to be aware of the person's underlying risk factors, such as mental illness, previous attempts, substance abuse, impulsiveness, isolation, depression, or general lack of well-being. If someone you know has several of these risk factors and then encounters a serious life difficulty. Providing immediate support and care can make a world of difference. Simply being there for them, offering love, presence, and reassurance, can go a long way. It's not your responsibility to fix their problems or to "save" them. But showing them that they are seen, heard, and valued can be incredibly powerful in helping them navigate their darkest moments.

If you perceive there is a possibility that they are at risk of suicide, then ask them if they are thinking about that. If they express having suicidal thoughts, gently ask if they have a plan and the means to carry it out. Simply talking about it can be incredibly helpful. When left unspoken, thoughts and emotions, especially negative ones, can become overwhelming and dangerous. Psychology tells us that speaking aloud helps us to organize and process our thoughts.

Next, provide them with simple and clear information on professional resources that will help them. Also, if possible, consider connecting them with someone who has direct experience with suicide, such as, an attempt survivor and or a suicide-loss survivor. Depending on what they express, it may be wise not to leave them alone. If you feel that the circumstances require it, calling 911 may be appropriate.

Then, ask them if they are open to doing some proactive planning to improve their general well-being. If they are open to it, encourage and support them in taking actions that can positively impact their life. There are many ways to heal, improve, and elevate our life experience. Many have immediate benefits for improving mood. Every small step helps. Support them in getting started immediately.

Finally, don't forget to take the planning steps we laid out in this section. Create a crisis plan. Having a plan in place is empowering, and the very act of developing it can be a positive, hopeful, and healing step forward. Doing it tells the sufferer's own being that they are worth fighting for, that escape through death is not the only option, and that there is help and support. Making a plan is a powerful declaration that, when the hardest times come, in whatever form, you will choose life. That you are going to stay in the light. Making a plan affirms that you are valuable, worthy, and supposed to be here.

Osho once said, *"You are not accidental. The world needs you. Without you, something will be missing in existence, and nobody can replace it."* If you've ever felt like life may not be worth the pain, you understand how deep one can sink, how it can feel like a bottomless pit. But just as falling further is possible, so is rising. Healing and renewal are always within reach. You are worthy of a wonderful life within yourself and in relationships with others.

Missing the rest of your life is not what you want. You just don't want to feel so bad within yourself and in this world anymore. You do have the power to overcome these dark times. You were never meant for misery. But the solution is not an end to your life. The solution is you, the real you. The one that hasn't been able to be known.

If the internal suicidal monster tragically overcomes someone, they lose what is most precious. Their life and all that was yet to come. Just as Osho said, then there will be something missing in existence. What's missing is felt most by those who were closest to the deceased. The following is a simple experience illustrating the impact of this absence. Just one of countless.

About two years after Cindy's death, my kids and I went to the graveyard to visit Cindy on her birthday. We brought some flowers and a card. The card's printed message expressed all the beautiful aspects of a mother's love for her children.

The kids added their own messages on the card. And there, sitting on the grass, they took turns reading them aloud to her, their voices soft and trembling with emotion. Zuko, about age ten at the time, read his, "To Mom, I wish I was there with you, but I can't be. I am sad that you have to leave us. I hope you are happy in Heaven, where you are perfect."

Then Brisa, about eight years old read hers: "Dear Mama, I love you and I wish I was at your birthday, and I miss you so much. You are the best mom in the world, and I hope you are happy with God. And I wish you could be here, and I wish you could see me and Zuko, and Dada soon. And I miss your food that you made; it was the best. Thank you for when you were there for me and Zuko, and Dada." And, of course, she drew a big heart to accompany her message.

We sat there holding each other in silence for a few minutes. Before leaving, I placed the card in its envelope, sealed it, and set it gently against the flowers. As we walked up the hill toward the car, a heavy weight settled over my body and soul. I paused, turning back to look at her grave. The sun was blindingly bright, and a breeze stirred the air. I imagined how the birthday card would soon catch the wind and tumble away into the nearby brush, becoming lost. Just like so many feelings and words we would have for her. For the rest of our lives, no one to say them to, no one to feel our emotions. All to be vainly expressed into the wind.

The hole she left for these two kids can't be measured. It is immense and permanent. If you, too, go into that grave, incalculable loss will occur. For you, for your loved ones, and for all those who you would have touched in the future. That grave will receive all of us one day. For now, you are meant for life, and this world needs you.

SECTION THREE

SUICIDE-LOSS SURVIVOR RECOVERY

CHAPTER TWELVE

AFTERMATH

"What you're enduring is one of the most horrific ordeals possible in human experience. In the weeks and months after a suicide, survivors ride a roller coaster of emotions unlike any other."

-Jeffrey Jackson, A Handbook for Survivors of Suicide

AFTER CINDY'S BURIAL, IT TOOK ME A FEW MONTHS TO FEEL UP TO GOING BACK TO HER GRAVE. If it was just for me, I think it would have been a long time before I went back there. During that first year, I was desperate to feel alive again, seeking out anything that brought me even a moment of relief. Returning to her grave didn't call to me. It wasn't that I didn't care or that I didn't miss her; I did. But I wasn't ready. I just hadn't needed to go there as part of my healing. But I had our children to think about. So, the first two visits to her grave were to do what I thought was best for the kids. When your mom dies, you go visit her grave and bring flowers.

There is an undeniable reality that when you are there at the grave, you do feel closer to them. I guess it's just knowing that their body is right there. I was struck by how well Zuko and Brisa handled it all. Zuko would sit in quiet contemplation, yet always kept a watchful eye on me. Once he saw my tears begin to well and fall, he would give me a small, empathetic smile and then hug me. Then, as if it was a contagion, his tears would begin to drip as well. He has always had a huge heart and is highly empathetic. Brisa, being younger, was much less mentally present and would find ways to distract herself. She mostly ran around, coming back periodically to ask questions about death and heaven.

Cindy's gravestone is flat and at ground level, like all the others in that section of the cemetery. On this first visit, we found her gravestone half covered in dried mud. The sight of it made me feel sad for Cindy. She deserved to have a clean and dignified gravesite. I also felt embarrassed having the kids see her grave looking like such a mess. But there was an eerie symbolism to this dried mud covering half of her name. Her death was such a tragic debacle, under such feelings of shame, and carried out alone in the darkness. The fact that Cindy was never really able to make herself known in life. She seemed far from ever even coming to know herself. It was as if even her gravestone was trying to hide itself and not be known. Then, as I continued looking at the dried mud and then around at all the other gravestones, which were totally clean, sadness turned to indignation. She didn't deserve this on top of everything else that had gone wrong. I cleaned it off as best I could, but all I had were my hands and a small twig for scraping out the letters.

Now fairly clean, I stared at the engraved granite marker, looking at her name and the two dates indicating birth and death. After someone is gone, there isn't much more that can make you totally present with their death than staring at that piece of granite with their name etched onto it. A flood of memories rushed through my mind, spanning the entirety of our past, the beautiful, the painful, the joyful, and the devastating. I saw her at 15, laughing on her porch in the

Dominican Republic with her family. I saw her walking through the San Diego Zoo with our toddlers, their tiny hands in hers. I saw her in our home helping the kids brush their teeth before bed. And then, I saw her having sex with her lover in my bed, and then hanging there in the garage, where I found her. It was a lot still. A lot to process, as they say. I was still in some mental and emotional overload.

We said a prayer before leaving, which felt more like we were trying to talk to Cindy than it was to a god. Zuko prayed first, so sweetly and lovingly, of course. Brisa didn't feel comfortable, so I finished praying. The words used would indicate that we mostly wanted to tell her that we loved and missed her, and that we hoped she was okay.

There is a curious aspect to where she is buried. From her hillside grave, I can look about a mile away toward an adjacent hill and see my childhood home. I chose to bury her in my hometown because, first of all, I wasn't going to send her body back to the Dominican Republic as her family would have wanted. Her children deserved to have her close, and I believe she would have wanted that, too. Aside from her hometown, this place was the closest thing to home for her. It was where we spent the first six years of our marriage and where we returned regularly to visit my family. She loved my siblings and father, and they all loved and had fully accepted her from the beginning, except for my mother, with whom a good relationship never developed.

As the kids went ahead, walking back to the car, I stopped and stared at the street where I grew up. I thought of how I lived there for so many years, so young and innocent, and how this future of ultimate relationship destruction and tragedy was waiting for me all along. I thought of how the young me could have never imagined what scene was going to be playing out across the way on that cemetery hill on some future day. I can tell you that that young me thought he was going to do it right. He thought he was going to have a happy family. All who come from really broken families want theirs to be the whole and joyful one they never had. It was my strongest desire of all, and nothing was more important to achieve. So, standing there in my current nightmare family reality, I felt pretty damn miserable. I felt something far beyond disappointment for what my attempt at making a family had turned into. I was supposed to give my kids a better life than I had. And now they had something even worse than me. That's a depressing feeling. I felt so sad and so ashamed. On our way out, I stopped by the cemetery office and asked them to fix whatever was causing mud to cover her gravestone.

The second visit came a few months later, just before Christmas. Once again, I went primarily for the kids, and much like the first time, the experience was a mix of emotions. The grave was still getting covered by mud. Frustrated but somehow not surprised, I cleaned it off once again.

This section, though written for the grieved, is also extremely valuable to the individual feeling desirous of the assumed reprieve of death. With how common it is for the suicidal to feel that the ones they care about would be better off without them, the realities in this section about the effects on loss survivors will reveal a very different reality. Far from being beneficial, the costs are high and prolonged. And even if the belief isn't that others will be better off, there likely exists an innocent ignorance about what losing someone to suicide does to loved ones.

The loss of a loved one to suicide, as opposed to natural causes or an accident, creates very specific suffering and challenges. Suicide, being a self-inflicted death, creates unique psychological trauma, differing from other kinds of grieving processes. In the months following my wife's suicide, I experienced a jumbled and chaotic play of every possible negative emotion. I could write them all out, but it would be extremely cumbersome, as it is literally ALL of them. A few of the most prominent are grief, frustration, anger, and guilt.

Trying to describe the feelings of losing a family member is the most poignant reminder of the limitations of speech. Any possible vibrations of the vocal cords could only convey a shadow of understanding. This may be why talking to others who have experienced something similar is helpful. Between two loss survivors, there is an inherent understanding that the other knows something about how they feel and what they have been faced with. To be known and understood is so important to us, and there is a wide gulf between two people who do not share the suicide-loss experience.

Death is hard enough on its own. Suicide puts the experience of death in a blender, mixing it into a cup of misery that its survivors are then left to drink. The pain that the suicidal person wanted so badly to escape does not go away. They simply pass it on to their loved ones. This, among many other things, is worth considering before you decide death is the best answer to your pain.

I can attest to the truth of this dynamic. Without my consent, when Cindy murdered herself, pain as a commodity was handed to me and my children, which was not ours prior to that event. It was not the exact pain she was experiencing, but the pain's impact on me was the most life-draining, oppressive darkness I have ever felt. I do not think that Cindy, and many other suicides, fully consider this inevitable result when deciding to die. Intent on stopping temporary suffering, and running from themselves. They make a choice that can never be changed, reconsidered, or regretted.

Though every suicide is ultimately a tragic victim. It is also true that the act is one in the furtherance of darkness and of bringing chaos and hell. For the family and loved ones left behind, it is a terrible act of abandonment. It is a total abdication of responsibility, virtue, and honor to one's own life and those they love. In relation to the higher human aims of positivity, meaning, purpose, expansion, and mutually uplifting relationship, it is a most spectacular failure. This is one of the reasons it hurts us survivors to our innermost core. Though endlessly unique, nuanced, and personal, suicide is still always, clearly, and excruciatingly an endorsement of death. It is a dreadful thing to wrestle with and could drive the bereaved mad if one isn't careful.

There is a question that often lingers for suicide loss survivors. If the victim had known that they would be ending their suffering at the cost of passing it on to the people who loved them the most, would they still have made that trade-off?

Of all the ways to heal from losing someone to suicide, acceptance is at the heart of it. Through much suffering, you will find your version of peace at some point, but it's a messy process. You may feel you've reached it, but suddenly find yourself back experiencing the loss as if it just happened. The loss is permanent, and the circumstances are too devastating to ever erase from memory.

I will never be able to erase the images associated with her suicide. Nor can my feelings ever return completely to what they were prior to the event. Still, my emotional and mental state vastly improved with the passing of time and in my process of healing. Humanity's capacity for destruction is equally matched by our resilience. For loss survivors, my hope and intention with this book is that you not only cope but grow and become an even better version of yourself because of the darkness you've experienced.

You may have noticed that I am using the term "suicide loss survivor." There is some ambiguity in terminology regarding those impacted by suicide. Does "suicide survivor" mean someone who attempted or was suicidal and survived it? Or does it mean those who have lost someone to suicide? Many of us find it helpful to be more precise in the terminology. It makes things much clearer if we refer to the family and friends who have lost someone as "suicide-loss survivors" and those who have survived suicidality or an attempt as "suicide survivors."

Though suicide itself is the most significant problem confronted in this book, the negative effect on loss survivors cannot be overstated, and the scope of the problem is immense. Each suicide is estimated to result in an average of six loss survivors. This means that worldwide every year, approximately six million people become newly bereaved loss survivors.

CHAPTER THIRTEEN

IMPACT

THERE ARE VARYING DEGREES TO A SUICIDE'S IMPACT. The effects of a suicide, or any death for that matter, is relative to the closeness of the relationship with the deceased. Immediate relatives, such as spouses, children, parents, siblings, and very close friends will be seriously impacted. For others outside of these close relationships, such as acquaintances and co-workers, the impact is normally much less severe, and their lives continue with little disturbance.

We can empathize with those who lose someone close to them and feel a sense of sadness for the person who died, but lacking a very close relationship, a death will typically have minimal life-altering effects on us. How many times do we hear of death and horrors occurring all over the world? We acknowledge it for its tragedy, and then we go on with our daily lives. We are not designed to suffer the weight of death for people who are not close to us, much less all the awfulness in the world.

Coping with the suicide of even one loved one was an overwhelmingly exhausting experience. It seems the mind, in an instinct for self-preservation, tries to limit which burdens and stressors it will bear. We can only process so much pain and for so long. I'm sure this is something we would like to ask those whose pain was too much to bear and who died because of it.

So, even if you know someone who dies by suicide. Unless you have a close relationship, you may not feel a significant impact. And by significant impact, I mean intense physical, psychological, and emotional distress that is by no means short in duration. This is natural, and there is nothing wrong with you. You are not callous or unfeeling; it is simply healthy human nature. If a suicide impacts someone you care about, you can make a big difference in their life by loving and supporting them in their pain.

Close Relationships

Suicide is a significant and shocking event for anyone who knows the victim, but for immediate family members, the experience is literally paradigm-shifting. Our closest relationships represent connection and stability foundational for a healthy life. Just strains in an important relationship can be draining and very painful. Death in these circumstances permanently shatters a huge part of our personal world. We feel a deep loss for the deceased. They were part of the most important goodness of our life, intertwined with our own meaning, and suddenly, they are gone.

Accompanying our own feelings of grief and loss are feelings of strong empathy for the person who died. Knowing them so well, we effortlessly conceptualize all that they have lost. We imagine their now-erased future and see everything that they will never experience. This is a lot of pain to associate yourself with. If the deceased were someone who had a great many years of life left ahead, the level of tragedy rises because their loss of potential life is so great.

The type of relationship, whether a spouse, child, parent, friend, etc., creates different types of pain and difficulties for the loss survivor. One thing they all share is the grief associated with the death, and that one of the worst possible inter-relational outcomes has occurred. The total and permanent severing of the relationship.

Suicide loss survivors are profoundly affected in two critical areas: emotionally and socially. For spouses and children, they are affected in a third critical area, which is economically. Obviously, becoming a single parent, as I know well, significantly impacts the economic stability of a household, especially one with young children. A missing parent creates a massive void of not just emotional support but of time, energy, and care for children.

- **CHILDREN** lose one of the two most important people in their lives. This is a catastrophic event for a child. Their world is flipped upside-down and turned inside-out. The stress and trauma can be severe. Those left to care for them bear a heavy responsibility. I hope all I share in this book regarding my children helps to convey the magnitude of this tragedy.

  When I was in the initial throes of feeling Cindy's death outside the garage, while first responders worked to save her, the majority of what came out of my mouth were the names of our two children. That and several variations of "oh god." Apart from Cindy, the kids were the overwhelming concern of my heart. They were completely innocent and now had been dragged into the suffering of Cindy's worst monster. It was as if I were experiencing right then and there all the pain and sadness they would feel throughout their entire lives for having lost their mom.

That parental empathy took no time at all to tear my soul to shreds. Little compares to the desire of a parent to provide for and protect their children. And here was one of the worst things I could imagine happening to them: the death, let alone the suicide, of their mother. And there was nothing I could do about it.

I spent several minutes on the ground as the most intense of anything I had ever experienced wracked my body and mind. It was like a violent car accident for the soul. My inner being careening chaotically out of control, flipping and rolling wildly over and over again, slamming into ruin and then engulfed in flames. All you can do is hang on as you're taken helplessly along for the ride. Nothing before then had reached even one percent of the negative intensity felt in those moments.

I do not know what it is like to be a child who has lost a parent to suicide. Most of us never will. I have to believe those who end up in this position are strong individuals and likely gain a certain wisdom about life that the rest of us will never grasp.

Because of their young ages at the time of Cindy's death, I chose to shield them from the weight of knowing she took her own life. Instead, I let them believe she had passed due to a heart condition. But I always knew that one day, the painful truth would have to come to light. When would I tell them? I didn't know. Whatever time they could live without the heavy burden seemed valuable.

Young children see the world as revolving solely around them, and therefore, they wouldn't be able to see her suicide as an act that had nothing to do with them. They naturally would have felt that they were at fault and that she wanted to leave them. I refused to let them suffer this way. I wanted them to continue to grow and mature without the additional pain the truth would have caused.

Keeping the secret from my kids was one of the main reasons that I thought I would never write this book. Paradoxically, they are also among my principal motivations. So that when they learned the truth, they'd at least have the complete story. I also wanted them to have immediately available the most powerful learnings and realizations I had gained during my process of healing. The kids obviously knew I was working on a book, but thought it was just about overcoming suffering.

As time passed, my fear of disclosure eased. Watching them thrive has brought me peace of mind. Ultimately, they deserved to know the truth, as it is part of their story. Fate, it appears, set the time for when I needed to have that important talk with them. This book's release forced the conversation. Six years after Cindy's death, I shared the whole story with them. There were some tears when I reached the saddest part, but they received the news calmly. Knowing the truth hasn't rocked their worlds as I had feared during those initial years. They have continued to be exactly who they've always been. Absolutely wonderful.

- **PARTNERS** lose the person they were most intimately connected to in all areas of life: the past, daily life, family, finances, love, and expected future.

  I experienced the loss of my wife four times within the span of 12 days. First, when the affair announced the collapse of our 16-year marriage. Second, when I found her hanging in the garage. Third, when the doctors told me she was completely brain dead. Then, the fourth and final time was when I held onto her after the life support was removed and her body shut down for the final time. These experiences made the phrase "walk through the valley of the shadow of death" seem tame compared to the final leg of my journey with Cindy. Through shocking turns and excruciating events, I emerged on the other side of that valley alone.

- **PARENTS** lose their child. A loss I cannot fathom because of the bond, depth, meaning, and love intrinsic to this relationship. Parents of suicide victims suffer even higher levels of guilt because of their natural position of responsibility over the child. In addition to all the complicated grief, the fear of other family members committing suicide becomes a recurring issue for parents. Becoming overprotective of remaining children is a common response. My sincerest and deepest sympathies go out to those parents who have been faced with the unimaginable.

- **SIBLINGS** lose what was supposed to be a close, lifelong relationship. Someone they are most likely deeply identified with and have been in the closest association. These losses cut to profound depths.

- **CLOSE FRIENDS** lose an important and special person. The friendship existed because there was a unique and valuable connection. Close friendships are sometimes even more important relationships than those with siblings. Many friendships are so special and positive that they last a lifetime, wholly voluntary, existing beyond the innate ties of family. Do not underestimate the impact on someone who loses a close friend to suicide.

In any relationship, suicide causes all kinds of serious damage. It's not just the total separation that causes pain. It's also because they did something profoundly hurtful in the midst of your relationship. With no opportunity for closure, that pain lingers and can cast a shadow over your entire experience of them. The bereaved person's sense of who everyone was and the meaning of the relationship can be put into doubt and thrown into chaos. It can feel like a betrayal.

Deep attachments are created with those we make meaningful relationships with. Some even say it's a memory that becomes recorded in the whole body. When the attachment is deep enough, suicide is excruciatingly painful because it cuts out a piece of the survivor's existential world. It is a tearing away of a part of yourself.

Recognizing and validating the magnitude of this tragedy and the feelings that accompany it is the beginning of the road to healing. There really isn't much else in our life experience more awful than death. Almost all other negative circumstances we can encounter have a temporary nature to them, and at the very least, there can be hope and possibility for resolve, remedy, or restoration. With death's finality, there is no possibility of returning to what was or resolving the problem. Life is forever changed. Any resolve and healing are left to the loss survivor to deal with and figure out alone.

If you lose someone very close to you in this way, you are going to have relentless and disruptive thoughts going through your mind as if a hamster was running on a wheel in your brain with an IV dripping caffeine directly into its bloodstream. It can feel as if you have lost most control over your thoughts.

In reality, your thoughts have been hijacked. Your brain's primary function is to keep you safe and alive. When suicide strikes your intimate world, it shatters part of your brain's understanding of that world. Any sense of security and stability you had with your environment vanishes. Suicide is such an extraordinary act that the loss survivor's brain is thrown into significant chaos. All the symptoms associated with trauma are commonly experienced. It is very common to experience depression-like symptoms. A loss survivor's sadness can even devolve into full depression and, even more sadly, suicidal thoughts.

The physiological effects on loss survivors are also significant. The "fight, flight, freeze" response of the instinctual, sympathetic part of our nervous system gets activated. Close exposure to death triggers this response. Stress hormones are initially dumped into the body and then continually trickle for a prolonged period of time.

A year and a half prior to my wife's death, my father passed away peacefully in his sleep. He was in hospice care, and the end was fully expected. However, when death arrived and I stepped into his room, saw him lying there, a surge of adrenaline and stress hormones flooded my body. An intense energy coursed through me, with nowhere to go, and there was nothing I could do with it. No threat to physically fight or need to escape from. So, being all bottled up inside, I felt like I was going to jump out of my own skin and punch holes in the wall.

A few days later, when I analyzed what had happened to me that morning, I realized that it was the "fight or flight" response. Even though my father was already dead, and any action would have been futile, my body still recognized the situation as DANGER, DEATH, DO SOMETHING!

When I experienced Cindy's suicide in real time, my body revved the fight or flight needle to redlining. The initial effect felt as if poison fluid was blasted throughout the inside of my body, which is probably somewhat accurate, as both adrenaline and cortisol would have been released in response to the life-and-death situation. I felt myself vacillate between raging energy, like I wanted to throw a couch, and then debilitating weakness, where I felt like collapsing.

Every suicide will be unique, and depending on the particular circumstances, the trauma and impact will be different as well. For example, was the body discovered in place by the loss survivor? How disturbing and or gruesome a scene? Was the victim still in the process of dying when found? What was the relationship? Elements such as these will all contribute to the level of trauma experienced by the loss survivor and should be recognized and understood.

Being patient and hopeful after the suicide of a loved one is difficult on its own. If you lose someone in your family, then you will also have to deal with the effects it has on the others in your family. I empathized deeply with my two young children and felt the weight of their loss every day. Every time they were sad or upset, even over the smallest things, it pierced my heart.

For nearly a year and a half, any time they experienced pain or sadness, I couldn't help but feel a surge of anger toward Cindy. This made some sense when it was something directly related to her death, but it didn't matter what it was. Somehow, it seemed like she was always to blame if they weren't feeling good. During those moments, I cursed her name under my breath or in the depths of my mind. It wasn't a good feeling, and I'm not proud of it. But in hindsight, I realize it was natural. The anger was going to be felt one way or another.

It was particularly distressing to see how it had changed my little girl. Before her mom's death, she was sunshine incarnate, so alive and joyous. After that, she became much quieter, regularly sad, and prone to angry outbursts. She had never been one to throw fits, but now they were happening regularly. Her afflicted emotions blasted outward at stores, in the car, or while getting ready for bed. During those months, it was as if there was a little rain cloud over her all the time. It broke my heart to think that she may have been forever changed for the worse. The term "scarred for life" seemed a real possibility.

A couple of weeks after Cindy's funeral, the kids and I moved in with my brother and his family, and I returned to work. Fortunately, it was a big house because not only did my brother Mark, his wife, and their three young daughters live there. Another one of my brothers, John, along with his wife and three children were also living there temporarily. It was the best place I could imagine for my kids and me to be at the time. We were all close; therefore, it was a supportive environment for us. My kids had aunts and uncles who loved and could help take care of them. Having six cousins with whom they could endlessly play and interact was also an amazing blessing.

I had a cell phone available for my kids so that they could contact me, and so I could directly check in on them. Brisa, however, began to call me many times throughout the day while I was at work, to the point that I couldn't accommodate all of them. I tried my best to comfort and reassure her. I encouraged her to be patient, told her that I would call her when I could, and that I would always come home. As a father, it was difficult not to answer every call, but something had to change. She needed to adjust to a more reasonable number of calls while I was at work or away. Setting that boundary was necessary, but it still weighed on me heavily.

When I didn't answer, her many voice messages began to build up. After a couple of weeks of this, I realized it would be better if my family held onto the phone and only let her use it for emergencies. I didn't want the phone to be a crutch and a distraction. Keeping her from being present and participating in her daily life.

Brisa's messages were so emotional. They offered such a raw, unfiltered glimpse into her wounded soul that I found it difficult to erase them. To this day, I've kept a few. Listening to them feels like a time warp, pulling me back to those first agonizing weeks in the aftermath. Some parts are barely understandable due to her voice breaking, consumed by anguish. Sometimes, she maintains decent composure, but that is the exception. None of her tones are defiant or angry, just unbridled expressions of sadness and physical pain. Here are some excerpts from those messages spanning several weeks.

"Daddy, I took a nap, and I had a bad dream. Daddy. I miss Mommy. Can you come home? I don't want you to be gone."

"I don't feel really good. I feel like I'm gonna throw up. I'll see you when you get home; I don't feel good; I have to say bye; I love you, bye."

"I miss you a lot, and I love you. I don't feel good. My tummy really hurts, and my head hurts, and I'm dizzy. Ok bye bye."

"When are you coming home? My tummy really hurts. Just remember that you're the sweetest Daddy in the world."

"Daddy, I called you to say I miss Mommy. I love you, bye, remember that."

The themes were pretty consistent, as you can see. If Cindy could have only kept present in her mind the suffering she was going to put her sweet baby through. Back when I was listening to these messages in real-time, it tore up my heart. It also induced great anger at Cindy for causing all of this for Brisa. My own guilt was also still far from being resolved, so when the little innocent person for whom you feel the most responsible and protective calls you the "sweetest daddy in the world," it's a pretty sick feeling, to put it lightly. I felt like the worst father in the world.

In those first months, when the pain was at its rawest, I'm sure the kids saw something different about me, too. No matter how much I tried to be strong and present for them, a shadow lingered over me. I carried an unmistakable weight, an aura of grief and unrest that must have been impossible to hide.

Experiencing each other's pain is a heavy weight to bear among surviving family members. We were like loose rocks on the side of a steep hill. When one slipped, the close bonds caused the hillside of our family to tumble downward. Tears might as well have been an unstoppable contagion. Thankfully, as time passed and with intentional healing work, Brisa regained her original, lively, and bright way of being. As did I and my son. Their healing was my healing, and vice versa. We rose together, just as we had fallen together.

CHAPTER FOURTEEN

TRAUMA

Experiencing the suicide of a loved one is TRAUMATIC AT A BASELINE. "Traumatic" may even be too weak a word to describe this situation, given how the word *trauma* is now thrown around in today's world so casually for any uncomfortable experience. Suddenly losing a loved one can be one of the most painful and severe types of trauma. Earlier, we talked about a pyramid that ranks the hardest experiences a person can go through. Here, you truly find yourself at the upper echelon.

With suicide, someone you love has been murdered. The fact that it was carried out by their own hand doesn't make the murder any easier to deal with. It makes it more stabbingly horrible in distinct ways, leaving the bereaved enveloped by a strange and twisted nightmare. The discovery of the body at the scene would add another layer of trauma. Witnessing the act itself would mean much more trauma still.

Trauma is differentiated from other bad experiences based on a few major distinctions. It is characterized by causing *severe* emotional and physical disruptions. These disruptions then last in varying degrees of intensity for a *prolonged* period of time.

In other words, if the impact on you is significantly life-disruptive and lasts for a significant time, then it's trauma.

Once here, in the emotional swamp of trauma, walking open stride, smooth and steady with the sunshine on your face, is no longer your reality. Down here, it's murky, dank, heavy, and slow going. It can feel as if you are living in a parallel existence compared to others around you, and that's because you are. You are still physically in the same world as everyone else, but spiritually, you have been pulled down to some lower plain.

Trauma creates new neurological connections and structures in the brain. Your brain was basically rewired without your permission. Just like when certain songs instantly remind you of a place or event, your mind forms lasting connections between experiences and emotions. Even after decades, that link remains because your brain has wired them together. And it doesn't even have to be a big moment, such as your first kiss; this can happen with any experience. I have a song that is anchored in my mind with a certain strip of road I was driving on during one of the times I heard it. There was nothing significant even happening at the time. Yet, every time I hear that song since then, I am reminded of driving on that stretch of road on that specific night.

If a simple song can leave a lasting imprint on your brain, imagine what happens when you lose a loved one to suicide. Because survival is our top priority, anything connected to life and death gets the deluxe mind embedding treatment. Then, our brain also demands understanding. So, this new area becomes the focus of your attention and thoughts, like a distress beacon and air raid siren flashing and blaring in your mind; disturbing, painful, and overwhelming. This is trauma.

When my decades-old bond with Cindy was torn asunder by betrayal and then self-murder, the effects on me were strange and awful. My well-being was effectively thrown into fluctuating levels of constant chaos. I journaled at the time that, during some moments, it felt like the bonds of my very molecules were being pulled apart. For weeks, I could not pinpoint or tell you that this or that specific part of my body hurt; it was everything, everywhere. My very life force felt like it was slowly draining away. My thoughts were no longer my own. Sleep wouldn't come until my mind was completely exhausted by warring thoughts and abhorrent images.

Everyone deals with trauma in their own way, and there's no single right way to heal. But no matter what, you deserve to move forward and find your way back to a healthier place. Trauma is temporary, unless you ignore it, push it aside, or avoid taking steps to heal. You can distract yourself pretty effectively for certain periods of time, and an illusion that you aren't in that emotional swamp can be created. We all need some distraction and reprieve from the pain now and again. I could feel better for short periods of time when I was in the company of a woman, some alcohol, or entertainment. However, even these weren't always effective escapes, and sometimes made me remember even more.

It's not a bad thing to give yourself a little reprieve from the trauma here and there. In the beginning, it can feel all-consuming. But when the moments of escape grow into a life lived in an illusionary world, things go from bad to worse. Many people try to escape through alcohol, drugs, or other things that change how they think and feel. This path of dependency on substances to self-soothe must be avoided, as it would have you losing your own life in slow motion.

Unhealed trauma is one of the greatest forces for life destruction there is. Trauma causes harm both inside and out. The sufferer may hurt their own life while also affecting those around them. You can see this everywhere in society, from some living on the streets to those in powerful positions. The negativity emanating from countless people with unhealed trauma spares no one. We all know what it's like to be at the receiving end of it. Do you think when a parent beats their child, they are really angry with and want to support the child's well-being? Of course not. They are really beating the shit out of themselves and their own pain. The child is just their avatar.

Inversely, when traumas are healed and overcome, they can be the source of our greatest self-transformation, leading us towards our highest selves. Those who have been deeply hurt have the chance to grow wiser and become better at supporting others who are in pain. When face with new challenges, we are more resilient. As the saying goes, "Smooth seas never made skilled sailors."

Society perpetuates the lie that multiple traumas should break you down further and further. We are supposed to think that the bad things that have happened to us make our life a tragedy. The reality is that each problem can further prepare us for the next. We can come to know joy more intensely precisely because of our travels into life's miseries.

Life only becomes a tragedy if you miss what is happening all around you due to remaining stuck in the traumas of your past. It's easy to fall into the mindset of being a victim, but that only leads to more pain. Life will always bring difficult challenges, and we don't get to choose which ones we face.

If you have lost someone to suicide, what has happened is truly awful and overwhelming. It is one of the last things you'd ever want to face. But remember, you were designed and are fully equipped to deal with yourself and your life in this new phase.

Instead of running from the trauma or entering into a victim role, take charge of your healing. Healing from your trauma means looking at it in its entirety, ideally with someone who can support you in the process. Talking about it is important. If you keep it inside, it can feel like a never-ending nightmare. Share your feelings with trusted family and friends, and consider seeing a therapist. Even just talking about it helps release the heavy emotions that build up inside. Talking helps us to organize our thoughts around the traumatic events. Writing about it can take you even further towards gaining a sense of understanding of your experience. The more you feel you understand, the more your mind will put the issue down.

Take the space and time to allow yourself to fully feel your emotions. As if lying on the beach, allow the tsunami of your trauma to wash over you. Feel its weight, its darkness, its chaotic force, and the sheer madness of it. You can only defeat a monster by facing it head-on. Ignoring or denying it doesn't make it go away; it gives the monster a place to stay in your mind and take deeper root inside you. And there it will remain, emerging at various times to make itself known to you and those around you in damaging ways. Forever hurting your life until it is fully faced and resolved.

Remember those neurological structures built in response to this event? Resolving and healing from the trauma doesn't mean they disappear. They will still be there, and that's why you will never forget. Healing means disconnecting, rearranging, and installing new, helpful structures.

I feel I was able to heal relatively quickly from the worst of the trauma through my intentional efforts, but I'm talking about the trauma itself, not the grief. Grieving is a unique process with its own set of challenges. I believe my trauma healed faster than I expected for three main reasons.

Number One: Early on, I became determined to reclaim my peace. I would not let the pain dominate my life. I would become better than ever for myself and my kids. This kept my mind and actions oriented in a positive direction.

Number Two: I sought to gain a deep understanding of all the elements that directly related to her suicide, starting with suicide itself.

Number Three: I took responsibility for learning how to heal and then dedicated myself to practicing what I was learning. Holistic well-being became the focus of my life. Also, writing this book has assuredly been a significant part of my healing journey. The final section of this book will discuss in more detail the most effective ways to overcome trauma and suffering.

CHAPTER FIFTEEN

RE-CREATION

AFTER TRAUMATIC EVENTS, WE "RE-LIVE" THE EXPERIENCE IN OUR MINDS MANY TIMES OVER. This can be so vivid that it is felt in the body. These experiences range from unpleasant to highly disturbing. We seem to torture ourselves with the event to no end. Yet, this is not self-torment. It is the body and mind doing what they are designed to do, which is to keep us safe. Something profoundly terrible has happened. Isn't it natural for your mind to focus on it intensely? The intrusive thoughts aren't your enemy, just as you are not at war with yourself. They only become harmful when you ignore or avoid them instead of acknowledging and exploring them.

Suicide is mostly carried out in private. Therefore, loss survivors may or may not discover the scene. Whichever is the case, the mind will recreate what it did not see in an attempt to fill in the gaps of what was not witnessed. There were times when my mind drifted back, trying to fill in the blanks of what happened before I found her in the garage. It was heartbreaking and difficult to relive over and over again. I didn't want to keep imagining it, but my mind went there anyway. I had to picture everything that happened on her final morning.

I watched as she got out of bed and got the kids ready for the day. I saw her make them breakfast as little Brisa chatted away at her. I could see the subtly disturbed and depressed emotions on her face as she went about the morning. She helps them pick out and then put on their clothes. Then, she drives them a block away to school. I watch as the kids give her goodbye kisses, then hop out of the van and say their normal loving "Bye Momma" and "Bye Mommy." Cindy remains for a little longer than usual, watching them as they walk away. Had she decided by then what she was about to do? Did she hug and say she loved them, knowing it was the last time?

Then Cindy returns home, and I see her sitting alone on the couch for a short while. I imagine the terrible feelings that must be going on inside her as the decision is made. She gets up and retrieves the rope. Then goes into the garage, ties one end to the pull-up bar, and then the other around her neck. She bends her knees, letting her own weight tighten the rope around her neck. In my mind, I see everything with painful clarity; I know her face better than my own, and every inch of that garage is burned into my memory. I remember exactly what she was wearing that morning: black sweatpants, a black tank top with the word "savage" on it, and no shoes.

I felt what she must have been feeling, all her emotions of enveloping anger. Anger at everything, at her lover, at herself, at "this fucking life", as I had heard her say before. I could feel the sadness, shame, and the dire hopelessness. I see her grit through the urge to stand up as the lack of blood flow to her brain begins to drift her off to what seemed to her like self-punishment, payback, and reprieve all combined. Then, all slight movements and tensing stop. And there she hangs alone in the dark. My mind's re-creation stops there, where my actual lived memory picks up the story of when I opened the garage door that morning.

Being swept up in this highly detailed mental re-creation of the whole event only happened to me a few times. For about six months, however, the trauma of seeing her hanging kept replaying in my mind, mixed with painful images of her and her lover together. These thoughts would hit me dozens of times a day, especially at night when I was lying in bed, driving alone, or during quiet moments. Anytime I wasn't actively distracted, my mind would take me back to those scenes.

Not fun, to say the least. It's quite horrible how the worst things seem to become seared inside our brain as if with a red-hot cattle brand. There were a few times when I felt so sick and exhausted by the intruding thoughts that while driving alone in my car, I yelled in total exasperation, "GET OUT OF MY FUCKING HEAD!", "LEAVE ME THE FUCK ALONE!"

You may want to resist the re-creations. You may feel you are wrong or morbid for having them. It is extremely frustrating to have your thoughts hijacked by tormenting things. But your mind will take you there, over and over again, anyway. I would suggest just going with it when the moment permits. Let yourself experience and feel what it needs. These episodes will pass. Patience and time are your friends here.

Your mind is simply trying to understand what happened and process it in the best way it can. Your brain wants to learn from this painful experience so it can protect you in the future. That's probably the principal reason memory exists. The afflicting thoughts and images will subside when a couple of things happen. You will go over and over it so much, and enough time will pass that it will start to dissipate as your mind will naturally move on to other things. And you will analyze it to such a degree that you arrive at some sense of understanding and acceptance.

CHAPTER SIXTEEN

UNDERSTANDING SUICIDAL INTENT

When someone kills themselves or attempts to do so, information about the severity and nature of the act itself can be helpful in several ways. If someone attempts suicide and survives, understanding the nature of the attempt will help you and the victim confront just how grave an issue is being faced. Are things more to the side of a cry for help, attention, or possibly manipulation? Or is this code red, pull the fire alarm, and immediate professional help is needed?

In the case of a completed suicide, understanding the severity of the intent is one more important part of gaining some understanding and resolve for the loss survivors. There may be other ways, specific to your situation, where information on the severity of intent will be helpful.

The following are aspects of the suicidal act, and then different descriptions as to its severity. Applying this to someone's attempted or completed suicide can help you more clearly understand its nature.

- Expression of the desire to die. (No expression / Some expression / Clear expression)

- Extent of premeditation. (No premeditation / Some premeditation / Significant)
- Arrangements made in preparation for death. (Insurance, will, letters, gifts, goodbyes.)
- Communicated suicidal intentions. (No warning given / Some indication / Warning expressed)
- Alerted someone who could possibly help. (No one alerted / Some kind of communication / Clearly alerted possible help.)
- Steps taken to prevent intervention. (None / Some steps taken / Serious steps taken)
- Proximity to people. (Done in isolation / Done near others.)
- Lethality of means used. (Highly lethal / Somewhat lethal / Low lethality.)
- Role of an intoxicant. (Intoxicant used to facilitate suicide / Intoxicant may have impaired judgement and reason / None used)

If you are familiar with someone's attempt, maybe even your own, or a completed suicide. As you read these descriptions, I'm sure you instinctively applied them to your situation. If analyzed as a whole, one can make a fairly sound judgement about the level of severity regarding the act.

Understanding how much intent was involved can help when a loved one struggles to accept what really happened. A parent, for example, may desperately want to believe their child didn't truly mean to take their own life. A spouse might convince themselves that it was just a cry for help that went too far. These thoughts are natural, but facing the reality of the situation is an important step in healing, whatever the truth is.

Or perhaps it's the opposite scenario. Maybe a spouse has convinced themself about their partner's clear suicidal intentions, but when measured against this scale, the level of intent appears to actually be quite low. When analyzed using these descriptions, the severity of the person's intent becomes much clearer. Truth and clarity are always superior to misunderstandings or distortions.

Suicide notes can also certainly provide important information. Although, as mentioned earlier, most people who die by suicide do not leave a note, about three out of four do not. When they do leave a message, it often reflects their deep pain, feelings of not being good enough, or the belief that they are a burden to others. Often wishing loved ones well and attempting to alleviate blame from family and friends. They often express that they are sorry for any pain their suicide will cause, and that they believe it is for the greater good of others that they die. Unfortunately, many times, important questions are left unanswered.

Suicide notes must also be analyzed with the understanding that the person writing them was not in a healthy mental state. Their ability to think clearly, conceptualize the future, and make rational decisions was deeply affected by their emotional distress. Just like we sometimes say things in anger that we later regret, writing can also be influenced by impulsive and intense emotions. It's important to remember that a note left behind may not fully reflect the person's deepest truth or the clearest expression of their soul.

CHAPTER SEVENTEEN

GRIEF

GRIEF IS ONE OF OUR MOST POWERFUL EMOTIONS AND A DEEPLY PERSONAL EXPERIENCE. With death, it is a sacred process where the loss is felt within the heart, mind, and body. Grief hits hard at first, then can linger indefinitely.

In the initial days of my journey with grief, it was an emotional earthquake where all I could do was hold on. It first hit shockingly and traumatically, finding Cindy's body in the garage, the suicide in real-time. Then, a day and a half later when the doctors told me she was brain dead with no hope of recovery. Then, five days after that, when the time came to remove the life support, and she passed as I held onto her. I would categorize these as "traumatic" experiences of grief. It was like falling off a cliff, hitting a ledge, but then falling further, only to hit another. Then falling one last time and ending up lying broken on the ground. Once she was really "gone," the continual *falling* and acute trauma ended. Only then could the full process of grieving the departed finally begin.

Death hurts whenever or however it shows up. The grief felt due to the death of a loved one must be experienced to be understood. The depth of the emotions is indescribable. Everyone is different, and all relationships are unique, which is why each loss is a truly personal experience. When loss comes, your journey will indeed be a winding road as you progress through your grief. The simplistic and formulaic five stages of grief model: denial, anger, bargaining, depression, and acceptance, has long been shown to be inaccurate for many people's experiences. Experiencing grief is now clearly known to be decidedly individual and unpredictable.

Trauma and grief are sneaky and unpredictable stowaways within us. They usually don't knock or announce their arrival, nor come when it's convenient. Sometimes, it makes sense when you are already feeling low with some current circumstance, and it comes to pile on and compound the sadness. Other times, you can be in a peaceful or even joyful moment, and then suddenly the disruptive feelings arrive like a thief in the night.

It is an ever-evolving process, living with tragedies of great magnitude. There is no set timeline, though the old adage of "time heals all wounds" does have great merit. Though time can only help, it cannot erase. Life is forever changed, and to find peace, one must learn to flow with these emotions, practicing patience in the process. Moving them through and out of you when necessary and making room for feeling into them when time and space allow.

The loss is a part of your life story now. Missing and grieving them has become a part of your journey. Denying this would only be to your detriment. Continuing to feel pain for your departed loved one does not mean you are unhealed or un-whole. You are alive and experiencing, and as such, you will feel as you need.

Feelings of grief have two main parts. One part is the pain and sadness you feel for their loss. The loss of their life and all that they will never experience. The other pain is the loss their absence brings to you and others. The connections we build with the people we love run deep, as if they were a part of our very soul. We became accustomed to their presence, sharing life with them and enriching each other's worlds. We felt a measure of fulfilment by how we were able to love, support, and serve them, and there was surely much that we received from them.

Loss and grief can turn a person bitter, angry, and depressed. But as with all challenges, this is another that gives us the opportunity to gain more wisdom and develop deeper compassion, gratitude, and love.

Life is change, and death is a truly massive one. We are constantly changing, and the same goes for human relationships. People come and go from our lives as part of an ever-evolving process. Birth and death are clearly two of the most dramatic ways in which this coming and going takes place.

We easily accept that strangers and acquaintances will come and go, but with those we care about most, we seem to believe these people will always be in our lives. The truth is that the person you are grieving was always eventually going to leave one way or another. All things are impermanent. The truth is that whatever time we had with them was a gift and was never owed to us.

When someone you care about is in serious grief because of death, it is an extraordinary time for your relationship. Although grief is something we carry inside ourselves, the love and support of friends and family can make the burden a little easier to bear. In my experience, just knowing that people really cared and were willing to be supportive in whatever way I needed made a big difference.

For a little guidance on interacting with someone in grief, consider the following ways to communicate with them:

"How can I support you right now?"

"I'm available to just listen if you want to be heard."

"I can't imagine what you are feeling right now."

Try and allow the person to feel and experience what they need to without trying to *make* them feel better or give too much advice. Try not to make it about you. There will be opportunities in the future to be supportive in other ways, but when the grief and pain are fresh, it's often best to just love, listen, and ask how you can best support them.

The following are examples of the kinds of statements that are **NOT** supportive:

"Try to focus on the positive."

"You have so much to be thankful for."

"This is part of God's plan."

"You need to be strong."

"It could be worse."

These things simply don't need to be said. The person's inner dialogue is already likely to include thoughts like these, among countless others.

With the wonderful experiences of connection and love comes the eventual pain and grief of loss. It is the cost we pay. Grief becomes a part of all our lives in time. With suicide, it arrives far too early. Patience, presence, and love will be your most supportive companions on this journey you are now on. Hold these virtues close.

The following shares part of my early journey with grief:

One night, just several days after Cindy's funeral, I lied in bed, my mind and body racked with the effects of the combined traumas of the affair, suicide, and the resulting upheaval of our entire lives. Cindy was the one in the grave, but I felt like it was my body decaying, as if the light inside of me was slowly dimming.

I was hurting so deeply for her, we had to leave our home, the kids left their school and friends, my career goals were derailed, and life in general changed dramatically to accommodate new realities of single fatherhood. Everything felt in disarray. That night, my anger and grief reached a boiling point.

I had dedicated years to building a life with Cindy, and right before the chaos struck, we seemingly had it all. From starting out our lives together in a one-room shack in her parents' backyard. We had the kids, the home, career, health, friends, and family. Now look where it all ended up. Where was I? My wife was dead, leaving me alone with two grieving kids, and living in a bedroom at my brother's house, betrayed, humiliated, and traumatized. At the time, it seemed as if everything had been destroyed.

As the kids slept soundly beside me, I tossed and turned with little hope of any sleep. My thoughts then shifted to my children's little hearts and minds. More than anything, I grieved for their loss. I couldn't stop thinking about their future, knowing they would go through a lifetime of big and small moments without their mom. I knew that immense heartache and suffering were now theirs because of this sudden new reality.

I gazed at their serene sleeping faces. Feeling the awe a parent feels at their child's innocent perfection. Such an utter contrast to the current darkness around them. These were my two babies. The ones who, above all, I was supposed to protect.

Then, the feelings became too much to bear. Like a warehouse full of fuel drums, where one is ignited, cascading explosions of grief, frustration, rage, and fear all compounded to expand out of control. All of the horrible, tormenting feelings exploded. The savage pressure filled my body, pushing me to the breaking point.

So, there in the pale moonlight, inches away from the faces of my sleeping children. I screamed the most dreadful, tortured, face-contorting scream. Torrents of pain poured out of my open mouth as my whole body trembled. All without a sound. Just as with the deepest of my pains and with anyone's plunge into hell. All was to be buried, wrestled with, and resolved on an intimate path and personal timeline.

Today, years later, I look at those same two peaceful faces under the same moonlight. Sweet feelings of gratitude have long since replaced those early days of relentless agony. It's impossible not to smile as I gently kiss their foreheads, saying a silent goodbye as I leave for work early each morning. They are alive, they're safe and thriving in all the ways that matter most.

Let the infinite love and wisdom of your heart dissolve your pain a little more each day. Your life still deserves to be lived. Truly, the greatest way to honor the departed is to honor and cherish the life you still have left. One day, we will all be "the departed." The people who love us will grieve, but they too, will deserve to keep living their lives to the fullest.

They say the amount of grief you feel is in direct proportion to the amount you loved and were loved by the departed. If there was never any deep love, there would be no significant grief. Love is an emotion that is sourced within us. Your grief can be softened as you realize that your love for them never has to leave your life. You get to keep loving them and remember the love they had for you.

CHAPTER EIGHTEEN

ANGER

JUST AS FEELINGS OF GRIEF COME AND GO IN VARYING INTENSITIES, the same dynamic plays out with anger. At seemingly random times, I would be overcome by extreme anxiety and feelings of rage. On several occasions, I found myself "stuffing" these feelings all day while at work. My body was like a plugged volcano full of pressure by the end of the day. When I was finally alone in the car driving home, this pent-up negative energy sometimes resulted in an ugly scene. I screamed at the top of my lungs the most horrible obscenities at her and at the whole situation. This was some deep, dark, and visceral pain.

Beneath the anger, I was feeling deep sadness, frustration, and rejection, along with the overwhelming grief for her death. The pain hit hard because I truly loved her and always wanted things to be okay between us. I had spent so many years of my life giving my love and making sacrifices for our relationship. And still, after all, she chooses to leave me, first into another man's arms. Then leaves our kids and me forever in a spasm of reckless darkness.

It was also a cruel irony that while I was out there dedicating my life to standing in the gap between chaos and order as a law enforcement officer. My own home spawned something worse than anything I had ever encountered on the job. My wife was murdered, so how could I not be furious with the person who did it?

When all of the negative thoughts assailed me, it felt like I was being stabbed by a hundred knives while being drawn and quartered from every limb. I felt so wronged, so unfairly treated, so abused, and so completely abandoned. It made me feel so sick. So, sometimes I screamed alone in the car, letting out all those emotions.

I shed a lifetime's worth of tears in the first few months following her death. Grief and sadness were the strongest emotions, but anger was there too. In those first months, I probably yelled terrible things at her ghost about a dozen times. Even though she wasn't there to listen, the most wounded and embittered parts of my soul demanded to be heard. Sometimes, it was so loud and harsh that it would leave my voice damaged and hoarse for the rest of the day.

There is another element at play here when it comes to these feelings of anger. There's most likely unhealed guilt and shame, and a lot of the anger is actually with ourselves as much as it is directed at them. Choosing love and compassion for all is the ultimate answer for regaining peace.

I'm grateful that I realized my pain needed to be fully acknowledged, especially by me. I allowed myself to feel it completely because it was real. It *was* a living nightmare. I hated that she took her own life. It hurt my children, and my world felt like it was falling apart. I deserved to let myself feel all of it, accept that it was real, and go through the emotions instead of ignoring them. Your pain needs to be felt and expressed too. Still, these expressions of anger should be handled with care to prevent causing suffering to others in the process. In most cases, they are probably best processed in solitude.

I want to make a note here of a lesser-known aspect of suffering traumatic loss. They say humor is a coping mechanism. Morbid humor is well understood to be a way humans deal with very hard issues. On two or three occasions, I had bouts of mad and hysterical laughing fits. Oh yes. Sometimes, the sheer absurdity of it all, how outrageous and unbelievable it all was. How disgustingly dark, destructive, and painful. How I was oblivious for so long as she was behind my back with that man, and then she killed herself a week after I found that out. Leaving me to suffer the aftermath alone with our two kids.

No part of me was laughing at her or the tragedy. My mind, overwhelmed, sometimes saw it all as maniacally insane happenings, like the kind of crazy you'd only see in the movies. Yet it had all happened, and there I was, along for the ride. It was a system overload. So, a few times, when I was alone. I found myself, for a few moments, loudly and uncontrollably laughing at the universe and all its awful capabilities. The kind of hard laughter that makes your abdomen and cheeks hurt, and makes you sound like a madman.

This reaction, even though seemingly strange and wildly inappropriate. It was a real human response and deserved to be felt, expressed, and allowed to be moved out of my body. I agree with Sigmund Freud when he said, *"Unexpressed emotions will never die. They are buried alive and will come forth later in uglier ways."*

Going through the extreme range of feelings was indeed quite an extraordinary thing. From my experience, anger was the emotion that faded the fastest. As I grew in compassion and forgiveness, both for my loved one and myself, the anger, along with other painful emotions, slowly lost its grip. It may sound cliche, but if you truly want peace in your heart, you have to keep choosing love.

CHAPTER NINETEEN

SURVIVOR'S GUILT

Have you ever been out enjoying an event with your friends while your partner is home watching the kids, and you feel a little bad about the fact that you're out having a good time while they are stuck at home? Well, multiply this feeling many times over, and you may have some conception of what survivor's guilt is.

Accurately described as feeling bad about feeling good. Survivor's guilt isn't just about you being alive while they're dead. This unique kind of negative feeling creeps up when you are enjoying life. It's felt in moments when you are laughing, experiencing something wonderful, and loving again.

It can feel like you're only supposed to be sad and heartbroken now that they're gone. Like, if you smile or have a good moment, you're somehow betraying their memory or not grieving how you're supposed to. But let's be honest. There will be more than enough suffering and sadness. Therefore, you deserve every experience of goodness possible. In fact, you will develop a deeper ability to savor life and its sweet moments precisely because of the loss you have felt so intimately.

The most difficult aspect of survivor's guilt occurs when there are any feelings of relief associated with the suicide. You might feel like a horrible person for having these thoughts, but you're not. Though grief is the strongest feeling, it's natural to have other emotions too, especially if their life was filled with pain and struggle for a long time before they passed. Surely you too suffered along with them in many ways. But do not misinterpret your feelings. You are not feeling any sense of relief because they are dead. You hate the fact that they killed themselves and are gone. Any tinge of relief felt is just your mind and body recognizing that some significant difficulties have ceased to be an issue. You were likely living in great unease and turmoil due to the impact of the suicidal person's behavior. You may have been living in constant worry for them. This emotional dynamic is just one more reason why the grieving process for suicide-loss survivors is so messy and difficult.

The guilt associated with losing someone to suicide is no small thing. Because they seemed to choose to leave, we can't help but wonder if we could have stopped it. We think that if we had just helped them in the right way, they could still be here.

For the first few years after Cindy's death, I would feel this sense of guilt in the background as my life progressed in positive ways. If you are feeling this, it is natural, but your feelings are misplaced, just as mine were. Empathy for the deceased is proper to feel, but not guilt. Even though someone you loved died in this terrible way, you still deserve to live fully and as free from that negative impact as possible.

After leaving the meeting with the doctors, the one where I was informed Cindy was brain dead, and that it was now my responsibility to let her die. My brother escorted me outside to the front of the hospital. He knew this was a grave and devastating moment. I started to feel overwhelmed with terrible guilt and despair. I kept telling him how I could have done things differently, said something differently, and kept her safe. Because of the negative things I said to her about her affair, I was now holding myself responsible for causing her suicide.

Placing his hands on my shoulders, my brother said one of the most impactful things anyone ever told me in the aftermath. "You had a right to your feelings." He made me look at the reality that anyone would have been upset over an affair, and that I had a right to express to her what kind of impact it had on me.

Surely what I told her had an impact, but she had hurt me deeply. Was I supposed to keep all that inside and not be heard or acknowledged by her? Of course not. Still, I rightfully regret certain ways in which I expressed things to her. Could I have done a better job communicating my feelings? Of course. But I managed the best I could at the time. Did my expressions of sadness and anger about the affair cause her to die? No. Suicide was an issue she wrestled with long before I met her, and very well could have plagued her for life. Her responses were her responsibility.

If you're carrying guilt, I encourage you to stop blaming yourself. You wanted them to live. They made the heartbreaking choice. Your love for them and mistaken belief that you could have been in control of their life are preventing you from letting them take full responsibility for themselves. Stop holding onto the lie. You are not responsible for their death.

CHAPTER TWENTY

ASSIGNING BLAME

Just AS WHEN ANYTHING GOES WRONG, IT IS NATURAL TO SEARCH FOR SOMEONE TO BLAME. Suicide creates a victim in the person who is dead, and where there is a victim, then there must be a perpetrator or even perpetrators. Even though they died at their own hand, our hearts don't want to make them the murderer. If there is someone else, anyone else we could possibly blame, it lessens some of the negative feelings we feel about the departed. If it were true that someone else was responsible, it would, indeed, lessen the horror of the reality that they killed themselves. It would simplify our grief so much more.

There is usually no shortage of possible targets to blame. The spouse, the ex, the boyfriend or girlfriend, the parents, the doctor, the psychiatrist, the kids at school, the employer, the government, the military, religion, etc. Many times, there are indeed things the bereaved can point to. Real acts that could have been negatively impactful to the victim. Or so-called sins of omission, the things that were not done which should have been. If a sports game is significant enough to pick apart afterward, imagine the Monday morning quarterbacking that takes place after suicide. Everyone's actions are meticulously analyzed. We do it to ourselves and to anyone who was a part of the victim's life.

I know I put myself through this. I kept looking back, searching for anything I did wrong, especially in the days before she died. And being the closest person to her in relationship and proximity, I also had the greatest potential to either help or hurt her.

The need to blame someone after suicide can cause serious relationship problems among loss survivors. Spouses of suicides are particularly vulnerable to being targeted for blame because of the close relationship, so much so that murder is often considered a possibility.

Cindy's mother and I had been very close since I met the family 18 years prior. But the pain and grief eventually led her to blame me for her daughter's death. She decided to believe that I should have kept her on life support indefinitely. Needless to say, this virtually destroyed our relationship. It is a tragic additional consequence that is not talked about much. Any death can strain a family to the breaking point. Suicide can tear a family apart.

I didn't want to blame Cindy, but I also didn't want to carry all the guilt myself. So, I effortlessly found someone else who could be held responsible. If not for him, Cindy would still be here, her ex-lover. After all, their affair was the reason I had decided to get a divorce. Both events seemed to be the two falling domino pieces immediately preceding her death. Easy, case closed. This man was the one who threw a wrench into our little family. But of course, it's not so simple.

Ultimately, I really needed to accept the truth. Yes, Cindy's affair with him was part of the final chain of events leading up to her death. But even in that, she also had full responsibility. She voluntarily chose to go down that deceitful road. It is so sad that the affair happened, and that its fall-out led to her final choice to take her own life. But those preceding events are just the content. And the content could have been any number of different things. The *context* is that Cindy had a suicidal fuse that had the potential to be lit. Her struggles with suicidal thoughts and other personal issues were already there, and many things could have triggered them. Her lover does bear full responsibility for his despicable behavior, but that is where it ends. Suicide was Cindy's issue long before his negative impact ever entered our lives.

If we're honest with ourselves, we know that people hurt each other in many ways all the time. But taking one's own life isn't a typical or reasonable response to that pain. Something much deeper was happening inside the person who chose suicide. Ultimately, we cannot blame others, as this will impede our healing. The truth is always necessary for real resolve. If someone else was at fault, then it would be manslaughter or murder. If it is a suicide, then responsibility lies with the person who chose to die. Believing anything else is not the truth. Even though you can point to many things that could have been different. The fact is that the victim had an underlying problem, which was ultimately not your responsibility nor anyone else's.

CHAPTER TWENTY-ONE

SUPPORT INSIDE & OUT

YOU ARE ALWAYS YOUR OWN GREATEST ADVOCATE. No one can truly know the pains and struggles you bear. This is okay and means that you have the privilege of having ultimate responsibility for yourself. We still naturally look to others for help and, many times, to save us. Support from others is hugely important, and we will get to that in a moment.

It is also true that the only person who can really heal your mangled heart and mind is you. Though the impact of your pain was initiated from outside you, your experience of it all was created wholly within. Did Cindy go into my body and rattle my brain and squeeze my heart? No. My perceptions and response to her actions created all that I felt, all I thought, and all my anguish. My brain and body did all of that within me.

This doesn't mean I shouldn't have felt the way I did. My emotions were natural; they were part of loving, losing, and living in this world. But they were my feelings, not hers. She was not me, and I was not her. Just as I had created all those emotions when everything fell apart in our relationship, I also had the power to create a new experience for myself moving forward. An experience that would lift my life to a better place.

In a world of wild swings between chaos and order, our well-being is inevitably made unstable and continually disrupted. It must begin this way, as we all start at level zero in regard to awareness and self-mastery. As newborns, we are wholly dependent on the outside world, and this continues for years. But as we mature and grow wiser, we become more and more the creators of our own life experiences and are able to manage our own well-being.

Instead of being oppressed by the world. When negative things happen, you can recognize them for their inevitability and remain in control of yourself, remembering your truest nature. Feelings of pain, frustration, sadness, anger, and all others can be consciously managed. We will feel them, but must not allow them to rule us or remain for long. They are *our* feelings, after all, and as such, are always ultimately ours to control. This is not ethereal, woo-woo mumbo jumbo. This is reality. It is our choice if we want to take ownership of our experience or not. The person with the greatest power to heal our wounds is us.

It is also true that we are designed to support each other. Others can be an immense help on your healing journey. The love and support I received from friends and family following Cindy's death was one of the most beautiful experiences of my life. It is illustrative of who we are as human beings to see how the heights of love and altruism counteract the darkest depths. Altruism is the belief in or practice of selfless concern for the well-being of others. It is the opposite of selfishness or narcissism.

The impact that so many people had on my children and me was invaluable and is recorded forever on my heart. I am now better able to support and love others in times of crisis, both because of what I suffered and how I was helped by others. Some of life's most meaningful experiences happen when you have the opportunity to assist others in their times of trial. People want to help you with yours. Let them.

When the worst moment of my life struck, a close friend of mine was there within minutes. Kevin appeared right beside me as I lay stricken in my front yard outside of the garage, where the paramedics were working on Cindy. An acquaintance had been driving down the street and saw what was happening and called our mutual friend. He was there at the literal moment of destruction, as my being was falling through the abyss. He put his arm around me and looked at my face. And through his tears and horror, he told me he was so sorry, but that he was there and loved my family.

His love and care had to have gone a long way to keep me grounded in some sense of order and goodness. In that moment, despair, rage, chaos, and death were blanketing all reality. My friend's presence was a lighthouse in a storm that was so suddenly violent it could have swept anyone away.

There was a stranger who arrived there almost immediately as well. A woman who was a volunteer crisis counselor. She goes to the scene of tragedies to be supportive of anyone in need. I had never before seen her in my life, but there she was, totally present, sincere, and reaching out to me with support and empathy. And that's who was there. A close friend and a total stranger. It was profound. The best of humanity, known and unknown, was right there as a counterbalance of order to the otherwise wholly chaotic situation. Writing about them being there, even years later, wells my eyes with tears, and their tenderness still echoes within my heart.

Before I even got to the hospital, there were friends, family, and co-workers waiting, and for seven days, several people were always there. Even though I had to go home every night to be with my two kids, there were always some friends and family who stayed the whole night with her. Tears again come to my eyes as I write this, not of pain but of the loving impact they all had on me and still do.

I could write many pages regarding all the experiences I have had with my family and friends, and even strangers who have been part of my healing journey. It's enough to say that it all meant a lot. Every kind and supportive word, every conversation where I could share my thoughts and feelings, and receive wisdom.

When something is deeply troubling us, sometimes we just need someone to listen. Other times, we might hear something helpful or encouraging. Hard times are when relationships are most needed and can become even stronger.

Professional support is also available and invaluable to you. Even though you may be strong, independent, and resilient, seek out people with experience and expertise who can provide you with life-changing help. Why deny yourself what professional resources can provide?

One of the most important ways of seeking support is to pursue our own personal growth. Before this traumatic experience, I was largely complacent in this regard. I assumed I was relatively wise and experienced enough to do well in life and handle any problem. But her suicide so deeply affected me that it triggered a major transformation. Staying the same was impossible, and I didn't want to go down the path of depression and self-destruction.

That left me with only one choice, the path I wish I had followed all along. To heal my deepest wounds, overcome my worst conditioning, and more fully embody my highest self. I am so grateful for all the resources available for furthering self-realization and well-being. I also sat with a therapist in the months after her suicide and had important conversations about my experience. It all mattered. It was all priceless.

If the suicide of a loved one has impacted you, your life experience has been hit by a metaphorical meteor. Change is upon you. Accelerated healing and exponential growth can be yours by prioritizing the evolution of your well-being. Be your own greatest advocate while at the same time seeking outside support.

CHAPTER TWENTY-TWO

THEY DID WANT TO STAY

THERE IS A WEARINESS THAT GROWS WITH TIME WHEN FACING DEPRESSION AND INNER STRUGGLE. This dynamic plays out across all human experiences. We all know well the terms "breaking point," "reached the limit," "done fighting," "ready to give up," "lost all hope," "throwing in the towel," "accepting defeat," and many more.

Although we idealize perseverance, patience, commitment, and enduring through hard things, all these negative phrases of defeat exist for a reason. For everyone, there is some point in any situation where something changes. Where, for whatever reason, the will to fight and to keep up hope seems to be lost. A long enough period of time has the capacity to continually diminish hope to the point of becoming non-existent. People quit jobs, leave marriages, abandon friendships, and give up on cherished projects.

Suicide is the ultimate ending of efforts. For reasons, perhaps always too complex and unknowable, people give up on their own being. The ending of efforts is a part of being human. We have all given up on something. Remembering this shared human struggle might help ease some of the anger and judgment we feel toward those we've lost to suicide.

For Cindy, this was no short fight. Death allured her as a resolution for what distressed her since at least the age of nine. Dying at 34 means she endured, persevered, and tried her best to live for 25 years. I am so thankful for all of those years she chose life over death. I and many others wish she could have kept persevering for at least another 25 and then another, and then another. It is a powerful reframing of thought to go from being full of anger at their leaving to being grateful for all the years they stayed.

Contrary to your feelings of abandonment and rejection, they more than likely did not want to leave you. Do not discount how many times the person's concern and love for you kept them alive. It is well known that many suicidal people are motivated to stay alive by the important and meaningful relationships they have. Their love for you may have saved them more times than you realize. Just because it didn't save them in the end doesn't mean they didn't love you or that your relationship wasn't important to them. Remember, in a suicidal crisis, their thoughts become impulsive and narrow, making it hard for them to see beyond their pain. The darkness just tragically ended up engulfing them.

Cindy's act was certainly an impulsive one in the end. Every single thing in the house, including all her belongings, was left as if it were any other morning. She said no goodbyes nor left any note. Not even a final online post. She gave nothing away, nor did anything out of the ordinary. When she actually decided to go, virtually no time passed before she was tying that rope.

One of the most distressing thoughts I had was "How could she leave our kids?" I truly believed that her love for them would always keep her safe from that darkness. The fact that it didn't was both heartbreaking and hard to understand. But several months later, while reading through Cindy's social media posts, I found something that helped me resolve this issue. October 25th, 2018, three months before she killed herself, she posted three pictures of our two children and wrote, "*2 of the biggest reason why I'm still breathing, why I still wake up every day; they're the reasons I control myself from doing stupid shit...I'll always be there to protect you both!!*"

Parents often refrain from suicide specifically out of concern for the effects on their children. Even though Cindy couldn't keep her promise to always be there for them, her own words revealed the truest intentions of her heart. My kids and I can find comfort in knowing that leaving them was never what she wanted. You, too, can also rest assured that your relationship was precious and valuable to your departed loved one. It likely gave them much more time alive than they would have had otherwise.

As discussed earlier, suicidal people do not even really want to die. It is an escape from pain and suffering that they are desperate for. They just became so clouded in their perceptions due to many aggravating reasons, resulting in a terrible choice that could then never be taken back. As statistics show, if they had survived the attempt, they likely would have been so grateful, reporting much regret for getting so close to losing their life.

If your loved one had had the opportunity to survive, they would likely be able to list many reasons why they love their life and want to keep living. This is simply and so tragically one mistake that is permanent. Know this. Their truest selves did want to stay. They did want to live. This is important for remembering who they really were. A beautiful life that sadly became lost.

CHAPTER TWENTY-THREE

INWARD DIVE

About a year and a half after Cindy's death, I was still feeling much guilt and responsibility. This pain was a constant burden on my heart and mind. I had learned a lot about suicide and the factors involved. I came to a realization that I should not carry the guilt and responsibility for her death. I knew I had always done my best. But the personal anguish and frustrations persisted anyway.

There was a belief system that got cemented into my brain about how I should feel about myself in regard to it all. I could acknowledge over and over again that I didn't have control over her decision, and that I shouldn't beat myself up about it. Still, I continued to carry a lot of guilt and shame. It seemed that this weight would now be forever a part of who I was. However, my higher self was not okay with this life-suppressing anchor around my neck. I always maintained an enduring desire to heal from the trauma and pain. This desire led me to an intentional act of self-restoration. To rid myself of this lie that had encapsulated me.

I had been learning to practice and experience more internal awareness through things like mindfulness, breathwork, and meditation. I also learned about EMDR, which stands for Eye Movement Desensitization and Reprocessing. I also discovered how our brains create physical connections based on our memories and beliefs, making them very hard to change.

I also knew that suppressing memories and trauma was not the way to achieve real long-term healing and recovery. The common human tendency for self-preservation would have us avoid conflict and then try to forget any horrible events as quickly as possible. It is natural to run from the pain. After all, with the brain's mighty power, just recalling traumatic events can create the same unpleasant physiological responses in the body as the real experience.

I learned that our bodies sometimes can't tell the difference between real experiences and thoughts. You can see this in how your body reacts to dreams. If a thought is strong enough, your brain treats it like a real event and forms connections based on it. This means you can have an inner event and physically change neurological wiring, hormones, and even gene expression in your body.

One day, finally fed up and tired of the weight of it all. Not wanting to feel like this for the rest of my life. I decided to be bold enough to try something totally new and strange to me. All of the wisdom I had gained about the mind gave me the will and hope to take action. I knew trying to run from the trauma would be futile and result in an endless fight, like trying to knock down a blow-up punching bag clown. You know, the ones weighted at the bottom that no one has anymore, but you've seen on TV and in movies. Punch the pain, demand it go away, and it will briefly, deceptively fall back and away. But that trauma clown will come back up again and smack you right in the face, over and over again. Trauma is a merciless opponent.

I realized it was time to change tactics. It wasn't just time to change my approach; it was time to stop fighting myself altogether. In fact, I needed to be my own hero. No one else could rescue me from my pain and guilt over Cindy's death or make it disappear. I was responsible for myself. It was time to go back. Back to "face the demons," as they say. Not to contend with and destroy them, but to dissolve them with truth and love.

Now, what I did, I wouldn't recommend just trying on a whim, and not too soon after trauma. Some period of time is needed to reflect on your experience and think about it deeply. Consider learning more about how the brain works. Begin practicing meditation. Develop your ability to feel deeply throughout your body. Practice stillness, intentional solitude, and conscious breathing.

I can't promise you what worked for me will work for you because there are so many variables. Both you and your struggles are very unique. What I can say for sure is that the principles of psychology I employed are effective and powerful. They are readily accessible to anyone choosing to employ them. Who knows what spiritual elements are at play here as well. There are so many mysteries about our beings that we will never fully understand.

To create the healing change I needed, I decided to face the source of my pain. Looking for the exact moment when the deepest darkness set in. How did I do that? The only way possible was by traveling through my own mind, into my memories, and back to the past. I know this might sound unrealistic or even silly, but stay with me for a moment. Just hear me out before you decide.

In June of 2020, I was a single father living alone with my kids. One evening, when they were at their cousin's house, I found my moment to attempt this healing work. I wanted to go into deep meditation to access my memories as clearly and realistically as possible. I had heard about sensory deprivation tanks that use salt water at a salinity and temperature, which creates a feeling of floating in the air. The salinity keeps you buoyant, and the temperature matches your body so that you don't even feel it's there. In complete darkness, with all distractions gone, you can fully relax and enter deeper meditation. Since I didn't have a special tank for this, I improvised. A warm bath in a dark, quiet bathroom would have to do.

So, I got into the bath, lay back, and did my best to clear my mind, focus on my breath, and just be. I didn't really have an exact plan of what I was going to do. I was just totally open to the possibility that something good could come of this. So, there I was, eyes closed, alone with my breath in the tub. Each time my thoughts started to wander, I would set them aside and return to the simple process of breathing. To just be with myself, fully, in the moment. Feeling all of the sensations of my body. Noticing the sound of the air going in and out of my lungs.

I'm not sure how much time passed in meditation. But with my underlying intention being a journey back to my trauma, at some point lying there in the tub, suddenly I was getting out of my bed a year and a half earlier. I was back there, waking up on the morning of Cindy's suicide.

I had been tossing and turning for the last couple of hours. A little earlier, I had heard the sounds of her and the kids leaving the house for school, and then when she closed the door upon her return. I tried sleeping a little longer, but after failing to fall back to sleep, I decided to get up. The morning was cold, so I went over to my closet and put on sweatpants and a hoodie. As I went out of the room, I expected to see Cindy somewhere in the house.

I was a little anxious about seeing her because I had sent her several texts in the middle of the night as I lay sleepless and anguishing over the affair revealed just days earlier. The messages were full of strong emotions and some harsh words. In the morning, I regretted sending the texts. So, I texted again, explaining that I was just overwhelmed with emotions, and apologized for my words. I promised to do better at controlling my feelings for the sake of the kids and moving forward in a peaceful manner. She hadn't responded to those last few messages. I was desirous to talk with her and apologize in person. I didn't want her to feel bad and suffer any more than she already was.

Looking around, I find the house totally quiet, and I don't see her anywhere. She's not in the kitchen or the living room. So, I go and look in the master bedroom and bathroom and don't find her there either. Maybe she was lying down in the kid's bedroom. I opened the door only to find an empty room. I go and look out the front window and see both of our cars there in the driveway, so she must be home. We have a home gym in our garage. She was probably working out, I think to myself.

I open the door to the garage and see Cindy there, facing the other way. She appears hunched over in the dark. My initial thought is that she is sitting in the dark, sulking. This assumption vanishes in an instant as I turn on the light switch, revealing the real situation.

She is hanging, bent at the knees, just a few feet away from me. "No! Cindy!" I shout in shock, quickly taking her down and beginning CPR. The air I blow into her lungs comes right back out in an uncontrolled manner, making the most disturbing sound I've ever heard. *I've returned, back to the genesis of my worst trauma.* I keep working on her. I refuse to let her die. I can still save her.

Then, as this was all unfolding vividly in my mind as I lay there in the bathtub, I stop the memory from continuing to play out as it had. It was time to reprogram my mind with a new, healing experience. It was time to finally let go of my guilt and shame.

So, at this point in the meditative deep dive within my mind, as I was there at that moment, trying to save my dying wife. I allowed my Higher Self to enter the scene, the Chris untainted by all the negativity of the world. The whole and divine being who each of us truly are, free of shame, regret, guilt, and fear.

He approached, and gently reached down taking me by the arm, stopping me from continuing to pump on Cindy's chest. I lifted myself up and then pulled myself in close. So there, standing on either side of Cindy, my Highest Self of pure light and love embraced the devastated and broken Chris. Compassion, forgiveness, and love cascaded over me. I told myself, "It's not your fault," and said in all sincerity, "I forgive you."

Forgiving ourselves is often harder than forgiving others. I had wanted to forgive myself for many months. I guess when I went into that bath, my higher self was finally ready to move beyond the lies I had been believing.

Practicing self-love and forgiveness within a deep meditative state, right where my brain had stored the trauma, had a powerful impact on me. I rewired some connections in my mind that day, replacing pain with peace and healing. After this intentional meditation, the memory of that tragic day no longer held the same painful grip on me. In fact, it was the turning point when I stopped being pulled back there and suffering the moment over and over again. My healing took a big leap forward, and I was able to gain back control over my mind.

CHAPTER TWENTY-FOUR

YOU WILL HEAL

Two years after Cindy's death, I was watching my daughter attend her first day of martial arts class. She was full of life, running around with big smile as they played tag as a warm-up. In my mind's eye, I suddenly saw her as if it was Cindy there as an eight-year-old little girl. She certainly was at one point, and I let myself drift back in time and perceive it. I saw a totally sweet and innocent little Cindy living so vibrantly with no care in the world.

It made me think about her life as a whole. Seeing her little replacement creation so happy and alive reminded me that underneath all the complications of life, we all just want to feel OK. To be able to explore this life without being destroyed by it. For Cindy, all the gunk of life coated her essence of joy and love more and more until she didn't know what she was anymore. Her vibrancy and light withering into darkness and pain.

A sadness ached within me because I could fully perceive her as a precious little girl full of hope and limitless potential, all of which came crashing down. This was grief still showing up, as it did periodically. But what started out as terrible and complicated grief was now turning more and more into a loving memory.

Around this same time, I finally found myself at her grave alone. This time, I was there just for me. I don't know what exactly it was that brought me there in a different spirit. It was definitely some combination of both time and the healing work I had been doing. Whatever it was, I wanted to be there alone with her. After many months of pain, anger, and grief, I was finally ready to reconcile. Ready to come back to compassion and love for her and me.

I laid a blanket on top of her grave, and then I lay face down. As soon as I did, I melted. Through sobs and tears, I told her how sorry I was that she was gone, how I had fallen short in the ways she needed me most, and that I couldn't save her. Lying down gave me the illusion of closeness. Pressed against the earth that held her, it really was the closest I would ever be to her again.

Grief for death and loss, and unreconciled wrongs, feels like a river of searing lava circulating throughout your veins, concentrated mostly in the gut, heart, and head. Only ceasing its punishment if we are able to release it. Tears and lamentations are part of being human for a reason. It's one of the fundamental ways we move negative energy out of our body, literally, through liquid, sound, and movement. For many men and some women, crying is often deeply suppressed. Society often conditions us to hold back deep emotions to avoid appearing weak and show that we are in control. But there, completely alone, I was free to feel everything. With no one to witness or judge, I allowed my emotions and words to flow without restraint, and they did. It was a bittersweet release. An outpouring of things I didn't even know I had been holding inside.

I was thankfully in a state of being where all of the negative impact she had had upon me was no longer an issue. I had come to resolve the four areas that had destroyed my connection and peace with her. The negative treatment throughout our relationship, the affair, her suicide, and abandoning our kids. I had also fully recognized where I acted in ways that had a negative impact. Compassion and forgiveness grew for her as I took responsibility for my own lacking. I came to understand that she did the best she could, given the awareness she had at any given time. I knew she was never out to hurt me intentionally. I was able to go and visit her in peace and love, not just because I had come to forgive her, but because I was also well down the road of forgiving myself.

The affair was a brutal drop off a cliff to my soul, but they do happen, a lot. It's just one of countless ways to mess up in life. Learning about relationships and intersexual dynamics helped me to understand the issue well. Though I never cheated on her, no one is immune to such mistakes. Even though I would want to believe that I would always be above such hurtful behavior, who's to say it wouldn't have been me cheating if things had aligned in a way to present a situation that would have drawn me in? With enough time and disconnection, could my fidelity have reached a breaking point as well?

Being honest with myself helped me let go of my judgement of her. With my new awareness, I also realized that we were never taught how to understand the fundamental dynamics of sexuality, masculinity, or femininity. We never learned many of the basic tools needed for a healthy relationship.

Instead of being uplifting and wonderful, sex often becomes a destructive force in so many people's lives. A lack of understanding and harmful belief systems around sex often results in a lot of unnecessary damage and suffering. For Cindy and me, this was one of the most painful and frustrating struggles in our relationship. Mostly because I felt neglected, as I always had to be the initiator. Our inability to approach sexuality with awareness and wisdom played a devastating role in our family's destruction and her death.

Because of my efforts to understand the issue of suicide. I came to realize that she was ultimately a victim of forces she was unable to overcome. She would never have wanted suicide to be a part of her life, much less the end of it. And regarding leaving our kids, well, if there is some type of afterlife, I cannot even imagine the pain she feels for losing her time with them. And she would be even more pained if they ever felt that she wanted to leave them.

This is the eternal tragedy of the impulsivity and tunnel vision of a suicidal crisis. She did what ninety-nine percent of the time she would never have done, which was to lose her kids or have them lose her. Every day, I love my children a little deeper, knowing their mother would give anything for just one more moment to see them, hear them, and feel them.

So there at the grave, after the initial intensity of being alone with her for the first time subsided, I felt myself relax and stopped sobbing. I turned onto my side, and without warning, my mind's eye conjured Cindy lying there beside me. We didn't speak, only gazing at each other in quiet understanding. Though existing only in memory, I see every detail of her face with perfect clarity. For a few fleeting moments, I lay there with her, as if none of the nightmare had ever happened. For the first time, it felt like we were truly seeing each other for who we were. Not for who we had been in all of our problems, nor what thought the other should have been. We never got to experience each other like that in life, so it was nice to do it right there. Even if the location was so sad, lying right there on top of her grave. Even though I was looking at someone who wasn't even there, I felt like I was in the presence of her highest self. I can only describe it as feeling very good. It is one of those rare occasions where you can feel your soul healing in real-time.

I did not know beforehand the reasons I was going there that day. I simply felt compelled to go. After being there, it was apparent that I just wanted to be with her. I just wanted to be in peaceful presence with her as I hadn't been for so long.

I turned over onto my back and stared at the clear sky for a while. Come to think of it, the weather has always been perfect when visiting her grave. Then, without forethought or any intention, I again saw her with my mind's eye. She was walking on the grass in a simple dress, her long hair hanging down. She was smiling, and the sun shone bright on her face.

I don't claim whatsoever to have seen any vision or the like. I knew clearly that it was my heart and mind creating and projecting what I was looking at. It didn't matter, though. It was comforting to see her. It was so good to feel near her and to feel at peace with her. The love and compassion I experienced that day washed away an untold amount of darkness. And as if mirroring the redemption of my heart and Cindy's memory, that day, I found her gravestone clean for the first time.

Several years of experiencing loss to suicide have taught me that there is no straight line to feeling "normal" again. No clearly marked trail to follow to the top of the mountain. Peace and joy will slowly return in the aftermath, but from time to time, the pain and darkness will show up. In times like these, sometimes the best thing you can do is just hold on and be patient. It's going to take time and effort, but you are going to heal.

Even though suicide throws loved ones into a terrible place and requires a long journey of recovery, studies have shown that the vast majority of those who experience loss and even severe trauma due to a suicide go on to live lives that are free of serious mental and emotional problems. With each day and moment by moment, try to be patient with yourself as you continue to heal. Believe in yourself and in your future.

SECTION FOUR

OVERCOME THE DARKNESS

CHAPTER TWENTY-FIVE

WELL-BEING IS THE ANSWER

WHEN WE ARE NOT LIVING IN ALIGNMENT WITH OUR TRUEST SELVES AND THE LIFE WE WERE DESIGNED FOR, it induces a sick feeling deep within. Life too easily becomes routine and a mushy grey of habits and tasks. Earning money, running errands, and taking care of the needs of others. The curiosity, brightness, and energy we had as a child often fades over time.

Our true potential often goes unrealized because we get weighed down by emotional and mental burdens. So many negative things can happen, leading us to believe the lie that we are not valuable, not worthy, and not meant for life. Suicide victims are surely those who most came to believe this lie.

Prevention is the holy grail for all who care about making a difference in the issue of suicide. So, what does prevention really look like? How can a high-risk individual be most effectively helped? What can truly change their heart and minds away from these lies and, therefore, the draw towards death?

Focusing on the risk factors and working to reduce or eliminate them can seem like the best strategy. However, this is akin to removing a weed by only pulling off the stem and leaves. The risk factors reflect much deeper issues. Underneath the layers of you name it, anger, addiction, or depression, is an inability to create and maintain a pleasant life experience.

So, instead of ripping off the stems and leaves with simple behavior modification or more shame. Let's seek healing deep in our roots. When it comes to suicide, well-being is truly the answer. It is what we all yearn for.

Well-being isn't just important because it feels good. Without it, we cannot connect with others at our best or share our unique gifts with the world. We become disconnected from ourselves, and all of life is severely diminished, including our longevity.

Well-being is a natural by-product of living with a love for life. And what is life but the continual experience and exploration of the self and the world? There is no remaining stagnant as a human being. We are creatures of movement and change. We can either be expanding joyfully or deteriorating further in misery.

A few years after Cindy's death, I experienced further traumas. My life reached a point where enough terrible things happened that I was at real risk of losing myself. The wounds were so bad, and the pain seemed like it would never end. All that I am about to share in the rest of this book is the wisdom that personally saved me. That which continues to sustain me and lift me higher.

After intimately witnessing a life becoming completely lost to suicide and feeling my own slipping away, my greatest desire became to prevent this outcome from happening to anyone else. It is my "why" for writing this book.

Now let's journey together on the path of intentionally creating beautiful well-being. You deserve nothing less. Here we go!

CHAPTER TWENTY-SIX

WHAT HAS HAPPENED TO US?

IF WE ARE GOING TO EXPERIENCE A PROFOUND CHANGE FOR THE BETTERMENT OF OUR LIVES, we first must understand what has gone wrong and why we find ourselves in our current state of suffering.

Our culture, and the majority of those we have a recorded history of, seems to do an effective job of cultivating dysfunctional societies and unhappy individuals. Though people with severe suicidality represent a small percentage of humanity, the level of unhappiness and disturbed experience for many of us is only a difference of degrees. Evidenced not just by simple observation but by hard statistics.

According to the CDC, in 2023, many U.S. high school students struggled with their mental health. Here's what they reported:

- 40% felt sad or hopeless for a long time during the past year.
- 20% seriously thought about suicide.
- 16% made a plan to take their own life.
- 9% attempted to kill themselves.

The number of people on antidepressants, anti-anxiety, and other psychiatric drugs is truly incredible. Data from 2020 revealed that in the U.S., there were 76,940,157 people taking these drugs. With much more time on the current trajectory, will it eventually be all of us? How many tens of millions more people would it be if we added all those who use alcohol and illegal drugs to cope with their unwell state of being?

There's another undeniable thing we often use to numb our pain and chase temporary happiness, food. The CDC reports an obesity rate of around 40% in the U.S.

The endless stream of content we consume is another way we try to escape from ourselves. We don't even need statistics to realize how many hours we spend lost in screens and entertainment. Movies, shows, sports, online videos, social media, and video games have the potential to virtually steal a person's life. And in the case of teen suicides, aggravating factors involving social media are regular catalysts. Many societal norms are out of alignment with what is actually conducive to our well-being. We are doing so much, so wrong.

So, what has happened to us? There are five main areas that are the root cause of our suffering and limitation. They are: modernity, early developmental conditioning, societal conditioning, experiential wounds, and lack of wisdom.

Modernity

Being human comes with challenges, no matter when or where we are born. But today's world also has unique problems that make life even harder. In many ways, the modern world is an unnatural place for our bodies and minds. Like a fish trying to live outside of water, we struggle to thrive in this modern environment. We were designed for a life far different from what is the norm in current culture. Our diets, daily routines, social and familial structures, along with many other aspects of modern life, are strange and new, and it is all hurting us deeply.

So, how can we know what kind of life we are most suited for? First of all, we can look at the long history of humankind for some answers. Humans, anatomically the same as us, have been present on Earth for at least 200,000 years. If you were to travel back all those years, take off all your modern clothes, and put on a loincloth, you would look the same as everyone else, regional differences aside, of course.

During approximately 190,000 of these years, we lived in small groups as hunter-gatherers. As such, our bodies and minds became optimized and programmed to live in specific ways with regard to social dynamics, nutrition, physical activity, and essentially all fundamental parts of life.

It was only 10,000 years ago that we shifted into being an agricultural society. This shift to agriculture marked the beginning of a revolutionary transformation in every aspect of how we lived. Change has only accelerated since the technological revolution of the last century. It has all led us to the way we live now, which is obviously a universe removed from the hunter-gatherer type of life that made up almost all of human existence. This extremely rapid change in the fundamental ways we live is a change so great and sudden that it is an utter shock to our physiological and psychological systems.

For eons, as hunter-gatherers, we would have naturally been very physically active. Today's lifestyle is so inactive that we have to go to gyms and buy special equipment just to stay in shape. Yet, most people don't even do that. According to the CDC, 60% of U.S. adults don't get enough exercise, and 25% are virtually physically inactive. The devastating effect this lack of movement has on one's holistic health cannot be overstated. It is a legitimate catastrophe for millions of people's well-being.

As hunter-gatherers, nutrition functioned in concert with the natural environment, and this was more in harmony with our bodies. There were no highly processed foods, chemicals, artificial ingredients, or refined carbohydrates. Nor did sugar flow incessantly into our bodies. Upon observing hunter-gatherer tribes that still exist today, we see diets that are fresh and composed of a variety of plants and animals.

Sleep cycles that restore and regenerate our bodies and minds were enforced by the celestial laws of day and night. Even firelight is in the red spectrum, which doesn't interfere with our ability to sleep like modern blue light-emitting devices do. Electronic technology, in general, leads humans to continue awake far beyond what would be natural. The CDC states that 88% of US adults report losing sleep due to binge-watching, and one in three adults report not getting sufficient sleep. How many more hours of sleep are lost when gaming and social media scrolling are factored in?

Living in small, highly interdependent groups, our hunter-gatherer ancestors lived in constant interaction with their family and community. Loneliness and disconnection would have been a rare occurrence, as opposed to the isolation that is growing today. The well-known irony is that as we have become more digitally connected, isolation and loneliness have only grown.

Being connected to nature, its plants, animals, water, sky, and stars, and all the accompanying emotional and physical benefits would have been a natural part of daily life. Quiet moments for reflection were likely regular occurrences. Our ancestors were free from the barrage of the hyper-stimulation of today's world. Sure, there would have been dangerous moments of fight or flight. But today's constant barrage of information and stressors has many living in a perpetual state of fight or flight, making a peaceful existence virtually impossible.

Our innate masculine and feminine natures were also lived out in much more harmony. Whereas modern culture is often destructive to these. As discussed earlier, living in incongruency with our basic essences is at the root of many of our greatest suffering as individuals, within relationships, and in society. Ask any woman how profoundly her well-being improved after intentionally cultivating and embracing her femininity. Ask any man how discovering his masculinity lifted his soul out of much despair. The critical importance of this issue is evidenced by a current movement to rediscover our healthy sexual essences. Books such as "The Wild Woman's Way" and "The Way of the Superior Man" are popular because they reveal wisdom that has been all but lost in the modern world.

We are all born at a severe disadvantage due to having a body and mind that was meant for a different world. We are alive, but for so many of us, just barely. I'm not implying that the so-called "savage" past was the absolute best way to live. Life back then was far from perfect. Just like today, it had both good and bad aspects.

Time and progress have been a double-edged sword. It hasn't all been bad. There are wonderful things about our current world and many things have improved. Though our current predicament sounds depressing and hopeless, there is a simple key to not only survive in this modern world where our ancient bodies and minds find ourselves, but to experience a thriving existence like has never before been possible. The modern way to describe it would be to "hack the system." This is done by taking advantage of the positive aspects of the modern world while honoring the core needs of our hunter-gatherer bodies and minds. If done with wisdom, this can optimize our physical and mental health as well as our relational connections.

Early Developmental Conditioning

At conception, we were created at the mercy of the genetics specific to our lineage. Certain traits and negative aspects of physiology are passed down to us. Studies have proven that even trauma can be generationally transmitted. While in the womb, the stressors and nutritional choices of our mothers also dictated how optimal our earliest development would be.

As newborns and children, we are powerfully shaped by our family. Most parents try and do their best in raising a child. Still, very often, there is sufficient dysfunction and emotional abuse that we come out of childhood with deeply detrimental conditioning.

Experiencing neglect, shame, harsh punishment, or witnessing a toxic relationship between parents are common childhood struggles that can have long-term effects. Other issues, like physical or sexual abuse, growing up with a single parent, or having a parent with mental illness or addiction, also deeply impact a child's development. A lack of support, validation, and acceptance can also deeply impair a healthy sense of self.

The detrimental mindsets and behaviors of our parents also have a great influence on us. Were they negative, defeatist, short-tempered, chronically worried, critical of others, depressed, or ungrateful?

Many of us come out of childhood with an imbedded belief that relationships are not safe. We believe that our value and worthiness depend on our performance and utility to others. That others' needs are more important than our own, and that our feelings and authentic selves are a problem.

Childhood wounds go deep and don't heal unless they are recognized, understood, and resolved.

Societal Conditioning

Beyond our family, we receive detrimental societal conditioning. Friends, teachers, aspects of religion, TV shows, movies, music, books, governments, and any other influential forces affect us in powerful ways. They, too, help to shape our ideas about ourselves, love, relationships, purpose, happiness, and success.

Is love like we see in Disney movies? Are we inherently unworthy and filthy with sin? Is success only achieved by a high level of material wealth? Do we have to hold certain political beliefs to be accepted? Is there a right or wrong way to look and dress?

Society is so often hostile to the individual. We learn to value the wrong things, respond in the wrong way, and see ourselves in the wrong light.

Experiential Wounds

We all get hurt by life at different times and in different ways. The way trauma and pain can severely limit our ability to live a thriving life, let alone stay alive, is a topic we cover extensively in this book.

Lack of Wisdom

Success in anything is directly related to the amount of knowledge we have for that activity. Living life is no different. The more wisdom we have, the better chance we have of creating the life we want. Unfortunately, most of us do not learn critical life lessons from our families or society. Therefore, each of us must take responsibility for our own continual learning and growth.

Because there is no avoiding these five major problems, it is up to each of us to overcome them, heal our wounds, and learn how to make well-being a way of life. The cost of not doing this is a severely diminished life at best and, at worst, misery and premature death.

Nothing about today's culture is set in stone or sacred. There are many ways to live, and different ways society could function. You just happened to be born into this one, but that doesn't mean you have to follow it without question.

Following the crowd sweeps you down a river of life that is not even your own. The conditionings downloaded to us by wounded people, dysfunctional families, varied religions, and arbitrary cultural values can carry us to places that aren't best for us.

Living in integrity with your highest self always means breaking old patterns and abandoning mindsets that don't serve you. The process is painful as there must be a death of the old false self for the real self to emerge. But as you discover your deepest truths and live by them, inner peace is found. And as you grow in compassion for yourself and understand more and more the difficult journey required for self-realization. You will inevitably feel the same compassion and deep empathy for others who are at their own stage of this journey, emerging from the dark fog and into their own light.

CHAPTER TWENTY-SEVEN

BREAK-UPS & DIVORCE

IN THE MIDST OF WRITING THIS BOOK, in an effort to help others with their hardest trials, ironically, personal life tragedy and trauma once again struck at the heart of my life. My second major attempt at love and marriage failed, while at the same time, suffering a huge financial loss. I lost hundreds of thousands of dollars that I had built up over many years of owning a home. Right when I thought I had gotten up and dusted myself off from the impact of Cindy's suicide, boom, punched in the gut and thrust back into the darkness.

Of all the different life challenges I have faced. The most devastating have been the endings of my two serious relationships. Relationships where my whole heart and life were invested. I am quite sure that in this, I am not alone. Losing a close relationship hits us in a way that nothing else does. I've faced major disappointments in my career, dealt with long-term health issues, and even been deeply betrayed by friends and family. But none of those struggles have affected my mental and emotional well-being as much as losing these two relationships.

I am again going to spill my personal guts about this because I want you to make it through this particularly devastating trial in the best way possible. I want you to be empowered such that the end of any relationship is never the end of you.

To be completely vulnerable, I will say that this divorce ended up being the catalyst for my most prolonged and profound period of emotional pain. It had a shockingly devastating impact on my sense of self-worth. Putting the most fundamental part of my being in dire jeopardy.

When I looked back a year later, I realized why it rocked me to my core. The divorce and verbal attacks from my ex were heart-wrenching to experience but were not the true source of the pain. It just happened to be the catalyst that brought to the surface all of the unresolved wounds from my *entire* life. It pulled the pin on all of it. All my insecurities, abandonment wounds, limiting beliefs, shame, and deeply buried frustrations and sadness.

In addition to some negative religious and societal effects, I was still working to resolve a lifetime of psychological harm from my mother and the 16 years of neglect, emotional abuse, betrayal, and abandonment experienced with Cindy. It seemed that with this divorce, the time had come for *all* of that to be recognized and *fully* felt. My body and soul were like, "We are going to feel and deal with all of this shit right now. It's time."

Since Cindy's death, I had been pursuing to heal my soul and even wanted to gain some measure of transcendence. So, sure enough, life presented me with the very opportunity I needed to confront the two things I was most fearful of and dependent on: money and intimate relationship. With my deep abandonment wounds and a scarcity mindset, I needed to completely lose these things in order to finally overcome my unhealthy relationship with them. To finally learn that even without them, I was still valuable and worthy. I was still OK. When I started writing this book, I had no idea that it would ultimately feature two major relationship losses. I had expected to be sharing how great life was going in my second marriage, but life has endless ways of surprising us.

I want to be open about my experiences with relationship loss because when it comes to emotional, physical, and mental pain, this is where life often strikes at our most vulnerable. When it can feel as if we're falling into darkness with nothing to grab onto. So many suicides occur during the severe pain that ensues after breakups. The two "Long Dark Nights" of my soul occurred after each of my marriages ended. I felt such intense inner torment that I can now empathize with those who feel that it is too much to bear. Even as I did all I could to care for my well-being, months of pain kept coming and coming. Many times, it felt as if I was doomed to feel that way permanently.

It was shocking and disheartening how much the second loss affected me. Since Cindy's death, I had been on an intense personal growth journey, and I had grown in many ways. So, it was humbling for me to be kicked so hard in my soul again. It was a stark lesson on how, no matter how much growth and self-realization occur, there are fragile parts of our beings that remain vulnerable to life's more traumatic experiences.

My second wife and I thought we both had struck gold with each other. We had similar life stories, and so much seemed to be in alignment for us. The excitement and passion of our new relationship was intense; it felt amazing. But I've since learned that this kind of rush can sometimes be a warning sign of future problems. At the time, we were convinced we had found our perfect match. But no amount of love or excitement could make up for the deep differences we discovered. I have made the mistake of rushing into a serious relationship twice now.

Both times being taught a brutal lesson about the need to really get to know a person and yourself in any new relationship.

There is also always the reality that no matter how emotionally healthy we are individually or how much effort is put into a relationship, nothing is guaranteed. Building a life together as a couple is already one of the hardest things to do. Trying to blend our families, her four children and my two, was so draining it felt almost impossible. On top of that, we started our life together during the COVID shutdowns and extended school closures of California, which made everything even more challenging.

In hindsight, I don't doubt that we loved each other, had the very best of intentions, and gave our best efforts. But with the deep differences, significant past wounds still healing, six children's individual issues, and many different outside pressures, we struggled mightily to maintain harmony. Things came to a head when multiple new crises all hit at once, piling onto the existing problems, and we broke under the pressure. Once again, my expected future collapsed, and once again, I had to dig my way out of the emotional rubble.

Again, my tendency for unhealthy attachment went from problematic to catastrophic to my well-being. Though I took all of the blame upon myself, the reality is that everyone plays a part in a relationship, either failing or continuing. From choosing a partner to the ability to overcome difficulties, and how one shows up each day.

For a long time, I hoped that even if we couldn't stay together, we could still treat each other with kindness and move forward with respect and goodwill. Unfortunately, this did not happen. Ending contact was one of the hardest things I've ever done, because the last thing I wanted was for us to end badly and to lose someone again forever. I truly thought that would never happen to us. But no matter how hard I tried,

I couldn't make anything right or make peace with her. After a year of trying, I eventually realized that letting go was the only way to heal and move forward. It became abundantly clear that there was nothing left for me there but pain.

I had to accept with the fact that I was now just going to be another monster in her story, no matter what the truth was. I later read a supportive quote about how you can do 99 things for someone, but they will only remember the one thing you didn't do. I also had to remind myself of one of life's most basic lessons. That other people will have their own opinions, and not everyone is going to like you. There are billions of people on this planet, and we can't harmonize with everyone.

Now, having personally experienced the pain of dark treatment after a break-up, I plead with everyone to choose the higher path. Relationships don't always work out, and that's just a part of life. People are different, and sometimes, no matter how hard you try, things just won't last. If a relationship ends, try not to tear the other person down. Letting go with kindness is always the better choice. This is why understanding, self-awareness, forgiveness, and compassion are crucial in all aspects of life. Without them, we become bitter and darkness spreads.

Though the relationship ultimately ended up spawning the worst experience of my inner life, still, I am grateful for her sincere efforts to love me and my kids. It had only been 10 months since Cindy's death when I met her, and the kids and I still had a lot of grief to go through. She had been amazingly understanding and compassionate with us in regard to that trauma. I experienced what it felt like to be deeply desired and valued by a woman for the first time. She was very supportive and believed in me writing this book. At a critical time in their lives, Zuko and Brisa received support and love from someone they were able to call "Mom." During the crazy COVID-19 years and school closures, we supported each other with the needs of six children.

One of the most important parts of healing is to let understanding evolve into forgiveness. Like all people, we both had our strengths and weaknesses. We both are on lifelong journeys of discovery and growth. Mistakes, difficulties, and endings are built into the process. Sometimes, even with the very best of intentions and most sincere efforts, two people do not always find enough harmony to keep their lives moving forward together. There is so much complexity and so many variables at play. The ways we were made for each other only got us as far as our incompatibilities allowed.

This relationship loss caused the Lie and the darkness to threaten me like never before. My ego and shadow-self had every justification to take the wheel and speed straight into Hell. Alfa Holden seemed to be speaking about my experience when she wrote, "*I hurt in places that you brought back from the dead. Now I have to lay them to rest again.*"

I hurt so badly that it required my full intentional effort in practicing self-care in order to heal. To make it through, I meditated, practiced breathwork, sat in ice baths, screamed into pillows, did hot yoga, worked out, held onto my children, cried, dived deep within my soul, sought wisdom, kept writing this book, and so much more.

It was my most epic internal battle, and many times it felt like I had been too damaged to heal. Thankfully, instead, it ultimately turned into the most intense time of self-discovery, healing, and growth I have ever experienced. Through it, I learned to finally forgive and love myself as never before.

Why Does It Hurt So Much?

So why do break-ups and divorces often create some of our worst life experiences? I dare to say it goes all the way back to what we talked about at the beginning of the book, that inescapable chaos and order dynamic. Just as a relationship can be created into being one of life's greatest joys, it must also have the same potential of deteriorating into our most profound miseries. We can only fall to lows that mirror the highs.

When all your love, energy, resources, and time are invested in a relationship, only to have it all fall apart, the negative impact is powerful. Your well-being is assailed from so many angles. Our deepest vulnerability comes from our need for meaningful connections. We rely on others to meet important social, emotional, and physical needs. Romantic love, in particular, gives us daily reassurance and affection, reminding us that we are valued and chosen by someone who loves us. When the relationship ends, the source of all this fulfillment is suddenly gone.

Lost is the intimate companion and friend with whom we grew accustomed to sharing daily life. If many years were shared together, the quiet and isolation can be downright disturbing, as if exiled into loneliness. Abandonment is one of our most primal fears. If one has unhealed abandonment wounds from childhood, this sensitivity can be severe. So, when someone does not choose us and leaves. We must go through the severe pain that abandonment induces.

As a relationship develops, a massive mental structure of who we are, what our life is, and will be is created. Not much else has more of an impact on how we conceptualize, plan, and envision our lives than the person whom we choose to love. When it fails, when it all comes to an end, it's no wonder the change is brutal. All of these important and wonderful things are a lot to suddenly lose.

Another source of suffering after a breakup, often not discussed, is the empathetic sorrow felt for the other person. No matter the circumstances of the ending, both people had believed in a future together, and both invested the most vulnerable parts of themselves. It is natural to feel extremely sad about the suffering the other person is going through as well.

Our ego often sees the end of a relationship as an indication that we weren't good enough. If the other person becomes hurtful, something that happens often, we may end up hearing the worst things possible spoken against us. When someone with whom we likely shared all our history, deepest pains, and vulnerabilities intentionally hurts us, it is felt as one of life's greatest betrayals. *"The worst pain is getting hurt by a person you explained your pain to."* -Anonymous. I can attest to the fact that receiving vitriol from someone with whom you were just in a loving relationship rips your heart out.

Pain is often at the source of the worst of humanity's actions, releasing the most vile parts of our shadow selves. While in severe emotional pain, people say and do things they later regret. The pain of a break-up is one of these times. However, our higher selves, acting in compassion and love, would always endeavor to minimize the damage at the end of a relationship. It is such a tragedy that what is already a terrible experience is often made more excruciating by final, vicious departing words. When this happens, we must understand that it comes from deep inner turmoil and pain.

To heal and move on, it helps to remember each other as you were at your best. The highest truth will always be that which was shared in love and kindness. Not the dark things that emerged during what is one of life's most difficult and painful times.

Break-ups regularly trigger all of the negative emotions and thoughts associated with suicide. A loss of belonging is principle among them. When you feel chosen and loved exclusively by the person you love, it is the biggest affirmation of value you can experience. And we all want nothing more than to matter. When we have a partner, we tell ourselves, "Out of the entire human race, this person wants me. I am the most important person for them."

When someone leaves you, it can feel like the deepest insult to your self-worth. Their decision to end the relationship may send a painful message to your inner self that you aren't valuable and were worth discarding.

Feeling like a burden, the other insidious emotion associated with suicide, is built right into the breakup deal. If someone we love leaves, we can feel utterly unwanted and unlovable. Why did they leave, our hearts ask? How can one not feel like a burden to the other person's well-being if they decided life was going to be better without us in it?

Being abandoned also taints the whole experience of the relationship. It makes you question everything good you ever experienced and heard from the beginning. "What did it all really mean then?" We ask ourselves. "Who was this person that I fell in love with? Did they ever really love me, or was it just the idea of me?" Now, all of what were once sweet and cherished memories become embittered, tarnished, and questioned. The loss doesn't only hurt our hopes for the future. It also moves backwards into the past, stealing even that goodness.

When a break-up has you feeling that the world and your happiness in it have ended, consider the following wisdom. It can bring you back to your true self and help you move toward an even better future.

You Are Worthy of Love

Accept that no matter what you did, however hard you tried, and everything you sincerely felt, you will most likely end up the villain in their story. This is just part of how many people cope when moving on. It's unfair, I know. But they will say and do whatever helps them feel better, and the best thing you can do is ignore it and focus on moving forward.

Their opinion and story about you don't matter anymore. Your relationship is now in the past. This is one of the reasons ending all contact is almost always necessary. The negativity is usually relentless and serves only to cause more wounds and prevent healing.

Just because a relationship didn't work out doesn't mean there is something wrong with you. No other person defines your worth. Making a life together is not easy, and we aren't all made for each other. Life can be chaotic and take many winding roads. Never believe that dark voice that tries to tell you that the ending of a relationship is a condemnation of you. Your worth is innate and cannot be taken away. You deserve to be loved. Believe in yourself and in the greater story of your life.

Appropriate Responsibility

There is never just one person responsible for negative impacts in a relationship. Sincere apologies are appropriate for both people during and at the end of a relationship. Don't underestimate how powerful and healing this can be. We can recognize our own mistakes and where we could have done better. And even if the other person doesn't do the same, we can be strong and honest enough to acknowledge it to them.

Be careful to take only responsibility for your part and no more. Idealizing the other person and the relationship will keep you stuck. If you are self-critical, you will likely take on more than your fair share of responsibility for the problems in a relationship. Remember, forgiveness is for them and you.

Let Yourself Grieve

You are supposed to feel sad and have all kinds of difficult feelings. This is because you bonded and loved. The pain after a break-up can be excruciating. It gets exhausting to feel all of it constantly.

There is a certain amount of pain and grief that you are handed when you lose someone or experience something traumatic. Picture a large bottle full of all the negative energy. This bottle is now yours to carry until it is emptied out. When you don't let your pain be felt or expressed, when you don't feel you understand your experience, it remains trapped and persists.

Healing happens when you allow this bottle to be emptied out. This is done by first acknowledging the pain and then allowing yourself to feel it fully. Cry and talk about it to yourself and with others. Journaling is extremely helpful as well.

If you have been conditioned to think that crying is shameful or weak, consider the following. Crying is something only humans do, which means it must have a special purpose. For thousands of years, people have understood the emotional benefits of crying. Today, science confirms that crying helps relieve stress and ease emotional pain, making it an essential part of the healing process. It triggers the release of endorphins and oxytocin, which are powerful tools our body uses to help us return to a peaceful state.

You may mistake your urges to cry as a problem or a sign that you are not healing. The opposite is more likely the case. Your inner being wants to heal and move beyond all the pain. Think of each time you cry as a little more of that bottle of pain being emptied out.

In my experience of grief for Cindy, there were a lot of tears. In the months after the separation, there were also many occasions where I could feel that sharp pain within my chest, and often, simply crying was the best antidote. There are many practices one can do in the process of healing. Crying is one of the most basic built-in tools we all have.

Return to Love and Gratitude

It is natural to go through a period when most of your thoughts get focused on the negative. This is OK. Let yourself be angry with all the things that hurt you. Feel the sadness, the terrible disappointment, and the hurt. Then, eventually, evolve toward remembering what was good. The love you shared was genuine and holds meaning even if the relationship is now over. This isn't about wishing for a return to the past. It's about letting love and gratitude dominate *your* heart again.

The poet Rumi wisely said, *"The wound is the place where the light enters you."* Beautifully describing how our pains are also doorways to growth. This quote also created a powerful healing image for me. On several occasions while in meditation, I visualized blinding white light pouring into my wounded heart and pushing out all the darkness.

Take charge of which emotions you want filling *your* soul. Letting go of anger and seeing the other person with compassion and forgiveness will help you heal much faster than holding onto judgement and resentment. They put their hopes and hearts into the relationship as well. Everyone is losing something and starting over. Take the lessons you learned and use them to make your next relationship better.

Let Go of What is Gone

There is always the possibility of reconciliation and reconnection as a couple, but this is rare. It is most likely the case that an ending is permanent. If you find yourself yearning for your ex and holding out hope of being together again, try to remind yourself of the following. The person you were with no longer exists. No, not dead and gone. Just no longer the person that you had been in a loving, committed relationship with, and you are not the same person either.

Let go of what is gone and surrender them to their own future. A person who does not stay is clearly not meant for you. You are no longer responsible for them, and you no longer owe them your feelings. Wish them well, then go and live.

It took much healing work and many months for my heart to catch up to what my mind had known since the day we broke up. We were not right for each other, and moving on gave us the opportunity to create a healthier and happier life for ourselves.

Time Heals More if We Actively Live

You can sit in your home, depressed and swirling within your pain day after day. Or you can use each day to actively invest in making yourself and your life the best they can be. This brings multiple benefits. First, staying engaged in life helps shift your focus away from the past. Second, every effort you make to grow mentally, physically, emotionally, or spiritually will help you heal and create a better, more fulfilling life.

The end of a relationship can gift a huge amount of freedom, which can then be invested towards your well-being. What will you do with all this freed-up time? It is a time to take an honest look at ourselves and do everything we can to improve our lives. Get focused and dedicate your time to taking care of your holistic health. Get started on or improve your fitness. Improve your nutrition. Expand your relationship skills and understanding. Do new, fun, and interesting things.

Being newly single can feel tough at first. It takes time to adjust to being independent again. Be patient, stay positive, and keep an open mind. This phase comes with two incredible opportunities: you can focus completely on becoming the best version of yourself, and you now have space for someone even better suited for you to enter your life.

Time brings new experiences and new memories. Until enough new happens, the old relationship remains the dominant memory replaying in your mind and stuck in your body. In essence, without new experiences, it's like an old record has been left playing on an endless loop. This is why literally "moving on" is important. Get active living again, and the past will fade as the new replaces it.

Something that helped me see things with a healthier perspective was to think about the percentage of my life the relationship will represent. I was with Cindy for a significant period of time. But even 16 years is still less than a fifth of my life. When I did the math for the 2 ½ years I was with my second wife, it had a freeing effect. Those couple of years represented such a minuscule fraction of my entire life journey, around two percent. This awareness helped me to see the folly in letting such a tiny portion of my life become such an outsized and destructive force.

Putting the time with someone into perspective by no means magically heals the wounds or corrects the wrongs. It is offered simply as a mental tool, looking at reality, in a way that may give you an empowering perspective.

Surrender

Not surrender in a defeated, giving up kind of way. Surrender in the sense that you come to a full acceptance of the things out of your control. All that happened and all that now is. The universe is out of your control, and so are other people.

Try to understand what you can concerning what went wrong and what hurt you, so you can learn from it. Then, once you have gone in enough circles in your mind, give yourself permission to let it all go.

What happens existentially when a breakup or divorce occurs? Someone who was once not a part of your life came into it, was present for a time, and now they have left. You existed before them and continue to exist after. When it comes to the inner pain associated with the loss of a relationship and most other life struggles, accepting change ultimately brings peace. They are gone, and you are here. Be with your reality exactly where you are.

Keep Going

As a society, we can often underestimate how devastating relationship loss and abandonment are for many people. The truth is that for many it tears deep into the soul and wracks the body with profound pain. The energy is intense, and it will find release. We can allow that energy to wildly drive us towards self-destructive thoughts and behaviors. Or we can channel it through our core of love and use it to create an even better version of ourselves. We can choose to transmute the pain into wisdom and gratitude.

An insidious aspect to emotional pain is that it can drain the gratitude, love, and life right out of us. It can be one of life's greatest deceivers. Therefore, we must be conscious of how we react. Not many other life trials have the same power to either destroy us or motivate us towards a higher state of being. It is the very definition of a pivotal experience.

Refuse to let anything in life take you down the dark road. When life covers you in so much painful filth that you lose touch with the light, strive to get back to it. And until you do, try to be patient with yourself and life as the process unfolds. I have had to tell myself many times that tomorrow is a new day.

Life is where all possibilities and experiences are. Life is our only fundamental need. As long as there is life, there is still opportunity for everything we love and want.

CHAPTER TWENTY-EIGHT

PROFESSIONAL CARE

Healing and moving ever towards a better version of ourselves is a deeply personal journey. But experiencing it all, from within our own minds, can have us travelling very alone. During the toughest times, don't be afraid to ask your family and friends for help. You're not a burden. People care about you and want to be there for you.

Sometimes, when your emotional health is in extraordinary jeopardy, receiving support beyond friends and family may be necessary. For a person who is losing themselves to the point of having serious suicidal desires, getting professional care is vital. Professionals are professionals for a reason. They have specialized knowledge, skills, and experience that can make a huge difference for you.

The stigmas attached to going to therapy are silly and outdated with what we now know about our minds and bodies. Why is this the only area of our well-being where we feel ashamed or embarrassed to seek help? There is no stigma about getting a personal trainer for support with our bodies. In fact, all efforts here are celebrated. The health of our minds deserves to be viewed in the same way.

There are so many resources available that can help. Your health insurance provider, community health centers, employee support resources, private therapists, social services in your area, school and university resources for students, group therapies, and religious-based services. Don't let money worries stop you from getting help; there are many free or low-cost options available. Every therapist is different, and with time, you'll hopefully find one who's a great match for you. If the first person you meet with doesn't feel right, do not give up on therapy and try someone else. The right person for you is out there.

About four months before my wife's suicide, she called me while I was at work and said she wasn't feeling very good and that she was interested in talking to a therapist. I was both surprised and happy to hear she was willing to do this. My experience with her was that she never wanted any counseling or therapy. I gave her the number to make an appointment, which she did. I was so proud of her and hopeful that this could be very helpful to her.

Sadly, after one visit, she told me she wasn't going back. She expressed disappointment with the "guy" and the experience. She said he just asked her a bunch of questions and that it wasn't helpful. She had a cynical nature about "professionals" in any field, and her brief openness to seeing if someone could help her closed after one short attempt.

She never did go back nor try any other therapist. Four months later, she was dead. Now, I don't know what happened during her visit. I can't really begin to pass judgment as to what went wrong. It seems apparent to me from how she spoke about it that there was an authenticity that was lacking for her. Cindy probably needed to feel a real connection or sincere interest from the therapist in order for her to feel comfortable being vulnerable, to trust the person, and therefore be able to talk about deeply personal issues.

She gave up on the process very quickly, to say the least. It is sad to think that if by chance she had met someone with whom she felt better, things could have been very different. Countless people are helped and lives saved because of good behavioral health care.

Earlier, I mentioned the time when Cindy was forced to stay at a mental health care facility for two weeks after a suicidal episode. Even though she didn't choose to go there, the calming medications and therapy sessions made a big difference in getting her through that crisis. It even marked the beginning of many years with no overt suicidal problems.

Recently, while going through some old boxes, I found a letter she had written to thank the people at the facility who helped her. I still had the original letter because she wrote it in Spanish. The English translation I made was given to the hospital. It reads, *"Hi, I want to thank all of you for helping me resolve and understand my problems. I feel so much better now, thanks to the good treatment and attention you gave me. My entire stay there was excellent. You helped me get my life on a better path."*

I witnessed firsthand how even a small amount of therapy and treatment was a tremendous help for Cindy in dealing with her internal struggles and suicidality. I can't say for sure, but I believe that if she had gotten professional help again, she might have made it through that difficult time too.

Still, there is an unfortunate reality to our modern medical system that one must be careful of. When the profits are limitless and the medical schools indoctrinate with a pharmacological-centric philosophy, everyone with any problem looks like a mental patient.

Countless people are diagnosed with mental illnesses of varying degrees, who are really just people experiencing the detrimental emotional and physical effects of living in a modern society in total misalignment with how they were designed. Many would also be "healed" from their diagnosis if they began to adopt core beliefs about themselves and the world that actually supported their well-being. This is, of course, in addition to ensuring that their physical body is being properly taken care of.

Some people can really benefit from medication. It can also be absolutely required due to severe conditions such as schizophrenia. But it's also true that prescription drugs can sometimes cause dangerous problems or side effects. That's why, as a starting point, everyone should try to care for their mental, emotional, and physical health in natural ways, such as through proper sleep, exercise, healthy food, and positive human connections.

Even though popping pills may feel like a quicker, easier fix, it certainly does not replace intentional healthy living. If you feel you are in dire need, then by all means do both. With time, if you do the work to improve your holistic health, you may realize the pills are no longer necessary.

CHAPTER TWENTY-NINE

CONNECTION AND COMMUNITY

THE PURSUIT OF SELF-REALIZATION AND INDEPENDENT WELL-BEING IS IMPORTANT FOR EVERYONE. All things outside of ourselves can fall apart; therefore, healthy independence is important. But deep down, we are naturally social and family-oriented beings. Any study of human history, biology, sociology, and anything else about humans illustrates our innate design is to connect both emotionally and physically with other people.

Studies show that when there is a significant lack in these areas, we suffer both physically and mentally. A higher level of social connectedness is also correlated with a decreased risk of suicide. Just as isolation and loneliness significantly raise the risk. For a vast improvement in your sense of well-being, it behooves you to develop, nourish, and enjoy meaningful connections with family, friends, and community.

In addition to suicide, loneliness or disconnectedness are believed to be responsible for most other "deaths of despair." Deaths of despair are those caused by self-inflicted detrimental lifestyle choices, such as alcohol related illnesses and drug overdoses. Death from heart disease or type 2 diabetes caused by obesity could also fall into this category.

Despite the enhanced connectivity created by modern technologies, isolation and loneliness are growing. Society is suffering more and more from a lack of meaningful human interactions and relationships. One study found that one in five Americans say they have no one they can talk to or look to for support in a problem or crisis.

To avoid slipping into isolation, we must be intentional about connecting with others. Spend quality time with your family. Eat meals, have fun, and go places together. Put away your phone and take a break from work so you can truly connect with the people who love and need you the most.

Friends and community outside our family are also very important, and you should make time for them too. It's easy to get stuck in a bubble with just your immediate family, but close relationships, both inside and outside the home, are key to our happiness and health.

The people we spend our time with usually influences us more than any other factor. This is why we need to create and maintain relationships with those who lift up our experience of life, while we too, strive to be that kind of person.

CHAPTER THIRTY

DISCOVERING SELF, PURPOSE & MEANING

As THE PRINCIPAL THEME OF THIS BOOK MAKES CLEAR, life is precarious and fraught with infinite dangers to our beings. When things fall apart and we are severely tested, we need to know who we are, and have a sense of purpose that carries us through. We need to feel that our life has meaning. As we discuss these three concepts, you will notice that they can be closely related and the process of their discovery often overlaps.

Who we are and what we truly value begin as inherently foggy ideas for us. This won't change unless there is an intentional effort to discover these things. The immense amount of conditioning from all the powerful influences outside of us naturally has us assimilate to our surroundings. Discovering who we truly are as separate from our families, culture, and the things we have come to identify with will happen naturally to some degree as we experience life and mature, but it will be limited without conscious effort.

Taking effective action towards discovering *the self* means actively living in every sense. It means continually learning and seeking new discoveries about life. Trying new things, like a new skill or hobby, and going to new places. Pushing beyond routines and comfort zones. Continuing to seek and develop new human connections, and engaging with the world as your authentic self.

Some of the most important things to learn about ourselves are:

- What brings me peace and joy?
- What kind of lifestyle do I want to live?
- How do I feel loved and valued?
- What are my triggers and weaknesses?
- What core beliefs are guiding my interpretations and responses to life?
- What things are most meaningful and important to me?
- What unhealed, unresolved wounds and traumas do I have?
- What are my fears?
- What do I want in an intimate relationship?
- How do I want to be remembered?

"Discover yourself, otherwise you have to depend on other people's opinions who don't know themselves." -Osho

Purpose & Meaning

A purpose is a vision or aim that motivates and guides our thoughts and actions. Finding purpose that supports your personal growth *and* has a positive impact on others is important for a life that feels fulfilling.

It's important to understand that our sense of self and what matters to us can change over time, and our purpose can change too. That's completely normal. We will have many different purposes throughout life. Meaning is needed because it helps us understand the "whys" of our lives. As the saying goes, "If you have a why, then you are able to bear any how."

Purpose can be discovered by accident, but to aid in the discovery, it helps to be in a continual learning state, regularly exposed to new ideas and activities. When you find yourself engaged in something that makes you feel intensely alive, happy, and aligned with what you find meaningful, you have most likely found a purpose.

Changing the world, attaining enlightenment, or reaching heaven are examples of pursuing what could be called very high purposes. You are more than welcome to pursue these things, but we can also remember that there is a beautiful life to be found in the much more seemingly mundane. Things that, for the most part, are easily attained. Living a life taking care of our basic needs, and experiencing the beauty of the universe freely available to us all.

Consider the following needs and see if this is a life that most of us are capable of living. Physical needs: safety, shelter, food, water, air, touch, and movement. Emotional needs: Self-love, human connection, being seen, heard, and valued. Spiritual needs: self-exploration and expression, purpose, living authentically, positively impacting others, and expansion of experience. Valuing these as our fundamental purposes sets our expectations exactly where they will best serve us.

As we search for meaning out in the world, we should never forget to continue the search within. We all understand the big meaningful things, like helping others or being a parent. But just as it is with purpose, we can also find meaning in the smallest moments and everyday things. Wherever you find yourself, whatever you are doing, there is inherent meaning, all due to the fact that you are alive to experience it. Every part of your life, large and small, makes up its whole, and your life means everything.

Simply living your daily life can be meaningful beyond measure. It is your mindset alone that determines the value of the life you are living. We can fall in love every day with all of the seemingly small things in life. Things we often take for granted, like taking a shower, eating a meal, and going for a walk. Imagine how blissful life would be if the great and seemingly insignificant were all given the same appreciation.

A diamond is rare but dull in comparison to the shimmer of the breeze and sunlight on water. Gold is scarce, yet the shades in a sunset are infinite and ablaze. Love withers, while the wind caresses, and the sun's warmth embraces without condition.

Self-knowing, meaning, and purpose are potent forces for positivity and resilience. They are like your raft, food, and water when your life collides into unwanted change and chaos. When everything else feels uncertain or falls apart, remember who you are and believe in your life.

Above all, never forget the one purpose we all share. After all the layers of life's complexity are peeled away, the purpose of life is simply to be alive. So, take some of the weight of the world off your shoulders and at the end of the day, give yourself permission to just live.

"A good traveler has no fixed plans, and is not intent on arriving."-Lao Tzu

CHAPTER THIRTY-ONE

SELF-COMPASSION AND FORGIVENESS

We HAVE EXPLORED A LOT ABOUT HOW THE OUTSIDE WORLD CAN HURT US. What about when the negativity is sourced from within? When it is us who have done things to hurt other people and ourselves? How do we heal from our own negative impact? This is where we need to practice self-compassion and self-forgiveness. We regularly forgive others, yet hold lifetime grudges against ourselves. If an enduring positive life experience is what we are trying to create, then we have to be at peace with ourselves.

None of us is perfect, so that's a basic reason we should have some compassion with ourselves. On top of this, we live in a tough world where it's easy to feel bad about ourselves. There's sexual shame from every direction, shame induced from abandonment, and from being demeaned and criticized. There's pressure to have incredible success in every part of life, measured by what society currently values, of course. We're supposed to be rich, have a great career, and be very influential. We're also expected to have the perfect marriage, honor roll kids, and constantly have amazing trips around the world. We are all repeatedly told while growing up that we can be anything we want and achieve any dream. We just have to work hard enough, and it will all be ours.

It's okay to want these things, in fact, who wouldn't? Life, however, is chaotic and will throw unexpected problems at us. It cannot ever be all roses and blue skies, let alone jet-setting, fame, the perfect spouse, and kids in Harvard. You could do everything "right" and, because of an infinite number of variables, never get close to attaining the "dream life" society says we are supposed to achieve. And obviously, we don't do everything right. Reality is that we are going to do a lot very wrong, and other people will definitely do us wrong. Life is also going to be just plain unfair many times.

Despite my highest intentions and best efforts, I've lost two marriages now and all my wealth. Did I ever imagine that life was going to be this rocky with these important issues? No way. My family was a mess growing up, and I was sure that I was going to do it right. More than anything I wanted to have a happy family and be financially secure. But things didn't go as planned.

When things go wrong, it's natural to want to blame someone. Many people blame others instead of taking responsibility. But for a lot of us, the problem isn't with blaming others. Instead, we place all our hate, blame, and shame on ourselves.

We know ourselves better than anyone else, right? Therefore, we know our imperfections and shortcomings better than anyone. We are easy targets. And because we can't escape ourselves, our minds continually go over and over what we did wrong or what we could have done differently. In the end, we are the only person we have control over, so it does make sense to look at where our responsibilities lie. But, and this is a big "but", the reasons for negative results are often more complex than we initially perceive. So many things and people are interacting in any situation. In the painful aftermath of bad experiences, it is so important to slow down and look at the whole situation with patience and compassion.

When things go wrong, it's important to reflect on what happened and be aware of our role in it. We need to take responsibility and feel the appropriate guilt when our actions hurt someone. This helps us apologize, fix things honestly, and learn from our mistakes. Most people don't have a big problem with this part. Most people don't have a problem with forgiving other people either. It's ourselves that we have a very hard time forgiving. If you look at any person who is genuinely suffering long-term, and you could see inside of them, you'd see a hurting, self-condemning little inner child.

The best way to truly forgive yourself and others is to understand that, at your core, you are good and worthy, even though you're imperfect and always growing. You've always wanted what's best for yourself and others, but you make mistakes and sometimes get off track. Still, you have always done the best you can, just as others do, with the emotional tools you have at any given time. Wisdom and maturity vary so much.

There is a powerful declaration that has helped countless people find patience and acceptance during hard times. "You are exactly where you need to be." This is helpful because it fully accepts what is, and from here, how you respond and move forward is all that matters. The alternative path of self-shame and condemnation would prevent your life from moving towards a better place.

So, when you find yourself carrying shame and don't seem to be able to forgive yourself, consider this practice. Imagine the three-year-old version of yourself standing in front of you. Now, realize that the little child is still you. Inside of us all is a child with deep wounds yearning for love and acceptance. Think about how you would care for and support your younger self. Then treat *yourself* with the same compassion you would show that child. If they messed up and were feeling bad, you wouldn't tell them "Yeah, you suck you piece of shit." Yet, this is often our inner dialogue. Instead, how about we tell ourselves, "You are good enough. I forgive you." When you're feeling down, give yourself credit and gratitude for all the many things you've done so well and everything you've been through.

An awareness of my wounded inner child was something I didn't have in the aftermath of Cindy's death. But during my next life crisis of divorce, this advice really helped. I actually spoke out loud to my hurting inner child Chris, and said with sincerity, "I love you" and "I am not going to abandon you. You are safe. I see you. I'm so sorry that things have happened this way." I have literally wrapped my arms around myself and given myself sincere hugs. I've reminded myself of who I am and the truth of my life. It was real and effective self-love in action. This stuff may sound strange, but loving yourself is not crazy and it's not a joke. When you are in the midst of horrendous inner suffering, it's time to seek help, but it's also time to save yourself. Who should be more responsible for our healing than our own selves? From whom do we deserve love the most?

Speaking to yourself out loud, declaring positive self-affirmations, and expressing compassion and confidence will bring about profound changes. The lies we come to believe about ourselves get embedded deep within and need to be confronted with the truth.

Let go of self-anger, regret, and condemnation. You deserve to be free of these life-draining things. You deserve forgiveness. Continuing to feel ashamed for past mistakes means you're falsely believing that you should be perfect or that your past self should have known what you know now. If you're actively working on bettering yourself, you're already living the best life you can, so be compassionate with yourself. At this moment, right now, you have enough, you do enough, and you *are* enough. Your journey is beautiful, even if it gets messy, like all the rest of us.

CHAPTER THIRTY-TWO

SELF-WORTH

IN A WORLD THAT MAKES US FEEL LIKE WE'RE NOT GOOD ENOUGH. Recognizing that we are intrinsically valuable and worthy is one of the most important truths we can learn about ourselves. This creates a secure foundation from which we can think, feel, and take on the challenge of existence. If you ever feel unworthy or like you don't matter, it's likely you've started to believe something about yourself or the world that isn't true. Beliefs that don't match who you really are. To move past these lies, let's take a moment to recognize a few important things together:

Your Existence is Beautiful

First of all, it is not wrong that you were born or that you are alive. There is no inherent burden you carry simply for being a human being. You are one of a kind and made for life. Your most fundamental right is to determine your unique path of exploration and engagement with this world. While you are alive, a blank canvas is gifted to you with each new day.

Prioritizing Self-Care

The people who need us deserve our love and care. We must be careful, however, not to endlessly sacrifice our own needs for others. Like the parent who runs themselves ragged serving their family. Everything they do is for the benefit of the kids and their spouse. At the end of each day, all their energy, emotion, and resources were spent on others, leaving them with little left for themselves. Like a drowning person who gives their life vest to another, when they were the one who needed it most.

Self-abandonment is unsustainable, wholly unfair, and not in the best interest of the whole. And we've seen what it can lead to. People can fall apart when their personal needs are neglected for too long. Though their intentions are good, in the end, everyone loses when there is nothing left to give. You have to be a priority too.

Ending the Self-Sabotage

Developing and maintaining our self-worth won't happen by accident. It has endless enemies and can remain a fragile thing. The world and other people will negatively impact us all the way until the end. The least we can do for ourselves is limit the *self*-inflicted suffering. You deserve to think and act in ways that support your well-being. Consider the following five ways to stop causing your own suffering:

1. Stop Comparing Yourself to Others

The old saying, "Comparison is the thief of joy," is 100% true. You are you, and there's no reason to compare yourself to anyone else. You could always find someone who is better looking, richer, smarter, or more successful. But that has nothing to do with you. You're on your own journey. You're living your life, at your pace, in your own way, and there's no need to measure it against someone else's.

No one can be more critical of you than you. Instead, try being your own greatest advocate and cheerleader. When your negative self-talk begins, remember that this is not who you are. Instead of letting the negative thoughts continue, tell yourself, "I love you, I forgive you, and I will do better."

2. Stop Telling Yourself that You Can't Change

You *can* change in amazing ways. Even if you've had negative habits or thoughts for a long time, you can still choose to change them. Every new day is a fresh chance to shape your life the way you want it to be.

Changing our habits and mindset is a challenging task. But if you set goals, take small steps, get support, and refuse to give up. You can reshape your whole life if you really want to.

3. Stop Hurting Your Life

Get out of that detrimental relationship. Set healthy boundaries with your friends and family. Abandon the habits that are creating temporary relief and pleasure at the cost of your long-term health and well-being. This could be countless things, from laziness to drugs, video games to alcohol.

4. Overcome Identifications and Attachments

Your self-worth has nothing to do with anything outside of you. "SELF"-worth, remember!? So, your partner, your job, your possessions, your successes and failures, other people's opinion of you, and all of the things outside of you need to be disassociated from anything to do with your self-worth.

All the circumstances and people around you are going through constant change. If how you feel about yourself is attached to any of these things, then you are at their mercy. This creates a lifetime of inner chaos. This would be like tying your sense of peace and happiness to the weather.

No matter what people say, what's going on in your life, or what you own, you are already whole, unique, and worthy. Your value doesn't depend on your past, your current situation, or what the future holds. To truly know your worth, you have to recognize this part of yourself, love it deeply, and promise not to turn your back on yourself ever again. Real self-worth and self-love don't come from the outside. It is simply who we are when we let all identifications, attachments, and expectations fall away.

Love Yourself

We naturally start out with a belief that others are responsible for our well-being. As helpless babies and children, how could it be any other way? However, relying on others as a source of love and happiness is an unreliable faucet of positivity at best. The flow is intermittent and sometimes shuts off entirely, leaving us holding an empty cup. Worst of all, when the flow turns toxic and sputters vitriol and hate, the poison gets inside us before we know it.

After going through enough ups and downs trying to get love from outside sources, we eventually learn there's a better way. Real, steady love starts with us. We can take full responsibility for caring for ourselves and giving ourselves the love we need. This doesn't mean we shut people out or become isolated; it just means that when we feel full and complete on the inside, the love we get from others is a bonus, not a requirement. And if others are negative or don't show love, it doesn't affect us as much, because we already feel whole and know how to meet our own needs.

Of all the ideas we have discussed, loving yourself as you would your own child will help you forgive and value yourself as you should. Instead of being your own harshest critic and punisher, you become your own greatest advocate. No matter how old you are, there is still a fragile soul in there that yearns to be supported, protected, affirmed, and valued.

What we do or don't do never defines our worth. Worth is infinite. Our actions affect our relationships; they can either help love grow or tear it down. Our actions also shape how close we feel to our most authentic self. But no matter what we do, our worth never changes. Nothing can take that away.

Peace is found after a long journey of searching in vain through experiences and people, and finally coming home to yourself. When you find your happily ever after within, nothing can ever take it away from you.

Ways to Practice Loving Yourself

- Forgiving yourself.
- Prioritizing your own needs (physical, mental and emotional).
- Loving your body by optimizing physical health.
- Valuing yourself.
- Respecting yourself.
- Celebrating and feeling gratitude for your life.
- Believing and trusting in yourself.
- Being honest with yourself and others.
- Letting go of what you can't control.
- Maintaining boundaries.
- Surrounding yourself with healthy people.
- Being kind to yourself.
- Seeing yourself as the hero in your story.
- Remembering your inner child and never giving up on them.

Beyond being an indispensable part of a thriving life, a solid sense of self-worth is likely the most powerful preventative factor against suicide. If your self-worth and self-love are lacking, you must invest in this part of you. Don't wait any longer. When you can sincerely tell yourself, "I see you, I accept you, I forgive you, and I love you", you have truly found yourself. We spend lots of time and effort showing this kind of love for others. We too surely deserve this kind of relationship with ourselves.

One of the most important things about self-love is how it enables us to experience any kind of suffering and still tell ourselves, "I will not let this take away my mental and physical well-being. This will not continue to diminish my life or those around me." Self-love allows us to move ever more quickly out of any darkness. We feel the impact, receive the lessons, and then return to the light.

CHAPTER THIRTY-THREE

PAIN IS FOR YOU

"We are born into a world so arranged that the price we pay for enjoying it. This is to say, we have sensitive bodies. Is that these bodies are at the same time, because they are sensitive, are capable of the most excruciating agonies."

-Alan Watts

Oⱽᴇʀᵂʜᴇʟᴍɪɴɢ ᴇᴍᴏᴛɪᴏɴᴀʟ ᴏʀ ᴘʜʏsɪᴄᴀʟ ᴘᴀɪɴ ᴀʀᴇ ᴛʜᴇ ᴍᴀᴊᴏʀ ᴄᴀᴛᴀʟʏsᴛs ᴛᴏ sᴜɪᴄɪᴅᴀʟ ɪᴅᴇᴀᴛɪᴏɴ ᴀɴᴅ ᴀᴄᴛs. Countless suicide notes and attempt survivors make this clear. Suicide never occurs when someone is feeling pleasant. It is the desire to end one's pain that becomes the push over the edge.

Since pain holds this key role in suicide, it is of the utmost importance to look deeper into what pain is. Pain seems like a simple enough thing, but do we really understand what it is? Is it wholly terrible and our mortal enemy - the thing we should fear most? When understood, pain becomes less frightening and loses much of its power. And most importantly, it would never feel so overwhelming or unbearable that we'd seek to escape from it at any cost.

How we deal with life's inevitable pain is one of our most critical choices. Pain is like fire. It's intense, it hurts, it's chaotic, and it has both the potential to destroy and create. With the wrong mindset of fear and resistance, our pain and suffering become the biggest reasons for our downfall. If we miss the lessons and the opportunities our hard experiences provide, and instead choose anger, resentment, and defeat, we move towards darkness. Our life experience becomes severely diminished as pain becomes our master.

We all have pain in our past, and there is, of course, much more still to come. It's time to let go of the belief that pain is our greatest enemy. Instead, we can learn to take back control and use our pain in a beneficial way, so it becomes something we can manage and even learn from. The truth about our relationship with pain is both simple and eye-opening.

Pain is an integral part of our life experience. A very unpleasant part, but it plays a critical role. The truth is, pain, both emotional and physical, is important for our survival and well-being. It is there to protect and improve our lives, quite the opposite of inspiring self-destruction.

One of pain's primary functions is the *escape action* it induces. This is what causes us to react quickly and instinctively when we're in danger, like pulling our hand away from a hot flame. The same escape action occurs with emotional pain. For example, if we're in an abusive relationship, the emotional pain we feel can push us to leave that harmful situation. It's our built-in alarm system trying to keep us safe.

In a very real way, suicide occurs when our pain's inducement to escape, meant to protect us, goes horribly wrong. Spiraling out of control in the worst possible way. For the suicidal, pain ceases to be the guide and protector it was designed to be, as *total* escape becomes the only priority.

To avoid this fate, you have to understand that the pain you feel is not you. Do not get lost in it or become identified with it. Hard feelings are temporary and do not define you nor your life.

Your core is happiness and peace, which is why these are your highest ideals and what you continually seek, and where you feel most content.

Emotional pain and distress arise to make sure you know that something needs to change. It is an inner tool that helps us manage ourselves within social dynamics. Just like physical pain tells you something's wrong with your body, emotional pain is a signal that something in your relationships or inner world needs care and attention. Sometimes, even your values and meaning systems need to be looked at and adjusted. At times, it may seem an unbearable misery, but this is the way it is supposed to be. Pain, with its varying degrees of intensity, is specifically designed to force action.

All the difficult emotions you feel, like sadness, anger, betrayal, disappointment, loneliness, grief, and shame, are all trying to help you. These feelings are like signposts, pointing towards where healing and change are needed.

In order to make the pain work for you as it is designed. The next time you feel it, slow down, breathe, and take a moment to step outside of yourself and try to objectively observe what is happening. Remind yourself that it is okay to feel. Remember that you have gone through hard times before and that this will be temporary. Then ask yourself: What is this pain teaching me? What is it revealing? How is this pain trying to help me?"

Your emotions are not an oppressor to be hated and feared. They are part of your innate knowing. They are sourced from your deepest inner wisdom.

If your emotional pain is associated with feelings of being a burden and a loss of belonging, be especially careful. Be aware that these particular negative feelings have the strongest relationship with suicide. These kinds of feelings can be especially painful and need to be addressed right away.

Remember: you are worthy, you do matter, and you do belong. If you're feeling anything different, it's because someone else has hurt you or because you did something that went against your true values, which led to guilt or shame. But even then, you can still heal and grow. Feelings don't define your worth. You deserve compassion from yourself and others. You deserve forgiveness and to be seen for all your good. You deserve every opportunity to continue progressing on your journey.

When it comes to prolonged emotional pain, know that there is a natural pace to healing that is unknowable. Trusting your heart's power to heal and being patient are important when dealing with life's larger difficulties. Any experience of pain can eventually fade and become a distant memory.

The philosopher Marcus Aurelius said, *"Do not disturb yourself by imagining your whole life at once."* Often, when we are feeling bad, we tend to wrap the whole story of our life in misery. We start thinking about everything negative we've experienced and we tell ourselves extreme things like, "My life sucks" or "Everything always goes wrong." These thoughts aren't true. Start noticing when this happens. When these thoughts show up, don't believe them. Watch them come, recognize they're not the truth, and then let them pass. You can even imagine them floating away from your mind and disappearing like a faint mist.

Emotional pain, as this chapter title declares, is *for* you. It is your friend. Your intense, impatient, highly demanding, and uncomfortable friend. Helping you to know that something is wrong or in jeopardy with your personal well-being or your important relational world. It will help you every time if you can just remain aware and not get lost in the wrong story playing out in your head. It's time to overcome the lie that emotional pain is an affliction. It's actually trying to gift you a better life, but only if you follow its guidance.

We must also remember, the good, the wonderful, and the light can't exist or have meaning without the bad, the painful, and the dark. If you enjoy pleasure, you can thank the existence of discomfort. We can only know life through its contrasts.

Throughout the book, I have attempted to describe the pain I felt in the aftermath of Cindy's suicide and the later divorce. Still, words will always fall short of capturing the breadth and depth of its impact. But it was the pain that motivated and guided me during the biggest turning points of my life. It inspired me to go on that timeless and critical journey inward in search of the truest version of myself. Now, my joy reaches higher because of the lows to which I fell. Trust in myself is unshakable because I faced death, chaos, and the real risk of losing myself, and still made it through. With pain, I now lead the way, instead of it leading me.

Pain has always been there to help us. We just needed to realize it. How we interpret and give meaning to our pain makes the biggest difference in whether it will be for our benefit or harm.

CHAPTER THIRTY-FOUR

BELIEF SYSTEMS SHAPE OUR EXPERIENCE

There is a statistic about suicide that illustrates how much our belief systems cause emotional suffering. No, not religious beliefs. When I talk about our belief systems, it refers to how we see ourselves and the world.

It turns out that children under 14 years of age are largely unaffected by suicide. In 2012, for example, suicides for kids ages 5 to 14 represented 0.7 percent of the total suicides in the U.S. And even within this age group, the vast majority of these suicides fell within the upper age range. Suicidal ideation and behaviors then sharply increase in adolescence, around the age of 14. What happens within our minds at this stage of development that results in feeling that death may be preferable to life? The answers are important because they also teach us about how much our mind shapes our experience.

As we grow into teenagers, we begin moving beyond a simple existence that was more instinctual and reactive. We begin to think and feel deeply into the experience of ourselves and the world, though the process of self-realization is still in its infancy. Still, as consciousness increases with adolescence, everything begins to be experienced more profoundly. Social interactions start to take on great importance, both the good and the bad.

Identifications, attachments, and expectations also really begin to take hold during this period. We start to assign meaning to who we are and our place in the world. This is also the time our "ego" begins to be strongly manifest. We begin to care deeply about what happens around us and how others see us. Disappointments, break-ups, losses, failures, and insults all become potential catalysts for severe and prolonged suffering. Notice how conflicts between teens and adults can sometimes lead to grudges that last for years. Whereas between two children, hard feelings were completely forgotten by the following day, if not within minutes.

Prior to adolescence, we accepted life more just as it was. We cried about hurtful events, then quickly and effortlessly moved on. Seemingly okay with a life that would not always happen the way we want. With a less established ego, life situations were not experienced as the deep threats and affronts they become in our teens and beyond.

Though our mental capacity grows, our ability to be fully present with life seems to diminish. Children get completely absorbed in whatever they're doing. They find joy, wonder, and thrill in the smallest things. But as the years pass, life feels more and more familiar, and we overlook how amazing everything still is.

Then, as if all these factors weren't bad enough, we develop a perpetual mindset that the future holds what will finally bring us happiness. Always anticipating the next thing, love, marriage, career, house, kids, etc. But even as each one of these is attained, we begin longing for what's still to come. Retirement, paid-off house, kids out of the house, going to

Heaven, etc. When we were children, the present moment was always more than enough.

Recognizing the nature of these changes in our minds can help us make sense of why life becomes so mentally and emotionally difficult. For many of us, maturing means carrying the pain of our past, feeling out of touch with the present, and imagining a future where we're finally happy. We all forget what we once knew without even trying, as children. That life is something best experienced in the here and now.

A particularly problematic belief system for those in severe suffering is known as "Black and White, All or Nothing Thinking." This common method of self-sabotage is a way of interpreting the world in absolute terms, where everything is viewed at extremes. Black and white thinking is known as a "cognitive distortion" because it inhibits rational thinking and certainly distorts the truth. Regularly using the words "always" and "never" can be a strong indicator of this mindset.

When black and white thinking combines with our inherent negativity bias, it results in catastrophizing situations, condemning ourselves and others, and as the old saying goes, "Throwing the baby out with the bath water." This mindset is particularly dangerous because life can come to be seen as *all* bad, that one is *totally* worthless, or that things will *never* get better. These, of course, are all untruths and unhelpful responses to life. Black and white thinking's inseparable companions are stress, anxiety, depression, and hopelessness.

Keeping our minds away from the extremes releases us from the enormous pressure they create. During difficult times, balanced thinking lessens despair and allows us to see the positives in situations and people. Keeping an open mind allows us to consider different alternatives and possibilities. Reality is a highly nuanced mix of both positive and negative.

It's deadly serious, totally ridiculous, and everything in between.

When I fully accepted that my life is both a tragedy and triumph, joy and suffering, pleasure and pain, and always will be. It felt as if the world was lifted off my shoulders.

Now let's look at two of the most empowering belief systems we can have.

I Am the Observer

Learning to manage our thoughts and emotions enhances our lives like little else can. Due to their ability to either lift us up or tear us down. The norm, of course, being a messy mix of both. To achieve well-being, we must free ourselves from what is the de facto chaos of our inner worlds.

The most effective way to do this is to think of yourself as the *observer* of your thoughts, feelings, and emotions. They are just like pop-ups on your computer screen, and just like with a pop-up, you get to decide what to do with them. Thoughts are also very comparable to dreams in that they are often chaotic, horrible, frightening, ridiculous, and even random. Our brains are relentless thought machines. Thoughts are running all day long and even while we sleep. It's likely that a majority of these never-ending thoughts deserve to be given little importance.

We are not our thoughts or emotions. Realizing this can completely change how you experience life. When you understand that your thoughts and feelings are not who you are, you stop being controlled by them. Instead of letting your old habits and automatic reactions take over, *you* take the lead. You become the one creating your life, not just reacting to it.

When unwanted thoughts and emotions begin to run out of control, follow these steps to help bring yourself back into peace:

1. Slow everything down.
2. Take deeper, slower breaths and observe your breathing for a few moments.
3. Acknowledge the thoughts and feelings you are having.
4. Clearly name the feelings, such as "I feel so angry, I feel betrayed, or I feel I hate myself."
5. Then declare the truth to yourself. "These thoughts and emotions are not me." This simple declaration creates the needed space between you and the negative thoughts.
6. Acknowledge yourself with calming compassion by reminding yourself, "It's okay to feel."
7. If the thoughts and pain are from anything in your past, declare, "This is the past leaving me."

This kind of self-awareness is the first step to freeing yourself from emotionally charged reactive behavior that does nothing but make things worse. Then, after you've prevented yourself from spiraling out of control, you can take action to further calm and heal by practicing the many techniques in this book for soothing the nervous system and self-care.

So much of our suffering comes from attaching our identity and therefore value to things, ideas, and people, and from believing things which aren't true about ourselves. So, whatever the problem is, it is incredibly helpful to remind yourself about your true nature. If it's a financial issue, declare "I am not my money." If it is a relationship issue, declare, "So and so is not me." If it is a problem with work, declare "I am not my job." If it is with painful emotions themselves, declare "I am not my pain." Doing this has a powerful calming effect because it's the actual truth.

Enduring happiness is for those who overcome the deceptive experiences, thoughts, and emotions and come back to the truth again and again. Our detrimental conditioning can never be fully erased, the insecure ego will never die, and pain cannot be avoided. Therefore, the only solution is to intentionally *manage* them. This means to always remain the objective observer of these forces, as opposed to their puppet.

Never Abandon Yourself

The most consequential belief systems you have in life are the ones about yourself. Whether these beliefs are supportive or detrimental determines the quality of your life. They create your relationship with yourself, and this determines the relationship you'll have with the world. For example, you'll be able to love others much more if you love yourself. If you don't value yourself, you will find little value in the world.

If you're struggling to feel at peace with yourself, it might help to revisit some of the ideas we talked about in Chapter 32, Self-Worth. Also, remember to picture that inner child of yours. What does that child deserve to feel and think about themselves? Now you can give yourself the love, care, and acceptance you have always needed and deserved. You can fully accept yourself exactly as you are, even as you continue to evolve. You can believe in yourself and forgive yourself. You can be kind and patient with yourself. You're worth acting in the best interest of your heart, mind, and body.

When our suffering and traumas breed horrible lies in our minds about ourselves and the world, feelings of doom and hopelessness can take over. We can lose touch with our innate desire to be alive, much less thrive. These lies must be overcome so we can heal.

The best way to get rid of a lie is to replace it with the truth. Sometimes that truth comes from someone else, and sometimes you have to keep repeating it to yourself until you believe it. One helpful way to do this is by using positive affirmations, repeating kind, true words about yourself.

A good way to start practicing this is by doing guided affirmations. There are many online video resources available by searching "positive affirmations." Or you can make it even more specific to your needs, such as "positive affirmations after a break-up." Guided meditations are a similar resources that are also wonderfully helpful. The following are some I consider to be the most important.

I believe in myself, I trust myself.

I am wonderfully unique and incomparable to others.

I forgive myself.

My worth is innate and cannot be taken away.

I have enough. I do enough. I am enough.

I am loved.

I am not my pain.

I am progressing towards the best version of myself.

I embrace change.

I am good enough.

I am grateful for all of the beauty in my life.

If you are going through an extremely difficult time and feeling low about yourself. I invite you to affirm these powerful truths to yourself every day for as long as you need to. Say them out loud and let them remind you who you really are. It may feel strange at first. It may feel weak and embarrassing. Just consider giving it a try. You'll probably be surprised at how good it feels.

Guided affirmations were particularly helpful to me because the death, divorce, and financial loss all combined, putting my sense of self in real trouble. Also, I made the classic mistake of trying to go back and "save the marriage" after it was clearly over. This set me up to be knocked down further. Once my experience changed from one of respectful, cooperative separation to that of being rejected, it attacked all my vulnerabilities. My inner child was now not worth choosing, not worth forgiving, and not valuable. All lies created within myself, but for several weeks, I was believing them without being conscious of how they were eating away at me.

Listening to and repeating positive affirmations helped rewire my brain out of the fog of self-deprecating lies. Remember the tunnel vision that can occur during times of emotional crisis. Affirmations are light that cuts through the darkness. They bring truth and positivity. I don't want to sound overly dramatic and call them a "lifeline", because I could have endured without them, but they really did help. They were so effective in lifting my spirits and helping me let go of the painful past that I found myself repeating them every day during the worst months. This practice surely moved my healing process along much more quickly. Think of it as free, simple, and effective therapy available anytime you need it.

I could have felt embarrassed or weak because I did these kinds of affirmations. Well, guess what? I was at a weak point. I am thankful that I loved and supported myself in all the ways I could find. For all the positive things that helped me get back to a place where I was again thankful for my past, peacefully in the present, and hopeful about my future.

An anonymous quote says, "*Your brain is a supercomputer, and your self-talk is the program it will run.*" More anciently, the Buddha said, "*We are what we think. All that we are arises with our thoughts. With our thoughts we make the world.*"

CHAPTER THIRTY-FIVE

YOUR BODY

AFTER OUR THOUGHTS AND EMOTIONS, our bodies are the next most important factor affecting our well-being. All experience includes our bodies as part of the equation. Sometimes we may feel like we leave our bodies, but the body is always there. Mental and physical health are so interconnected that a lack in one brings down the other. Just as improvement in one will raise the other. For the suicidally inclined, prioritizing physical health is a must.

We now know that many mental and behavioral problems, especially in young people, are often caused by poor nutrition, lack of movement, and harmful environmental factors. The quality of your life really does depend on how you move, what's on your plate, and in your glass. We've discussed just how important self-love is, and we can't truly love ourselves unless we attentively take care of our bodies too.

Food is one of life's great pleasures. But with all that's available out there, it's easy to make unhealthy decisions that hurt us. The good news is, today we also have more opportunities than ever to eat in a healthy way. Right along with the endless variety of junk, there is an abundance of healthy options. For optimal well-being, intentionally pursuing holistic nutrition is paramount. We need unprocessed, unrefined, organic, and nutrient-dense foods. For the majority of us, consuming a variety of healthy proteins, vegetables, fruits, grains, seeds, nuts, starches, and fats is ideal. Eating moderate amounts until satiated, not stuffed. Some supplementation can also be important.

Long-term well-being must be the priority, rather than short-term pleasure and convenience.

Gut Health

In recent years, the importance of our gut health and "microbiome" has become more understood. We cannot thrive with an unhealthy gut. It's where we digest our food and absorb all our nutrients. Eighty percent of the immune system is in the gut. A large portion of our hormones, including most of our feel-good hormone serotonin, are produced there. Mental health and the gut are fully connected.

Unhealthy diet, stress, alcohol, and overuse of antibiotics all damage our gut. In addition to avoiding these things, we can support our gut health with probiotic foods such as cold fermented sauerkraut, kimchi, kombucha and yogurt. A probiotic supplement may be helpful as well.

Hydration

Being well-hydrated is needed to keep everything in our bodies functioning properly, including our sleep quality, cognition, and mood. As soon as you wake up, start your day with a glass of water. Eight eight-ounce glasses of water per day seems to be the general recommendation. Of course, this will vary with factors such as body weight, level of physical activity, and outside temperatures. And no, coffee doesn't count as water!

Fasting

Daily intermittent fasting and periodic 24 to 72-hour fasts also have incredible proven benefits, such as increasing metabolism, reducing body fat, reducing inflammation, reducing blood sugar levels, and increasing levels of human growth hormone. It also boosts brain function and helps prevent neurodegenerative disorders. There is also research showing that fasting can increase longevity and delay disease.

We'd be missing out on an extremely powerful tool for our well-being if we don't make fasting a part of our routine. Go about doing it wisely and do your own research. Professional counsel from a doctor or certified nutritionist may also be appropriate before beginning any new diet protocol or fasting regimen.

Sleep

Deep restful sleep is so critical for well-being that we talked about this extensively in the book's second section, Surviving Suicidal Crisis. Please refer back to Chapter 8 to review.

Fitness

Physical fitness is fundamental self-care. When it comes to health problems of every kind, exercise is often the most effective preventative factor and can even be the most potent intervention. Physical activity not only provides long-term critical health benefits, but also has instant positive effects on our mood. It's a two-for-one gift you can give yourself anytime you want.

Sunlight

We need sunlight. However, with the sun's association to skin cancer, its important benefits are often overlooked and missed out on. Yes, too much sun obviously can have negative effects, but exposure to sunlight is also a foundational part of maintaining well-being. The sun is a fundamental part of life on Earth and literally enables our existence.

Benefits of sunlight include vitamin D production, helping regulate our levels of serotonin and melatonin, which affect our mood and sleep. Sunlight relieves pain, promotes relaxation, reduces depression, and boosts the immune system. Our bodies are designed to be in the sun. We are walking solar panels hungry for sunlight, but modern life has us indoors most of the time or covered with clothes when we are outside.

How fair or tan your skin is determines how long you can be in the sun without protection. For those with the lightest skin, ultraviolet (UV) radiation damage can begin between 5 and 10 minutes, after 30 minutes for those with tan skin, and after 60 minutes for those with very dark skin. There is a very helpful chart online from the National Institutes of Health, just search "NIH How much sun is too much?" Use the chart to find out how much sun is best for you each day.

UV rays are the strongest when the sun is at its highest in the sky, between 11 am and 3 pm for most places, and are also stronger near the equator and in mountainous regions. Keep this in mind and adjust your exposure accordingly. I am naturally very light-skinned, so I try and get my sun in the morning or late afternoon and limit my uncovered exposure to 15 minutes.

So, get out into that sun with as much skin exposed as your morals and the law will allow for the appropriate amount of time for your skin type. This practice of self-care will become one of your staples as you experience how good it feels.

Physical Connection

Physical connection is not a luxury. It is a fundamental requirement for our well-being. It should be prioritized just as much as the other basic needs addressed in this book. Plutonic and sexual physical connection are a basic part of a healthy existence.

Healthy physical connection looks different at different times in your life and in different relationships. Whether you're single or in a romantic relationship, your body still needs to give and receive touch, whether it's something as deep as sexual intimacy or as simple as a hug from a friend. All kinds of touch are important and have real value. Being disconnected physically from other people and even ourselves will leave us with a great feeling of lack.

If you are in an intimate relationship, you have the most expansive opportunity to enjoy this aspect of well-being and connection. You have a world of possibilities at your fingertips with this beautiful part of life. Physical touch is a critical aspect of any relationship and should never be neglected. Too often, couples get complacent and stop putting effort into staying physically connected. But in a truly strong and healthy relationship, physical closeness is always valued.

Most would agree that sex is a basic requirement for experiencing a deep and fulfilling connection with a partner. But without intentional effort to continually collaborate in a loving, explorative, playful, and curious way, physical fulfillment can wither and fade. Leading to, at best, discontentment, and at worst, a catalyst for the end of the relationship. Every one of us deserves to experience a lifetime of beautiful physical connection.

Sexual connection is one of the four pillars of basic physical well-being. Breathing, eating, drinking, and sex are all innate and also partially involuntary parts of our body's functions. They all function as part of our unconscious sympathetic nervous system. None of them are mere preferences, even though sex is often mistakenly seen as an optional part of a healthy life. All four are core functions of our bodies. Arousal happens without our consent, just as breathing, hunger, and thirst.

All four create powerful effects within us and not just mentally and emotionally. They all cause uncontrollable physiological changes in our bodies. I don't have to spell out here what the physical effects of arousal are, as they are anything but subtle. Just ask any teenage boy who wasn't quite ready to get off the school bus, because of what would be an embarrassing bulge. Parts of sexual function are so innate that unlike eating or drinking, our bodies will even carry out aspects of it in our sleep, if need be, as in the case of so-called "wet dreams."

Understanding this may help you better understand the importance of sex for basic well-being. Knowing that it is a core function of our bodies like eating, drinking, and breathing, at the very least, should remove a lot of any conditioned shame you may have with regard to your sexual needs. Now, of course, it needs to be managed in a healthy way that ideally results in a positive impact on you and others. It can surely be poorly managed, just as eating can.

When sex is a positive experience, it results in many powerful benefits for our well-being beyond the obvious physical pleasure, such as higher self-esteem, lower stress, and increased fertility. It reduces the risk of prostate cancer, heart attack, and even reduces pain due to the release of oxytocin.

All of the non-sexual forms of physical contact are vital for well-being as well. So, *responsibly* hug, hold hands, kiss, caress, shake hands, and fist bump as often as you can. We are designed to touch each other.

Beyond these basic aspects of physical well-being, the following are other great ways to elevate your health. All of which have become essential parts of my lifestyle of intentional self-care.

- Sauna
- Meditation
- Cold immersion
- Yoga
- Breathing techniques
- Massage
- Stretching
- Scientifically backed natural products such as certain essential oils, herbs, ashwagandha, and turmeric.

CHAPTER THIRTY-SIX

RELATIONSHIPS

CHILDHOOD TRAUMAS AND DETRIMENTAL CONDITIONING are often pointed to as the root source of most of our internal problems. I went through my share of emotional pain as a child, but I always found ways to cope with it. Except for the shame I picked up from religion, I generally felt at peace with myself. But everything changed after Cindy's suicide, and then going through a divorce. That's when the deeper impact of emotional trauma really hit me, wreaking havoc on my nervous system, hijacking my mind with negative thoughts, and inducing feelings of worthlessness and despair. No other problem or difficulty unleashed the darkness upon me like the ending of these two relationships.

Pretty much all problems, apart from the death of a loved one, pale in comparison to the suffering we feel when a relationship ends. It turns otherwise stable people into emotional wrecks. We now know the basic reasons for this from our understanding of emotional pain associated to relationship loss learned in Chapters 27 and 33. Now, hopefully going forward, we can avoid being reactionary victims to these emotions and spare ourselves from being dragged down into more suffering than necessary.

Now let's talk about how we can create as wonderful relationships as possible. Relationship wisdom is another one of the most helpful things you can pursue when it comes to your well-being. We are designed, inside and out, to live in close engagement with other people. This is where many of our most wonderful experiences of life happen. Where we learn things about ourselves and the world, we couldn't learn any other way. Family, friendship, and intimate love are vehicles that can lift us to some of the highest feelings of purpose, meaning, discovery, and bliss.

Learning to have great relationships means first unlearning all the horrible things we've been taught about relationships our entire lives. Funny how this is the case with virtually every significant issue, like finances, sex, health, and self-awareness. We get it all upside down and backwards at first, then we spend the rest of our lives paying the price for it. Untangling the mess our ignorance and bad information created for us.

The most important truth about relationships is that in order to have healthy ones, we must also be working on a healthy one with ourselves. We need to love, forgive, and accept ourselves independently. We also need to learn how to meet our own physical and emotional needs, because engaging in relationships from a place of lack and desperate need sets us up for all kinds of problems.

When we go into relationships lacking a well developed sense of self and in great need of the other person, deep fear will underly everything. This dynamic creates co-dependency. Co-dependence hurts relationships because it creates the false belief that someone else can make us feel complete, valuable, or happy. When we depend on others for that kind of validation, we constantly need their approval just to feel okay. As a result, we take their emotions, words, and actions personally and let those things dictate how we feel.

A co-dependent person also feels responsible for fixing or saving other people. This results in continually neglecting ourselves in order to prioritize others, believing this is the only way to be accepted or loved. This is often referred to as "self-abandonment" or "self-betrayal."

Co-dependence is a difficult and virtually universal challenge because we all start out our lives in a 100% co-dependent relationship. Particularly with our mothers, but also with the other people who cared for us. We needed them for everything and had zero independence nor sense of self. Then this natural baseline is often exacerbated further by dysfunctional families, which engage in both emotional abuse and neglect. We learn that being loved and accepted is conditionally based on how we perform. Religiosity often exacerbates this conditioning, as it also creates deep beliefs of needing to perform in order to be worthy. We often grow up in unsafe relationships where other people's needs are always more important than our own. We come to believe that fear, manipulation, shame, and control are intrinsic parts of being in a relationship. "Make the person you care about happy, or you will suffer", is the programming we receive.

To break free from co-dependency, we must understand where this conditioning came from and learn a new way of being within relationships. One of mutual respect, acceptance, and trust. Where there is safety and comfort to be our authentic selves, and both people are uplifted by being in the relationship. Why be in any relationship that does not function in this way? Sure, there can be suffering in being alone, but it pales in comparison to the hell you and another person can create together. A relationship should be safe and enriching. If it's not, you may want to take a hard look at the relationship and consider what is best for your well-being.

Many of our earliest relationships were harmful and unsafe, leaving us yearning for a happily ever after if we could only find "the one." Someone who will "complete us" and *make* us happy. This is totally understandable, but let me tell you right now. You have to reach into your brain and rip out this absolutely false and damaging idea of a "soulmate" or "the one." This Disney fantasy belief system has the power to mess you and your life up big-time. The myth of "the one" leads us to do very unwise things, including rushing into marriage, losing ourselves in relationships, continuing on in detrimental ones, and having our worlds crushed when "the one" cheats on us, leaves us, or dies. It's kind of hard to get over a break-up if you convinced yourself that the person was your once in a lifetime soulmate. Let me tell you, they weren't.

Instead, let's embrace a clear reality. People create their relationships one day at a time. There isn't just one person out there who was made just for you. There are actually countless people out there with whom a beautiful relationship could be created, contrary to fanciful ideas about "the one" we see in movies and hear in most love songs. We'd all be much better off if an ideal relationship was seen as when two happy people choose to be together because they enjoy their life more with each other. They work as a team, supporting, encouraging, and building a life together. Their relationship is a steady foundation that helps them face the challenges of the world. They know hard times will come, and they're willing to put in the effort to maintain a healthy connection.

Who you choose as a partner is a most consequential decision. Prioritize finding someone with the following traits to start with a foundation for success.

Green Flags

- Communicates needs.
- Sees past relationships as valuable learning experiences.
- Speaks about others and past partners with respect.
- Self-aware and takes responsibility for personal development.
- Honors your independence, separate interests, and connection with others.
- Shares or supports your fundamental goals.
- Patiently and constructively resolves conflict.
- Authentically apologizes.
- Possesses positive character traits such as kindness, empathy, resilience, humility, flexibility, and gratitude.

Red Flags

- Needy, makes their whole world about you.
- Blames past partners for all relationship problems.
- Doesn't clearly communicate needs, expects "mind reading."
- Projects their negative beliefs onto you.
- Unhealthy jealousy where they invade your privacy, control, and interrogate you.
- Unable to resolve conflict. "Sweeps problems under the rug."
- Lack of affection or physical intimacy.
- Disrespectful to you and others.

- Dishonest and unreliable.
- Black and white, all-or-nothing patterns of thinking.

Resolving Conflict

Even for very emotionally mature people, relationships will inevitably have difficulties. There will be disagreements, misunderstandings, different priorities, values that collide, and plain old bad days. Therefore, mistakes, conflict, and the need to resolve and repair will always be a fundamental requirement in relationships. It's during these times when a relationship can be either nourished or poisoned. If conflict is not resolved, then hurt, invalidation, and disconnection grow, destroying true intimacy. Learning how someone deals with hard times may be the most important thing to understand about someone with whom you will potentially spend your life.

Loving someone is easy when life is going smoothly and you're having a great time. It's how well you move together through offenses, grief, sadness, and misunderstandings that makes the difference between success and failure. The problem is that most of us were never taught or modeled how to resolve issues healthily.

When in the midst of a conflict, there are several things you can do to prevent any more damage from being done and begin the process of repair and resolve.

- First and foremost, *always remind yourself that the other person is not your enemy and the goal is mutual love and peace*, not to win or be right. Remind each other that you want the best for each other and the relationship. In other words, start from a place of positivity, connection, and trust.

- Be open to the very real possibility that **you could be wrong**. This is hard to do in the heat of the moment when everyone is highly triggered. Which leads us to the next one.

- **Slow down**! Just as with almost everything else in life, simply slowing down can make a big difference. Take a few deep breaths. Stabilize yourself. Observe your emotions. **Think before you react and speak.** Ask yourself, "Is what I am about to say likely to get the result I'm looking for? Or is it likely to make things worse?"

- Respectfully **take time and space from the argument**. If one or both of you are feeling too emotional to talk in a calm and constructive way, it's best to take a break and give yourselves time to cool down. Raising your voice is usually a clear sign that you're not ready to solve the problem together. That's when a time-out can really help. Here's a healthy way to do this. "I'm feeling some really strong emotions right now, and I need a little time to calm down before we keep talking. Can we come back to this in 20 minutes?"

- Really **listen to the other person**. Repeat back to them what you have understood so there are no further misunderstandings. This goes a long way to reaching a resolution. What they say has to matter and be acknowledged, or there will be no end to the problem.

- **Be aware of your non-verbal's**. Many sources say that ninety percent of communication is non-verbal. Whatever the percentage may be, it's clearly powerful. Just take the examples of an eye roll or a scowl. Ask yourself, "Are my gestures, posture, tones, and facial expressions conducive to healing the conflict? Or are they adding more fuel to the fire?"

- *Avoid using language that escalates emotions like "always" and "never."*

- *Avoid accusatory or condemning language by avoiding "you" statements.* It's much more productive and better received when we speak using "I" statements. Such as, "I feel disregarded when you do x, y, or z."

- *Stay on the issue at hand.* It is so tempting to bring up more issues once an argument begins. It's probably just human nature to think, "Well, while things are already bad, I might as well get this off my chest, too." Or we bring up something they've done to discredit the other person or deflect the focus from ourselves. This is always a bad idea, yet when we are upset, we do this over and over again.

- *Don't assume things about the other person.* Instead, ask sincere questions to gain clarity.

- *Focus on finding a solution.* One of the worst things we do in a conflict is go around in circles about the problem. Not only does this prevent us from resolving, but it also causes us to spend more time in a triggered state, and we often end up saying things that cause even more damage.

Healing Apologies

The following is what real resolution looks like in the aftermath of harmful behavior:

- **Taking responsibility** for the action, words, or behavior. **Being honest** about it and giving a genuine apology where remorse is clearly felt. This is only effective if done without making excuses, blaming, or justifying.

- **Giving the other person an opportunity to be heard.** Then **express real empathy** for the pain caused and **acknowledge their feelings**.

- Future **actions are taken to improve** the undesired behavior.

- Then, **be patient** with the **time it takes the other person to feel peace** of mind regarding the issue.

- Finally, **forgive yourself** and **move forward**.

Resolving problems is never fun, but it's actually an important way to build trust and strengthen your relationships. Even the healthiest relationships face challenges. Don't be fooled by perfect-looking lives on social media; every relationship takes effort behind the scenes. Growing through conflict is where the relationship gets better and where intimacy can grow deeper. To drastically improve your relationships, invite your partner, friend, or family member to practice these basic principles of healthy conflict resolution with you.

Cindy and I did not have the relationship tools to do this well. And after failing to resolve problems healthily in the first year or so, we settled into the horrible habit of giving each other "the silent treatment" for several days. Time would pass, lessening the anger, and we'd then go back to "normal" as if nothing happened. The problems swept under our rug became mountainous. This sad pattern only caused further suffering and wasted each one of those opportunities to confront and resolve our issues and actually make things better.

Boundaries / Preserving Self

Boundaries are an essential part of maintaining our sense of self and autonomy. Losing control over our own lives is an extremely oppressive feeling. Each of us deserves to live the life we want and be treated by others in a way that we deserve. If you are a "people pleaser" or have the "nice guy (or girl) syndrome", then learning to have boundaries is going to be especially challenging. But you cannot heal or have peace unless you get used to disappointing people and take back your power.

Basic Relationship Boundaries

- Treating each other with respect and kindness.
- Each person takes responsibility for their own behavior.
- Different ideas, opinions, beliefs, and feelings are accepted and respected.
- Supporting each other's needs and desires.
- Respecting each other's privacy and independence.
- Clearly communicate needs, desires, and feelings.

- Honesty.
- Protecting relationship privacy from family and friends.
- Mutually investing in the relationship.

Relationships are inherently challenging because there will always be different needs, goals, and ways of seeing the world. The remedy for this universal problem is for both people in the relationship to first fully acknowledge this dilemma. Then, as each naturally makes an effort to pursue their own needs and desires, they *also* support the other person in doing the same. The more intimate the relationship, the more important this principle is. This is a great challenge, to be sure, as many things will not be in harmony. This takes real self-awareness, maturity, wisdom, and acceptance. It requires a real sense of joy in another person's happiness and their unique way of being. You can't go wrong with the classic Golden Rule. Treat others how you want to be treated.

Lust, excitement, and commonalities will only keep two people together for so long. If you are in a relationship for the purpose of lasting love, then understand that love is experienced in the following ways: Support, validation, listening, presence, vulnerability, touch, empathy, patience, and acceptance.

Love is maintained by being vulnerable with each other. Being vulnerable means sharing your true feelings, your hopes, dreams, fears, insecurities, and even the parts of yourself you struggle with. This fosters a deep and meaningful connection. Vulnerability also helps trust to grow, and trust weakens one of relationships' worst enemies, fear. The fear that causes us to try and control, withdrawal from, or blame each other.

A relationship is like a garden in need of intentional effort and care, or it withers and dies. Both the big and little things matter in a relationship. Every day, you are unconsciously creating a story in your head about your partner and the relationship. The other person is also doing the same thing. What this overall story is will determine whether or not you are content in the relationship. The story is dynamic and alive. You and your partner have the power to create a story of discontentment, leading towards eventual failure, or one of growth, joy, and fulfillment.

So, intentionally make positive memories, keep your sexual life vibrant, be interested in continually getting to know each other, be generous with love and appreciation, and support each other's interests, hopes, and dreams. Keep growing as an individual and as a couple. Manage yourself with the utmost care when you feel the urge to condemn, criticize, and complain. Have regular conversations about your relationship to celebrate wins, express gratitude, and discuss areas that need improvement. Never forget how amazing it is to have a partner to share life with in such a deeply connected way. Every person deserves to be cherished and adored. Complacency and taking your partner for granted signal the beginning of the end.

Not much else in life will affect your well-being as much as your relationships. This area of your life deserves to be among your highest priorities. Being intentional with your relationships means that you make yourself in such a way that you show up more and more as your highest self. Loving your people deeply and fully, valuing, respecting, and honoring them.

"I love you" is a wonderful thing to hear and say, but what does it really mean? What we all hope it means is, "I see you. I hear you. I'm for you, and I choose you." When these four things are truly honored, we experience relationships as we hope for them to be.

Most <u>Harmful</u> Ideas About Relationships

- My partner is responsible for my happiness.
- My partner should meet all my needs.
- My partner should already know my needs.
- Passion and happiness are constant in a good relationship.
- Needing to be together *all* the time.
- It's supposed to be easy with the right person.
- My partner completes me.

These ideas set your relationship up for failure. They are gross misconceptions that must be overcome.

CHAPTER THIRTY-SEVEN

CONTINUAL LEARNING & GROWTH

AS HUMANS, WE HAVE AN INNATE SUSCEPTIBILITY TO BE DECIEVED AS TO WHO WE REALLY ARE. We all struggle between who we are and the negative way the world makes us feel. There are endless ways the world can distort our sense of self. Inevitably, people will harm us physically and mentally. Disease breaks us down, and even some of our personal choices cause great self-inflicted harm. As time passes and more negative experiences pile on, our true selves can be progressively buried deeper and deeper under layers of pain, frustration, and sadness.

The Shadow Self and the Ego are influences, but we are goodness and love at our deepest core. That is why we endlessly seek positive experiences. We strive to live a life in harmony with our true nature. For our true selves to win out, we must pursue a path of continual learning and growth. Society might lead you to believe that this is important for the purpose of acquiring more status, wealth, or receiving more love.

The real reason to continually learn and grow is that it cultivates our self-awareness, helps us see the world with greater clarity, and leads to greater resilience. It also gives us the opportunity to discover more of what we love. What if you have an interest or natural talent that is never discovered simply because it never had the opportunity to be born? How many wonderful things are missed out on simply because you never picked up the paintbrush, volunteered with that group, read that book, or went to that dance class?

To continue evolving, we must remain curious, open-minded, and willing to learn from diverse sources. The world is overflowing with different religions, philosophies, cultures, and ideas. Novel interactions and exposure to new ideas are paramount. You don't know what you don't know, and once you think you know it all, growth ceases. Too often, we get comfortable in a routine existence. It's been said that the "comfort zone" is where dreams go to die. It is also where we may miss out on the life we were meant for. We feel most alive and fulfilled when we're living on the edge between stability and challenge, pushing ourselves, learning, and accomplishing new things.

Remember the puzzle pieces of truth and wisdom that are scattered and hidden out there in the world, which we discussed? It is only through expansive experiences and continual seeking that you are able to keep finding these precious pieces.

"As long as you live, keep learning how to live."
- Seneca

CHAPTER THIRTY-EIGHT

SPEAK & LIVE TRUTH

"Truth is not what you want it to be, it is what it is, and you must bend to its power or live a lie."

-Miyamoto Musashi

Of ALL THE WAYS ONE CAN ENSURE AN UNHAPPY AND ANXIOUS LIFE, living out of integrity with our deepest truths is probably the most effective. Not being who we truly are and not following our heart towards the life we truly want.

Unfortunately, our families and society don't just indoctrinate us with all kinds of ideas and ways of living that aren't really our truths. It also exerts enormous pressure on us to conform. This phenomenon occurs at various levels, including those of a nation, ethnic group, religion, family, and even our one-on-one relationships.

It's natural to just "go along" to "get along", but conforming too much to your environment, when it is outside of your truth, is a slow death to yourself. It's not a bad thing to want to please others or to fit in, but if constantly done at the cost of yourself, this will lead to real unhappiness.

Not being true to ourselves is akin to living a lie. And lying is a fear-based behavior. We know that the truth doesn't always make everyone else happy, and in fact, very often results in conflict. But speaking and living your truth is the only way to align your life with your true values and desires.

When you start living your truth, it might shake things up at first. But whatever falls apart as a result are just the things that aren't really best for you, like when someone decides to leave a harmful relationship or quits a job that wasn't right for them. It may seem tough at first, but it's actually a step toward a much better life. It creates an opportunity for a new relationship or job that they will love.

If you are living outside of integrity with yourself, you will know it through your body and emotions. You may be able to convince yourself of all the lies you are living, but your body will continue to give you signals that things are very wrong. When our core essence says "No, stop or change course," its language is often stress, frustration, anger, and sadness. It's the opposite of the peace you feel when you're on the right path and living in integrity.

If things get really dire, and suicidal thoughts emerge, you can be sure that you are living in a way wholly outside of integrity with yourself. It's so unfortunate how this pain can be misinterpreted to mean a desire to stop living altogether, when it's actually a message trying to help you, not harm you. It's an unmistakable sign that something needs to change. Your body and inner self are shouting, "Please stop living this way!"

The following are important ways to live your truth:

- Say what you mean.
- Don't people please. If it feels wrong, you shouldn't do it.
- "No" is one of the most important words for living your truth.

- Be honest with yourself about reality. You must be able to recognize hard truths about yourself and the world.

- Take complete responsibility and ownership over your own life. This frees us from some of life's most detrimental mindsets, like jealousy, regret, powerlessness, resentment, and victimhood.

- Speak and surround yourself with goodness, because this is the highest truth of who you are.

Destroy the Lies Within

During my two most painful life experiences thus far, my suffering was made much worse due to the self-condemning lies that took hold within me. In the case of Cindy's suicide, I was placing most of the responsibility on myself. I believed that my kids' lives would be forever damaged because of it. I believed that she did it because she hated and wanted to leave me, and that she wanted me to suffer. It took a couple of messy years, but eventually I was able to overcome these beliefs in the ways I have described in this journey.

Almost four years later, the divorce from my second wife led me again into the pain of believing inner lies and threatened to have me forget who I was. I had all the symptoms of depression day in and day out with very little reprieve. It even induced a chronic anxiety I had never experienced prior. That feeling you get when you're falling was in my chest for over a year. What was making me feel this way? It's easy to just say, "It's a breakup, a divorce, of course it's going to be painful." The usual prescription for feeling better is typically, "Time will heal the wounds", "You've got to forget about it and move on," and so on.

You could lean on these ideas, but there is a much better way. A way to more fully heal what afflicts your heart and mind. To understand where our worst suffering really comes from, you have to look deeper inside yourself, into your thoughts, emotions, and soul. You have to discover what detrimental beliefs you have created in association with the hurtful event, which are now causing your pain to be multiplied and prolonged.

I gained more clarity on how to do this from reading a masterful work called The Way of Integrity, written by Martha Beck. The book takes you on a journey to resolve your deepest misalignments with your true self, using Dante's Inferno as an allegory. We learn that at the heart of our misery, we will find deeply embedded beliefs that keep us stuck in shame, guilt, and fear. Beck calls these toxic beliefs we carry "hell thoughts." She explains that these hell thoughts will afflict us endlessly, unless we identify and eliminate them from our beings.

This is done by first identifying your "hell thoughts." Then, you must begin the process of dispelling them. However, due to being deeply entrenched, a little effort is required to eliminate them. Beck suggests that you initiate the process by simply injecting doubt. More specifically, ask yourself if you're sure that thought or belief is absolutely true. As there are few absolutes in life, this strategy is wholly effective, and you start to see the cracks forming in the lie. Then, to fully dismantle the "hell thought," you write it down and below it write down all the reasons you can think of as to why it's not true.

Empowered with this newfound wisdom, I endeavored to apply it to my situation. In regard to my divorce, I began by peeling back all the layers of messy thoughts and emotions to reveal which beliefs were actually at the root of all my seemingly endless suffering. I thought to myself, "What negative things am I believing about myself because of this divorce?"

It didn't take long to find them. They were; "It was all my fault we didn't make it." "I will never find someone like her or more ideal for me again." "I'm going to regret losing her for the rest of my life." "I am going to be alone forever," and "I'm not meant to have a lasting love and relationship."

Of course, there's real pain that isn't just about these "hell thoughts." Naturally, I grieved the loss of a relationship I had made immense sacrifices for and with someone I loved deeply. And yes, it triggered my worst traumas of abandonment and shame when my efforts to stay together were rejected. But these were not the reasons for my most intense and enduring suffering. No, it was the distressing lies I was telling myself, without even being fully aware of them.

So, I wrote them down, and underneath each one, I wrote all the reasons I could think of as to why they were not true. The surprising part was that it wasn't even hard to do. I was able to write a long list under each one. It made it so clear that what I had been believing wasn't true. Then, with the lies shattered, everything inside me started to change, and I reached the healthiest state possible after such an experience. It was not *all* my fault. If I found her, of course, I could find someone else. I *have* healed, and I *am* made for love.

In this newfound clarity, I also made an important realization. So much of the pain and distress I had been feeling came during the time I was attempting to return to the relationship. Why was this particularly detrimental for me? Besides my past trauma of abandonment being triggered, returning to the relationship was out of integrity with what was actually best for me and my children. It was my weaker, fearful self and my ego that had me wanting to return to the known, rather than step forward into the unknown and a new future. When I realized that I did not want to go backwards, it allowed peace to finally settle over my being. With the limiting beliefs eliminated and my vision towards the future, my life was able to fully move forward. From there, amazing things really did start to occur.

Once you too, confront and destroy your self-condemning lies, they will lose their power and naturally fade away. Freeing you from the internal, self-inflicted chains that bind your life into a living hell. Let's look at how this applies to other situations apart from a breakup. I know that it has been a major theme here.

Let's consider a rape or abuse victim. The act of the rape or the abuse in real time is truly horrific, but what is it that has the victim suffering for extended periods of time, sometimes decades or a lifetime? There is the raw trauma for sure, but part of it is likely due to the beliefs that have become embedded in their minds associated with the experience. The beliefs that each person holds may vary depending on the particular circumstance, but they would all undoubtedly be beliefs that create self-shame, guilt, and fear. And they will all be lies, such as "It was my fault", "I'm dirty", "I will never feel better", "I am not safe", "I can't trust anybody", etc.

Whatever bad experiences led to your personal journey into the underworld. You can find your way back out by practicing what we talked about in this section and in Chapter 14, Trauma. To help even further, once you clear out the lies, you can replace them with positive and self-affirming beliefs, using the positive affirmations we discussed in Chapter 34.

CHAPTER THIRTY-NINE

MASTER OF YOUR LIFE

WHY IS IT THAT POWER IS SO SOUGHT AFTER AND SO VALUED? What is it about control that we love? If we're really honest with ourselves, the reason is pretty simple. We want things to happen in the way we believe they should. We think we know what's best. Deep down, we just want to feel safe and free, and having power and control seems like the way to attain this.

The universe, the Earth, society, friends, partners, and even children are never ours to control. Sometimes, things go our way for a little while, and it feels like we're in control. But eventually, life always shows us how little control we really have. With time, the forces of chaos and order always make their supreme dominance known.

Does this mean that we should abandon any ideals for power or mastery? Not at all. Power is one of life's greatest blessings. The power to think, feel, move, speak, and create. Power is an ability that enables you to engage with life in the ways that are most meaningful to you. So, if there is one thing worth mastering, it is ourselves, our own mind and body. The biggest challenges to overcome in this pursuit will be your compulsiveness, attachments, fears, preferences, and aversions.

Pursuing self-mastery is fundamental to a life of enduring well-being, and the reason is twofold. On the one hand, letting go of the need to control everything brings peace; you stop wasting energy on things you can't change. On the other hand, you are empowered to focus on what you can control, like your thoughts, choices, and actions. This is how you truly take charge of your life. Let's explore the ways this can be achieved.

Master of Your Feelings

To be the master of your life means to manage all the positive and negative emotions you experience effectively. Pleasure, excitement, stress, fear, anger, sadness, all of them. Both positive and negative emotions can be extremely problematic for us. Negative emotions are easier to recognize as a problem because they are so uncomfortable, and the kinds of terrible things they can lead to are well known. But positive emotions can be just as destructive as negative ones if not managed with wisdom. Such as when infatuation induced by a new relationship clouds sound judgment, the tantalizing attraction to another person besides your partner, or the enticement of tasty junk foods and drinks.

The so-called "seven deadly sins" are the result of seeking positive feelings. Pride, greed, lust, wrath, gluttony, envy, and sloth are all detrimental ways of experiencing pleasure or satisfaction. We fall victim to them because of their ability to create very strong yet short-lived positive feelings.

And they are indeed dangerous, and not because of the threat of some afterlife punishment. But because the punishment is self-inflicted, severe, and quite immediate. The positive feelings don't last long and come at a high cost to our well-being. If even just one of these negative traits begins to rule us, our light is diminished, and our highest self will fade.

Now, what about negative emotions? We can't let these emotions control our lives, so we need to manage them with wisdom. When strong negative feelings come up, there are two main ways to handle them. We can either "sit with them" or take action to shift ourselves back into a more positive state. We need to be capable of doing both, as each has its appropriate time and place.

"Sitting" with your feelings is a term used to describe the practice of fully acknowledging them, allowing yourself the time and space to feel whatever feelings are arising. As opposed to repressing or avoiding them, you allow them to flow freely. This may result in crying, screaming, or just sitting quietly. We discussed some of this dynamic earlier in the chapter on trauma. The important thing is that you do this with the awareness that all our feelings are important, and it is okay to feel them. Understanding that even though uncomfortable, they are just feelings. You do not allow them to overrun you or create negative self-beliefs.

The best way to prevent negative feelings from dominating is to see yourself as separate from them. That the pain is revealing something to you. And most importantly, remembering that feelings are temporary and won't last forever.

Sitting with our negative feelings is not always something we have the luxury of doing each time they show up. Sometimes we need to be engaged with family or work, and sometimes we may just be tired of feeling them and need a break. This is when we can use our practices for healthy emotional regulation. Especially the ones that have an immediate effect of elevating our mood.

We won't list them all as they are sprinkled throughout this book. But the following are several potent ones: connecting with people, moving our bodies by shaking, dancing, or exercising, breathing techniques, physical human contact, guided meditation, positive self-affirmations, and getting out into nature. Virtually any act of self-love and care can help change our thoughts and improve our mood. Sometimes, these might only offer temporary relief from pain. But unlike harmful distractions, these self-care practices are always beneficial as they provide some immediate relief and also contribute to long-term healing.

These two methods of dealing with negative feelings are vital because one who is becoming a master of their life will not go down the route of using destructive coping methods, such as repressing, or self-medicating with alcohol or drugs. As a person who chooses to live life with intention and awareness, you become more conscious of your emotions. You use them for your growth instead of your demise.

Enduring well-being is achieved when we break free from the enslavement of unconscious emotional reaction. This is why all self-improvement and much of spiritual practice prioritize self-discipline.

Maintaining an awareness of who we are is the cornerstone of self-mastery. Remember that your core essence is something apart from the cells and neurons that make up the biological machinery. Your brain and nervous system are an intricate configuration of raw materials from the earth, which is only animated because of the life-force energizing it. Realize that your body is the puppet, and your life-force is the puppeteer, and not the other way around. Becoming conscious that you are the master of your inner experience is the very definition of transcendence.

When I feel like I'm beginning to lose control of my thoughts or emotions, I remind myself that I am not my body, my mind, nor any experience. You can practice this in real-time by reassuring yourself in ways such as, "I am not these feelings of heartbreak." "Money doesn't determine my happiness." "This anxiety is not who I am." This doesn't mean dissociation; this is conscious transcendence.

Feelings certainly help guide us, but they are also chaotic and cannot be trusted carte blanche. They are caused by fluctuations of chemicals in your body associated with emotions like love, fear, and anger. When it comes to your thoughts and feelings, the best thing you can do is slow down and take the time to understand them. And please remember that thoughts and emotions are far from all or nothing. You can feel angry for A and B while also feeling grateful for Y and Z.

Thoughts and feelings are flowing all the time. The important thing is to remember that *you* are the master. You get to decide what to do with them. Even a couple of thousand years ago, this was understood. The Roman emperor Marcus Aurelius said, "*If you are distressed by anything external, the pain is not due to the thing itself, but to your estimate of it; and this you have the power to revoke at any moment.*"

Master of Your Story

Humans are storytellers, and every day we are unconsciously creating ours. The world sets the scene and brings in the characters, but it is us who gives the story its meaning and overall theme. Who we believe ourselves to be in the saga shapes our experience. If we are the victim, a failure, helpless, unlucky, doomed, or the villain, there's little chance for it to end well. We can all feel like this sometimes. But it's when things are at their hardest that we must continue to believe in ourselves and never give up. The story is your personal reality. To make it a wonderful one, look at life as an epic adventure and yourself as the hero, because it is, and you are.

You're Already the Master. You Just Don't Know It Yet.

In spite of the outside world's endless torrent of stimulus, the creation of our experience and, even more importantly, the interpretation, ultimately happens completely within. Everything you hear, see, taste, touch, or smell. Even the emotions of love, hate, fear, and pleasure. It is impossible for anything that happens outside of our bodies to create an experience within us. Making this one of life's major ironies because our basic struggle is dealing with the effects of the outside world.

To better understand this, consider the following. Let's imagine for a minute that you did not exist. The world would still be buzzing with an infinite number of stimuli. Innumerable sights, sounds, tastes, etc. But none of it would have any impact on you. Now you're suddenly in the world, and all your senses are open for business. You hear someone speaking to you. Where is this experience actually being created for you?

Well, the person's vocal cords vibrated, forming a series of compression waves in the air. These waves travel through the air with no specific destination. But then, like a satellite dish, your ear funnels those compression waves into your ear canal and to your eardrum. The eardrum starts to vibrate and passes those vibrations to three tiny bones in your ear called the malleus, incus, and stapes. Several more functions happen involving tubes of fluid, hair cells, the release of chemicals, and then electrical signals being sent up to your auditory nerve to your brain.

In your experience, how did this sound come into existence? The sound was only potential, a floating possibility until your eardrum and all the ensuing complexity *created* your experience. It all occurred because you were alive to bring the experience into your existence. This can be further understood by the fact that we are only capable of hearing sounds within the 20 and 20,000 Hz vibration per second range. Sounds outside that range are all around us, but we are not creating any experience of them.

How about the meaning of the sound? Well, since you create the existential experience of the sound, then its meaning must also be your creation. And so it is with all your senses and therefore the entire unfolding of your life. Outside stimulus can only inspire the creation within us. Your life is the experience you are making combined with the meaning you're giving it. Knowing this, would you allow anything to damage, much less destroy your life?

The world would have us forever believing that it is everything outside of us that makes us feel things. That it is the relationship that makes us feel loved. The betrayal that makes us feel hurt. The achievement that makes us feel happy. Yet, all of these feelings are solely created within us.

Knowing you are the only creator of your experience is powerful, because as the world's forces collide with you, you are able to be the gatekeeper of your heart and mind. You are able to be the meaning maker and the storywriter for yourself. Some of the deepest suffering and suicide happen when the world runs wild with a person, when the world is writing the story for them with all its negativity.

To further understand your power, consider the following example with the experience of grief. Think of someone close to you who has died. How did that experience feel? It was undoubtedly extremely hard and sad. Now, consider the countless other deaths that you have been aware of during your life. From news reports in distant countries, to fatal car accidents, you slowly passed as you exited the traffic jam it caused. How did these experiences feel compared to the loss of your loved one? Totally different, right? One can crush your heart while the other is forgotten within seconds. So, what exactly makes these experiences so different? It's your perceptions and ideas about the person and the meaning you make of it.

That was an emotional example. We can even look at the physical and see that, still, the experience is only created and managed by us. Why can one person sit in an ice bath for several minutes at 36 degrees and remain at total ease, while another would shriek and recoil with just one foot dipped in that cold water? Are these different species of humans? No. The only difference is how the mind is being managed. Was that example too mundane? Let's raise the stakes all the way to the max, and go in the opposite direction toward extreme heat, scorching heat.

Many of us have seen the iconic picture of a monk in an act of self-immolation, taken during the Vietnam War. Self-immolation means to burn oneself alive. This suicide was atypical, given that his intent had nothing to do with escaping personal suffering. This man had decided that this would be his way of bringing attention to an issue affecting his community. It was done in protest against the South Vietnamese Government's oppression of Buddhists during that time in 1963.

Though his intentions were noble, I wholeheartedly disagree with his method of protest. That being said, his act reveals a powerful truth about the level of self-mastery that's possible within each of us. There's a reason it remains one of the most iconic photographs of all time. It's extraordinary to behold. I will let the words of a New York Times reporter, David Halberstam, who was there at the time, describe it.

"I was to see that sight again, but once was enough. Flames were coming from a human being; his body was slowly withering and shriveling up, his head blackening and charring. In the air was the smell of burning human flesh; human beings burn surprisingly quickly. Behind me, I could hear the sobbing of the Vietnamese who were now gathering. I was too shocked to cry, too confused to take notes or ask questions, too bewildered to even think…. As he burned, he never moved a muscle, never uttered a sound, his outward composure in sharp contrast to the wailing people around him."

Now, compare this to how most of us retreat to the comfort of air conditioning after spending just a few minutes outside on a hot day. Yet, this man, Thich Quang Duc, had arguably the most intense of external stimulations of physical pain possible and didn't flinch a muscle or make a peep. He was human, just like you and me. The difference was that he fully realized and took complete ownership of the fact that he was the master of his experience. No matter how strong, they were still just feelings.

Given that the core purpose of this book is to free people from death by suicide, this example may seem strange or inappropriate. I would agree at first glance. But in this book, we are holding nothing back. There has been no tiptoeing around as we talk about life and death, misery and joy, and what it really means to heal and feel alive. In no way was this example an endorsement of any kind of suicidal act. Instead, it is shared as a striking example that reveals the human potential for ultimate dominance over mind, body, and emotions. Let's simply recognize the suicidal aspect of this example as another profound lesson on how we all respond so differently to life. I feel that it is tragic that this monk and others chose death as a method of protesting abuse and injustice. Though their motives were for good, the actions were the opposite of life-uplifting. Love, hope, and life would have been a better path.

The point is to help you understand that what happens within you is yours to decide. Your most basic right as an existing being is to choose your own path and be in control of yourself. Apart from this, we really have no rights to anything, no matter how much we'd like to believe otherwise. Everything can be taken away from us, and anything can be done to us.

Realizing that you have 100% control over your own life experience is the most freeing revelation that anyone can have. Liberating you from what would otherwise be a lifetime of oppression from the world around you. This is a truth that has been continually re-discovered throughout the ages by those who have been subject to the most terrible outside forces and still found their inner power.

You can only choose between two ways of being. One is a chaotic and precarious life at the mercy of all that happens around and to you. The other is where *you* are in charge and in control. The choice has always been there waiting for you. Though this creates the best possibility for a peaceful life, there is a cost that many are not willing to pay. And that is, you must take total, all-encompassing responsibility for yourself. You cannot be the master and creator of your life unless you let go of the idea that someone else is responsible for saving you, giving you what you need, or to blame. But so often, we just go on pretending we're OK, accepting the status quo, because we're stuck in our patterns or because we're too afraid to change. We will always be our own most potent limitation.

Healing and becoming our best selves is possible for everyone. It just requires dedication to this path. Every day is precious, so do today what is best for your heart, mind, and body. Then do it again tomorrow. Each time you slip off course, forgive your mistakes and wrong turns. Choose to love yourself the way you deserve over and over again.

Becoming the master of your life ultimately means that you consciously decide what to do with your emotions and actions. You give meaning to your experiences. You are writing the story of your life.

CHAPTER FORTY

HAPPINESS

Happiness is a universal desire. We want to feel good. At our core, we are made of love and joy. As such, we naturally want to feel these emotions in every part of our lives. If we looked closely at what we do each day, we'd see that most of our actions are in the pursuit of happiness. This is a force for good when it motivates us to build a better and more meaningful life. And if sought with care for others, it makes the whole world a better place.

Many things in life can bring us fleeting happiness, such as wealth, fame, power, beauty, success, and pleasure. None of which are inherently bad or a problem. All of them can be partnered with very positive things. For example, if pleasures of the flesh are connected to healthy nutrition and meaningful relationships, this is a win-win. Wealth and power can be good things if managed with love and are used to help others; that's a win for everyone.

Wisdom and experience teach us that the most enduring happiness comes from seeking peace, health, freedom, connection, belonging, and purpose. It comes from continual self-exploration and growth. By learning to engage and respond consciously to life, rather than compulsively reacting to it. It's a great joy to be the master of yourself, your thoughts, and your emotions.

Should Happiness Be the Goal?

There is a paradoxical dynamic when it comes to wanting happiness. Studies show that the more people want and expect happiness, the less satisfied and happy they actually feel. This reveals that our belief systems around happiness have a profound impact on our ability to actually experience it. Nathaniel Hawthorne wrote of this phenomenon, "*Happiness in this world, when it comes, comes incidentally. Make it the object of pursuit, and it leads us on a wild goose chase, and it is never attained.*"

If happiness is the focus of your pursuit, you'll always be chasing, but never finding. Over time, we realize that no matter how much love, money, success, or exciting experiences we have, it's never enough. We will always yearn for more. Also, because we're always evolving, what makes us happy changes too. The places we want to live, our relationships, possessions, and our purposes all go through transitions. Therefore, happiness is a moving target, and the goal posts are always shifting. Happiness is not a destination because, as the old saying goes, the joy is actually found in the journey.

To find joy in the journey, we must moderate our expectations for it. This mindset allows one to feel much more appreciation and acceptance, no matter what the circumstances. Instead of focusing on the idea of happiness, seek the best version of yourself and have a positive impact on others. Instead of striving for happiness, pursue the virtues of wisdom, courage, and moderation. Live to love and heal yourself. Then, happiness is no longer an emotion; it becomes who we are. As Henry David Thoreau said, "*Happiness is like a butterfly, the more you chase it, the more it will elude, but if you turn your attention to other things, it will come and sit softly on your shoulder.*"

Entitlement kills happiness. We must accept that we are not owed a constant state of happiness, only the opportunity to enjoy it when it comes. Try this and see how it feels: Give yourself permission to stop expecting a perfect state of happiness. Instead, accept that it's completely okay to *not* feel happy all the time. Take a deep breath, and allow that sense of acceptance to settle in. Just considering this is likely already inducing feelings of relief within you. You'll actually be happier if you let go of the belief that something is wrong with you or your life, if you don't feel happy all of the time. You'll free yourself from so much unnecessary stress, anxiety, and disappointment. Less expectation for happiness leads to experiencing more of it. Pretty simple hack, right?!

Happiness can certainly be an ever-growing part of our life experience. Practicing the principles described in this book will surely be of great help. However, the biggest secret in life is this: happiness is already who you are. That's why it's so hard to find out there. You already have it, like when you're searching everywhere for your keys, only to realize they were in your pocket the whole time. Everything you need to feel happiness is already within you, and it's always been there.

Happily Ever After Isn't Reality

People who seem to experience an enduring sense of happiness are not living in the absence of struggle. They are still subject to the ups and downs of the human experience, just like you and me. They are often people who have simply come to an acceptance of the fact that they will not experience happiness all the time. They understand that feeling down, frustrated, angry, fearful, anxious, and all other "undesirable" emotions will always be a part of life. That they will come, and they will go, and feeling them is perfectly acceptable.

Expectations create the groundwork for our later reactions. So, if we accept and even expect a life that will always bring some disappointment, pain, and loss, it lessens the negative impact when we are hit with it. No matter what we do or how much we wish otherwise, sometimes things will go badly. Transcending suffering or living "happily ever after" can never be attained, because we need unhappiness to experience happiness. As we've mentioned, there could never be an awareness, much less an appreciation of the positive, if there wasn't a contrast with the negative. Peace and happiness must have their eternal counterparts of distress and melancholy.

Just as it is with many other inseparable relationships, such as hunger and satiation, excitement and boredom. It is the ebb and flow that maintains happiness' tangible feel. This idea is not only true in a philosophical way, but it's also confirmed by science. In our bodies, there is no such thing as a non-stop high with our feel-good chemicals, like dopamine and serotonin. They naturally rise and fall.

Having a wonderful life never meant an absence of negative emotions. Each one of us is designed to have the full spectrum of feelings, as they are all necessary. Even the "bad" ones. Just like pain is for us, every one of the negative emotions has its purpose in our lives. To feel is a gift. It means you're alive! Let's normalize that being alive is more than enough to feel happiness.

"We exaggerate misfortune and happiness alike. We are never as bad off or as happy as we say we are." -Honore de Balzac

Love Is All Around You

Feeling good constantly is also a struggle because, as we move through life, the sources of love and happiness change, just as we change. At any given time, we seem to depend on one or a few things to induce feelings of happiness. Sometimes it's a new possession, a certain activity, a job, a spiritual path, or a person.

When in a romantic relationship, this single source of positivity almost always takes on an outsized role. We become so enmeshed and so dependent on this single person. When you combine the intense biological and energetic forces at play, along with our deep conditioning about finding "the one" and reaching "happily ever after" in coupledom. Our world can start to feel very small, focused entirely on one person. The joy and excitement we feel with them can become so strong that the other parts of our life, which used to give us happiness and meaning, begin to pale in comparison to the importance of this new, seemingly magical source.

While we are on the ride, it feels like the best thing ever. But when it suddenly stops, and instead we are watching someone else riding in our place, the experience instantly converts from ecstasy to misery. And as all the songs about breakups and broken hearts express, the world turns grey and lifeless, and pain becomes all we can feel.

When it comes to experiencing love and happiness, I made a wonderful discovery during my time alone following the divorce. No longer having an outside source of love and positivity from a romantic partner, I was forced to work on actually loving myself. I was in dire need of this as I had always depended heavily on relationships to meet my emotional needs. Even though I felt very lonely and craved the affection of a woman, I resisted the urge to jump right back into dating, avoiding the notorious "rebound." I was determined to take this opportunity of being single to develop independent happiness and fulfillment. It was time to really practice all I had been learning about healing. To learn what self-love was and to master my thoughts and emotions.

During this time, I had a particularly profound experience. One day, I was driving and listening to a song by a female artist with a beautiful voice. I had only recently discovered this song, though I had enjoyed other songs from this artist going back many years. I suddenly had this epiphany that she was singing to *me*. When this thought entered my mind, the experience of listening to it brought the enjoyment to a whole new level. How could it not, right? It's an extraordinary gift to have someone create a song and then sing it for you. This idea wasn't just simple fantasizing either. I could *feel* that there was truth to it. Just as true as the fact that I am writing this book specifically for *you*. Whoever you are, my intention is that it be for you, individually. I care about *you*.

As I applied this personalizing way of experiencing things to other positive things around me, the truth of this became even clearer. Simple pleasures, like the cool breeze on my face or the way the wind made the leaves on a tree shimmer, felt like they were meant especially for me. The sunrise, with all its grandeur, was being displayed as a special gift for *my* eyes. The sweet taste of a mango, and everything else I paid attention to, all felt like it was created for me to enjoy. Just as it is all especially for you. Maybe this was just my sense of gratitude deepening. Still, nature's creations and even what we create only have meaning when it is experienced. For any of its beauty and magic to even matter, it needs you and me.

Experiencing the world in this way provides positivity in abundance. There is so much beauty out there to savor and enjoy. Instead of experiencing it as a disconnected visitor or observer, realize that it is all especially for you and feel the goodness of creation embracing and loving you in endless ways. Anywhere and at any time, there is for you an infinite gifting. More than you could ever receive. We all know how just a single person can be the source of so much joy. Imagine what the entire universe is unconditionally offering you at every moment.

Love Never Dies

At a time when I was feeling especially empty and alone, I took some time to meditate, just as I had many times before. But on this occasion, a unique vision unfolded within. I found myself standing in empty space. A white floor was the only thing that gave any sense of order or direction. Everywhere I looked, there was nothing, and the distances were endless. I was alone.

After a short time, two forms began to materialize in front of me. Unexpectedly, my parents were now there with me, their presence comforting and full of love. Then my children take form, smiling and joyful. Next, my brothers and sisters appear, expanding the growing circle around me. Then one by one, now in quicker succession, all the people who have loved and cared about me throughout my life, from childhood until the present time, appear all around me. Close friends from school, workplaces, and all my walks of life. I look around at all their luminescent faces, overwhelmed as warmth and affection wash over me. Then, from between the crowd, Cindy steps out. My heart warms and my eyes well.

Many of our darker times occur because of a problem with one particular person or event, like a break-up or a significant disappointment. It's unfortunate how our minds work sometimes. We are loved and valued by so many people, but we let one person or problem make us forget. We get so focused on one thing that we lose sight of all the love and goodness around us.

This practice reminds me of the movie Ghost when Sam is about to enter into Heaven and is saying goodbye to his wife, Molly. He says, "It's amazing, Molly. The love inside, you take it with you." Never forget all of the love you have received in your life, and all of the people who care about you and to whom you matter.

Whether or not these people are still present in my life, all the love that they had for me was real. It still exists in my heart because it doesn't have to die. Why should it? Even as people come and go in the natural course of life, the goodness experienced together is a sacred gift. It can continue to be positive energy that remains within us. It can be timeless if you let it. You can become conscious of this truth and therefore never lose love and light once it comes into your life. It was given to you freely; take it with you. You are loved. There is always love around you.

Live a Life You Love

Visualize yourself as an old and frail person, in the final days of your life. You're sitting alone on a porch on a quiet afternoon, thinking back on your life. What thoughts will you have? What was most valuable? What will you regret? Some of the most common regrets those at the end of their lives express are, not staying closer with friends and family, working too much, not being true to oneself in order to please others, and not allowing themselves to feel more gratitude and joy.

We all know how the years can seem to pass by in the blink of an eye. So, live as intensely and fully as you can. Even as you appreciate your life as it is, continual expansion is fundamental for joy and meaning. It's hard to thrive while doing the same things every day: work, phone, TV, sleep, repeat. Too much routine can have you feeling that life is mundane, uninteresting, and dreary. We must regularly do new things as opposed to just watching them. Novelty makes life interesting, exciting, and keeps us feeling alive. We must be careful not to allow the need for stability and all our responsibilities keep us in too much constrictive order. The time to truly live is now. So, live a life you love.

CHAPTER FORTY-ONE

GRATITUDE

"A man never feels the loss of things which it never occurs to him to ask for; he is just as happy without them; whilst another, who may have a hundred times as much, feels miserable because he has not got the one thing he wants."

-Arthur Schopenhauer

IT IS NATURAL TO RUMINATE ON WHAT WE HAVE LOST, don't have, and all our negative experiences. We spend a lot of time dissatisfied with life as it is. We surely don't have everything that we want, and things could definitely be so much better.

If our energy is spent mostly in this, let's just call it "headspace," where negativity dominates, then you simply cannot be at peace. Instead, we end up feeling mostly negative emotions like bitterness, regret, sadness, frustration, and resentment. And often, these feelings don't stop there. The real danger comes when they grow into darker emotions like anger, hate, or a desire for revenge. That's when the pain doesn't just stay inside us; it starts to hurt others, too. People living in a personal hell are rarely satisfied to suffer alone. And as the old saying makes its truth known, the miserable can't help but drag other people down with them. This is why people end up being neglected, abused, and even murdered.

Most of us don't go quite so far down this dark route. Usually, people spread their pain in more subtle ways, such as through criticism, insults, and selfishness. And sadly, what gets totally lost is all the goodness and love that could have been exchanged instead.

So, why is it so easy to become entrapped within negative thoughts and emotions? Why is this a universal problem we all face? One reason is referred to as the "negativity bias." It appears that we are biologically programmed to focus on negative past events and habitually worry about the future. Our minds remember anything that feels dangerous or painful, whether it's something physical or emotional, to help keep us safe.

Some more reasons we become dominated by negative thoughts and emotions are due to some things we have discussed in past chapters, like living out of integrity with who we are, holding beliefs and value systems that don't serve us, seeing the world as black and white, having an unwell body, and detrimental relationships.

If you often find yourself feeling depressed and seeing only a bleak future ahead. Your brain's negativity bias, past trauma, and likely several unhealthy mindsets are all working together to hold you back from the life you're meant to live. This is one of life's most dangerous traps, and it can be especially harmful for those struggling with thoughts of suicide.

One of the best ways to overcome these challenges is to experience feelings of gratitude. Practicing gratitude shifts our focus to all that is good in our lives, which, when we are willing to look, is often a whole lot. This doesn't mean we put on rose-colored glasses and deny the reality of our problems and suffering. It means that we look at our lives honestly and allow the positive and the possibilities to be most prominent. Why not allow all the many good aspects of life to outweigh the bad?

Many of us, despite our horrible experiences and current problems, could probably see that a great portion of our lives have been relatively good, if not highly fortunate. Today, most people in the world have their basic needs met, like food, water, shelter, safety, and connection with others. It's easy to forget how amazing that really is. And on top of that, many people are living with more than just the basics; they have access to abundance and incredible opportunities in life. And it is indeed true that even the poorest in much of the world, even with their many difficulties, enjoy luxuries that kings and emperors of the past could have only dreamed about.

The world offers an endless variety of activities, places, entertainment, and cuisines. Incredible technological conveniences such as washing machines, cars, and smartphones. We travel great distances quickly and comfortably. There are countless educational opportunities, many of which are easily accessible. Incredible comforts that would have been mind-boggling just several decades ago, like air conditioning, heaters, running water, and toilets, are all just afterthoughts for us. We have modern healthcare, countless career opportunities, and access to limitless information. Most people in the world live with a high degree of personal freedom and are able to safely pursue the life they want.

If, after our basic needs are met, we still feel dissatisfied or ungrateful, we are likely allowing comparison to dictate our feelings. All things do exist in relation to each other, and being able to make comparisons, distinctions, and judgments is an important part of life. The downside to this is that comparison with other people's lives can lead to a lot of unnecessary suffering.

After basic needs are met, everything else is truly a luxury and will inevitably vary greatly from person to person. Money, status, health, talents, success, and relationships will never be the same for everyone. If we can't find contentment when our basic needs are being met, having more won't really make us much happier. And if you feel the need to compare yourself to others, it's more helpful to think about those who have less or are facing harder situations, which can remind you of just how much you already have. Why selectively compare with just those who have more? Comparison, however, is never an effective long-term way to create well-being. Focusing on your own life and seeing your journey as wholly unique and incomparable to others is.

Expectations and entitlement also play large roles in limiting our experience of gratitude and, therefore, overall happiness. We must realize that life is chaotic and largely out of our control. Call it fate, chance, or God, but life will seem both cruel and benevolent as the years pass. Some things in life will go the way we want, and some won't. To free ourselves from unrealistic expectations, we need to accept that life and others don't owe us anything and they never will.

The ancient Stoic philosopher Epictetus shared the following as a way to deal with the inequality and unfairness of life. *"Remember that you must behave in life as at a dinner party. Is anything brought around to you? Put out your hand and take your share with moderation. Does it pass by you? Don't stop it. Has it not come yet? Don't stretch your desire towards it, but wait till it reaches you. Do this with regard to children, to a wife, to public posts, to riches, and you will eventually be a worthy partner of the feasts of the gods."*

In our individual lives, there is always so much we could choose to be grateful for. We can be grateful just for being born and getting the chance to experience life. We can also be thankful for the simple things we often take for granted, like being able to think, feel, and move our bodies. We can appreciate what our parents or caregivers gave us, and all the love, kindness, and support we've received along the way. All the health we have enjoyed. For all those who contribute to society, dedicating their lives to building, repairing, teaching, protecting, healing, entertaining, growing food, raising animals, transporting, and manufacturing. We personally benefit from all of their talents and efforts.

How often are we grateful for ourselves? For how far we have come, all we have overcome, everything we have learned, and for all the love and kindness we have shown to others. How often do we recognize the wonder and beauty of the world and the universe? For these five senses, which let us become immersed in it? The way the sun shines down on all of us. We are all gifted with the same water to drink and air to breathe. Gravity keeps us all on the ground. Somehow, all of our hearts keep beating, and we wake up each morning. The most important gifts of existence are universally given, no matter who we are.

Even in the darkest moments when the present seems a nightmare, and it is hard to see any good. There can always be a small glimmer of gratitude for the possibility that the unknown future always offers. We can be grateful that tomorrow will be a new day, and with every new day we get a chance to create a better life.

Experiencing gratitude releases feel-good chemicals in our bodies like dopamine, oxytocin, and endorphins. These have instant effects that help lift our mood. The positive effects of gratitude account for one of the reasons praying feels good. Much of prayer is spent expressing gratitude. But you don't have to direct your thanks or appreciation to any particular god to experience the benefits. Gratitude is a feeling experienced anytime we think about the things we love, value, and appreciate.

The most counterintuitive thing about suffering is that when overcome healthily, it unlocks our most profound sense of gratitude. In other words, we need suffering to be able to experience gratitude at its highest levels. This occurs in the same way that loss allows us to more fully appreciate what we have.

Try starting and ending each day by intentionally taking a moment to practice gratitude. One of the quickest ways to feel better when you're emotionally hurting is think about things you're grateful for. Our minds aren't great at thinking about two different things at the same time. So, when you need a boost, try asking yourself what you're thankful for. You'll start to notice that more positive thoughts and feelings begin to flow.

Though it will always be a world of dark and light, suffering and joy, where you focus your thoughts is always your choice. You get to create the story of your life. Gratitude will inspire you to write a beautiful one.

For me, the pains and losses of the past few years were enough to bury my soul under a lake of alcohol or maybe even six feet of soil. I now understand how absolutely devastating and exhausting the darkness in life can be. Avoiding becoming lost in the darkness is a test we all face. Gratitude brings in the light, and where there is light, darkness cannot remain.

CHAPTER FORTY-TWO

LETTING GO

IN THE WORLD OF SELF-IMPROVEMENT AND HEALING TRAUMA, the term "doing the work" is a common phrase. It refers to what one does to heal from the past and live optimally in the present. Of all the advice and wisdom out there about how to feel better and live well, one idea is especially important: learning to *let go*. When we hold on to the past, try to control the uncontrollable, and stress-out about the future, we're existing in a very uncomfortable place. But even though "let it go" sounds simple, how do we actually do it?

Well, among the many things that help develop this way of being, engaging mentally, physically, and emotionally in the unfolding present is the most effective. This is why you hear so much these days about "mindfulness" and "being present." The positive effects are becoming more and more understood. That doesn't mean the present is always easy. Things like divorce, losing someone you love, or getting seriously sick can deeply affect you and change your life for a long time. But even as certain effects endure, we can still recognize that new life is constantly unfolding with each day and each moment. What has or hasn't happened is not the meaning of your life. *Right now*, the past has moved out of existence, and your fears about the future are only speculation. But what you can touch right now, what you can know for sure, is your life as it is happening right at this moment.

Consider Alan Watts' wisdom on the topic: "*You don't get attached to the past. You go with it, with life. Life is flowing all the time…and you are going along with it, whether you want to or not. You're like people in a stream. You can swim against the stream, but you'll still be moved along by it. And all you'll do is wear yourself out in futility. But if you swim with the stream, the whole strength of the stream is yours. Of course, the difficulty that so many of us have is finding out which way the stream is going. But certainly, as it goes, all the past vanishes, the future has not yet arrived, and there is only one place to be. Which is here and now.*"

CHAPTER FORTY-THREE

EMBRACE CHANGE

"Nothing is so painful to the human mind as a great and sudden change."

-Mary Shelley

L<small>IFE</small> IS WILD. We need strong tools - emotional, mental, and physical to help us face all the pain and hard times. So, as I wrote this book, my goal was to share what has helped me most in my own journey to overcome anxiety and sadness, and live at my best. Few other endeavors are as important, and it certainly can be a matter of life and death. This has not been a philosophical exercise for me. *All* the ideas and principles we have talked about have been an integral part of my own healing. Sometimes I wonder if they have even saved my life.

The order in which each principle has been presented is by no means an indication of importance. But as I now address the topic of *change*, I will, however, start off by making a special emphasis. Understanding and embracing change would be near the top of the list.

The very essence of reality is change; it is chaos and order in action. All things, including ourselves, are in a constant state of change. As life flows, the degree to which we are just along for the ride as just one person among billions, and as tiny specs in the vastness of the cosmos, may be difficult for some to accept. Almost all, and I mean *all*, of the control we think we have is an illusion. No matter how stable our life feels, other people or nature could change everything in an instant. Not accepting or understanding this results in disharmony with life. When change is resisted and resented, we place ourselves at odds with the entire flow of the universe and in conflict with the present.

Change is so hard because it challenges our ego's three biggest weaknesses: attachment, fear, and the need for control. Ironically, just as much as we dislike change, we also need it because change brings novelty. Why do we hike any trail other than the first one we ever enjoyed? Why do we try new restaurants? Why do we seek *anything* new? It's because for the body, mind, and spirit, expansion is essential nourishment. Change means excitement, mystery, discoveries, and new growth.

We love the changes that we see as positive. So really, when we are talking about the need to embrace change, we are referring to change that we consider undesirable, the change that hurts. First, let's make clear that embracing difficult change doesn't mean that we have to feel good about it. It doesn't mean that we don't feel the appropriate feelings it can bring. Embracing change simply means that we accept it, we take its hand and make peace with it. As endless changes occur, we respond by continually taking responsibility for ourselves and for what we *can* control. No matter what happens, we consciously show up for ourselves and others as our highest selves.

What about worst-case scenarios, such as a cancer diagnosis? Truly a tremendously difficult turn of events. Feelings of fear and sadness with hard change like this are, of course, natural. It's a life change that no one wants. Embracing change like this simply means accepting that this *is* something that happens in life, and our response to the news is what we have control over. With the whole universe out of our control, myriad things can happen. No matter what difficult change we encounter, our response is what either makes things better or worse, amplifies suffering or alleviates it.

The hardest change is often when we are experiencing what feels like the end of something. Death is surely an ending, and its total uncertainty makes it one of life's most difficult changes to face. Perhaps, as most of us hope, death isn't a complete ending, and instead just one more kind of change. No matter how our opinions may differ, our intrinsic connection with the universe is real. But what that connection transitions into upon death is a mystery we all have the privilege of wondering about.

Embracing change also means understanding that endings are, in fact, new beginnings. In life, creation always springs out of what is, for a time, destruction and change. The endings and the parts of your life that fall away are just part of a continual process of transformation. When things seem like they are falling apart, in the larger story of your life, other pieces are falling into place. It just takes time for the process to unfold.

In the journey of the self, change is what opens up the widest doors to new revelations. Toward becoming more free from the things we have become identified with and attached to. Everything is temporary, including you. Your thoughts and emotions, your desires, priorities, and goals. All around you is also in constant flow. People and your environment are like the seasons. Here for a time, until suddenly they are not. If we accept that impermanence is a natural function of life, then we will have a mind and heart that flows and finds peace with all the many changes, big and small.

We are both physical and energetic beings, and both are fragile. With enough strain and pressure, the physical body will break. Our spiritual nature, under enough stress, has its breaking points as well. Life pulls, strikes, and tears at us all. It is only with the ability to move, bend, and flow with life that the pressures can be managed. If your mind is rigid like a block wall, with your ideas, expectations, and beliefs are all cemented in place. When life comes with its greatest storms, when abandonment, heartbreak, betrayal, illness, injury, and death come. A rigid mental structure will crack as it cannot move with the changing forces, and we are at risk of collapse.

It is better to be like a living tree with deep roots in self-awareness and wisdom. A trunk and core made of love and a desire for growth. Vibrant branches that can flow with life, the way it happens. Our ideas and conclusions should be like leaves that can be shed and blown away, able to be renewed with even better ones. And just as a tree stands ever exposed to the changing elements, we too must expect and endure what storms may come.

When we understand and adapt to change, nothing in life is insurmountable. Your story is unfolding in real time with events unknowable. What will happen in the next chapter? Just keep going and choosing light and life. Your actions matter, but in so many ways, you are like a leaf in a raging river. You can't control what happens after death, much less what will happen tomorrow. You are a flicker in the universe's unending fireworks show. So, enjoy your life-burst while it shines.

LIFE & DEATH BY INTENTION

EPILOUGE

PART ONE

RETURNING ONE LAST TIME

When I did that meditative "deep dive" back to that moment of Cindy's death, I had returned there with the intention of healing *my* trauma, specifically, guilt, shame, and sorrow. A year and a half later, my healing continued to progress. I still, however, felt very saddened by those final memories of Cindy. My heart empathized with how she must have suffered self-anger and loathing like nothing I could imagine, made undoubtedly clear by her act of ultimate self-punishment. I knew this final event of her life was not representative of who she was and not what she wanted.

When someone dies, the story they leave behind continues to affect the living, and Cindy's final, terrible days dominated the way I felt about her. She would not have wanted that extreme darkness to be what the kids and I were left with. Nevertheless, Cindy's legacy had become frozen in this state. So, I decided it was time to return once again to that most dreadful moment. This time to allow Cindy's highest self to illuminate the experience with the truth of her being. I didn't want the girl who became utterly lost to be what forever remained of her.

The idea of doing another deep dive had been on my mind for several days before the right time came. The moment came on a sunny afternoon in October, about a week after what would have been her 37th birthday. At that time, I was remarried and had four stepchildren, so having a quiet moment alone at home was very rare. But this particular afternoon had left me with an empty house, allowing the quiet solitude needed for this endeavor.

The bath had worked so well on the prior occasion that I decided to try it again. I closed the blinds to darken the room and opened the valve to fill the bath with warm water. There was some Epsom salt infused with lavender, so I thought, well, lavender is supposed to be calming, so let's throw a little of that in there. Once it was filled, I took off my clothes and slipped in. Why do we always say, "slipped in" when we talk about getting into a bath, "I slipped into the tub." Wouldn't slipping be a bad thing? Anyhow, that's how we say it. So, I relaxed into the warm water and closed my eyes. Then I just breathed.

I try to let go of my thoughts, but naturally, random thoughts come uninvited anyway. Sometimes they carry me away for a little while, but then I remember I'm trying to meditate, and I let those thoughts fade away. Then my mind goes off again, to some unintentional place, but this time I come back to the void a little faster. I'm getting more present with just my simple existing self now. I think to myself, "Relax, let it all go and be with the stillness." I continue to breathe into deeper and deeper relaxation and presence.

My breathing is now smooth and rhythmic, almost hypnotic. Within the silence of the room, my breath sounds like light waves on a beach flowing in and then out.

Suddenly, as if my mind knew just the right moment to take the leap, down into memory and past living experience, I arrived. As if by time machine with no physical device, the past opens up, and I am back there, again, back at the worst day of my life.

Now, inside the memory, I'm lying there in bed. I didn't get much sleep last night. It was the seventh night I spent feeling heartbroken over her affair and the end of our relationship and family. The pain always felt worse at night. During those hours, I would text her, pouring out how hurt and devastated I was by what she had done. And that night, for the first time, I wrote to her that I hated her for it.

I regretted the way I angrily expressed my feelings, and I wanted to tell her in person that I was sorry. I go out of the bedroom expecting to find her, but I don't see her anywhere. I relive the memory as I did before, checking throughout the entire house, then making my way to the garage. I walk through the kitchen to the garage door and grab the handle...

At this point, I take control of the replaying memory and consciously stop it there. Like rewinding a video, I play it backward, all the way to the moment when I was still lying in bed. The time had come to experience this from a higher perspective, including from a different vantage point. This time it wasn't about me and my experience of that day. I was back there, this time for her.

So, I leave my exhausted body in the bedroom and move my awareness to the garage. Now, like a fly on the wall or an invisible ghost, I'm in the darkened garage observing the scene. Cindy is finishing tying off one end of a rope to the pull-up bar. Then she wraps the other end around her neck and cinches it tight. Then, bending at the knees, she lets her own weight begin the strangulation. The horrid energy in the room is so palpable it's hard to breathe. To describe her face as being in discomfort would be the ultimate understatement. Consumed by hopelessness and emotional pain, she resists the urge to simply stand up, able to bear the pain and terror of hanging by expecting it to be over soon.

I have a sense of what it physically felt like for her in those final moments. A few days after that morning, I stood in front of a bathroom mirror, tied a rope around my neck, and pulled it tight. I had zero intention or desire for suicide. Only a morbid need to know what it felt like. To gain even a little bit of understanding of what she was experiencing at the end. I can tell you that once the blood flow is shut off, it only takes a second to feel intense pressure building in the face and head. It quickly feels as if your head is going to pop as vision blurs.

I can only imagine the dark determination she must have had to resist that powerful instinctive urge to simply stand up and take the weight off her neck, releasing that panic-inducing pressure and easily stop the fast-approaching doom. It breaks my heart to know she felt the depths of something even worse and more desperate than pain. Something so dire, about herself, about the world, about being, that it drained the very life from her.

As I continue to helplessly watch the scene, something amazing begins to happen. Stepping forward out of the darkness, a woman emerges with brown and copper hair, hundreds of curly ringlets flowing down. She calmly walks toward the suffering and dying Cindy. Moving confidently and with an aura of dignified radiance, her face is calm and serene. Just her presence illuminates the dark garage, and we are no longer in the dark. This was Cindy's Higher Self.

Now standing above Cindy, she reaches down and gently lifts her to her feet and frees her neck from the rope. Not having the strength to remain on her feet, her Higher-Self lowers Cindy down and cradles her in her arms. Utterly depleted by both a broken soul and physically reaching death's doorstep, Cindy holds on like a child who was just found by her mother after believing she had been lost forever, and begins to cry. Her sobs of relief, shame, and gratitude are soft and subdued.

I continue to watch the extraordinary scene unfold, almost holding my breath, waiting to hear what will be said, but there are no words exchanged. There is just presence, just love, just life.

Exiting the mental journey, I feel myself back in the water and slowly open my eyes. Now, alone again in the tub, I take a few more deep, thoughtful breaths. I remained there for a while, allowing myself to take in what I had just seen and let the emotions reverberate through my body.

Following this experience, something in me changed. I felt lighter, and my head was clearer. Was that really how it happened that morning? No, but my heart feels something different about Cindy now, regardless.

If you are skeptical of this practice and say to yourself, "You can't just make up a new memory the way you want in order to replace a bad one." That is totally understandable, and I am with you. The way it happened really is and always will be the way it happened. However, there are parts of the brain that don't know the difference between fantasy and reality.

There are many scientific studies showing that the brain's "reality threshold" can indeed be crossed. Meaning that the lines between perceived and imagined experiences can be blurred. This is because the same regions of our brains that process perceptions also process internal images. If the experience in the mind is vivid or intense enough, it can be perceived by the brain as real. Take the example of how visualization helps athletes perform better. Under brain scans, imagining bodily movements activates the same circuits that actually moving does. An altered state of consciousness, which deep meditation can achieve, further impairs the brain's normal ability to distinguish between reality and imagination.

Beyond the science, the main point is that her suicide wasn't representative of the greater truth of her life or who she was. It would be a terrible thing to allow someone's lowest moments to become what forever represents them. Therefore, the intent of my inward journey was to deeply anchor a positive experience in the same place where the nightmare was, helping to heal my heart in regard to Cindy. And something highly positive surely became imprinted on the feeling part of my brain.

It was a healing revolution in my mind, to take that worst moment of pain and darkness and convert it into one of love and compassion. As I had done for me and now for her. The original memory threatened to leave a completely distorted legacy and portrayed an idea about her that wasn't true. If Cindy's true self, uncorrupted by life's pain and deceptions, could have miraculously broken through before the end, everything would have been different. Cindy would be alive, and there would never have been a need for a meditative journey to heal the past. It would have just been herself that day, deciding to stand up and take the rope off her own neck, saying no to the darkness and yes to the light.

We all have ups and downs in life. All of us get it wrong in big and small ways at different times. That's OK, because the truth is that life itself is wild, confusing, and messy. Pain and darkness will always threaten to blind us to the miracle of existence. If life is to win out, we must allow light to be the dominant force. We must constantly reconnect with the truth of who we all are. My meditative vision helped me see even more clearly that compassion and forgiveness for ourselves and others is the universal solution to suffering.

"Getting over the past" doesn't mean being able to forget or erase it. All of our memories, both good and bad, are valuable. They're like tiny gears in the machinery that make up who we are. Starting from birth, we are slowly being assembled, each experience adding new pieces to the person we're becoming. Ideally, most of the process would be crafted with care and wisdom, but we all get plenty of rusty and broken parts. However, when these negative experiences are well-processed and converted into wisdom, they make the evolving result even more of a masterpiece. The prolonged difficulties occur when our painful experiences remain unresolved. Many remain so repressed that we aren't even aware of how they are affecting our feelings and behavior. Part of the beauty of life is that we can continually fix and replace the damaged parts of ourselves. Our own mistakes and outside impacts damage us, but we are endlessly able to repair and refine.

My most detrimental experience deserved to be re-examined and reworked, just as yours do. What that looks like for you is unique to you. But leaving trauma just as it is allows it to continue hurting us. I'm thankful I was able to recognize how consequential my trauma was and then confront the nightmare face to face. Going back and transforming it from darkness to light, and from death to life. No one else could have done it for me, just as no one else has the power to heal you. Ultimately, it is within each of us to decide if we are going to rise or fall. For when darkness comes, *you* are the light.

As you put into practice the principles of well-being we have discussed, your life *will* be transformed. Doing this inner work will replace harmful beliefs with ones that empower and enhance your life. You will move beyond the trauma and negativity that has likely been a generational pattern in your family, as was the case with mine. You will rise above the pervasive dysfunction in society as you shed its destructive lies and false promises. The independent well-being of your heart, mind, and body will grow exponentially.

Become the creator of your life. It is *you* experiencing the ever-unfolding present moment and making the meanings and feelings about it all. It's time to take your rightful place as your *own* master.

If you have ever had yearnings to be close to God, to know and feel the source of creation. All you have to do is become aware of the infinite power and beauty of the life throbbing within you. Allow yourself to feel into your own existence like never before. Whether in the complete stillness of meditation or in total immersion in any activity. Feel the endless reservoirs of love and resilience within. Could there be any better description of the divine than what is in you already? With the power of your divinity, you may not be able to raise the dead or calm a storm. You can, however, lift your life and many others into a brighter existence. You can turn darkness into light and misery into joy.

PART TWO

PLEASE DON'T GO

A COUPLE OF WEEKS AFTER CINDY'S FUNERAL, the day came for us to move out of our house. With the truck loaded and my kids and family waiting outside, I walked back into the house one last time. I looked around at all the emptiness. Countless memories of so many good times with Cindy and the kids passed through my mind. Right here in all these now empty rooms. How strange it is, the way a little bit of time can change everything so completely.

I slowly walked through each room for one last look. When I got to the back guest room, where most of the affair had happened, I stood there for a while, lost in thought. Then suddenly, I started violently punching and kicking the empty space where the bed used to be. Filled with anger, grief, and guilt, I cursed them both for what they had done. Back then, I still saw the affair as the principal factor leading to her suicide. I was only in the primitive stages of what was to be my journey of recovery.

I then slowly walked back to the center of the house, where the kitchen was. It was an oppressive feeling, knowing I was walking out of that house for the last time. But leaving was a necessary step in the process of letting go of that life and beginning to build a new one. Emotions welled up, and I began to weep. Leaning backwards against the cabinet, I slowly slid down until I was sitting on the ground. Crying like the defeated, beaten down, and abandoned man I felt like at that time. I wept for my children, for myself, but mostly for her. "Why did you do it?" I quietly sobbed. "You didn't have to go." I continued crying there for a little while and then expressed my last words in our home that was now no more. "I didn't want you to go." My heart and soul broke again and again. You would think the pieces would have become too small to break any further, but in those days, pain knew no bounds.

Sometimes pain is so immense that its duration can't be estimated. For those with deep trauma, "healing, letting go, and living our best life" is what we all want, but will always be so much easier said than done. There are no quick fixes to the horrible parts of this life. The darkness out there can be so bad. It gets inside and borrows deep within.

The contrast between happiness and misery is a stark thing. On one side, feelings of happiness would have us wanting to live forever. And on the other hand, misery can be so crushing that ending our own existence becomes a real desire. This is why people tie ropes around their necks, put guns to their heads, and jump from bridges. The darkness is real. Feeling absolutely hopeless and worthless is real. Ending the dark feelings through a self-imposed death could be a breath away for all of us. The many millions who have died and will continue to die by their own choosing are not a different species. They are you and me, and we all deserve to live.

Life presents many adversaries, with one of them being a force that seems solely interested in our premature death. It is the elements of our experience that create an overwhelming feeling that life isn't worth living. This is quite paradoxical, given that it is also our trials that help lead us to our highest selves.

Our most painful and darkest of times trying to teach us the most profound lessons about love, goodness, and what truly matters in life.

One afternoon at the hospital, while Cindy was still on life support, my friend Kevin was kind enough to share something very wise with me. He told me that even though things were so sad and bleak at the time, he saw rainbows in our future. Out of all the kind and supportive things my friends and family said to me during that time, that one stayed with me the most. Maybe it was the beautiful imagery, or maybe because it inspired hope that not only would we endure, but our future could even be wonderful. Either way, he was absolutely right.

Life continues, as it always does, to be a mixed bag of light and dark. The repercussions from her suicide continue to echo. Still, many rainbows have come arching through our lives in different ways. I have experienced empowering growth in every meaningful way, and I appreciate life like I never could have before. Zuko and Brisa are thriving emotionally and physically. We always had a strong relationship, and everything we went through only made our bond deeper. My most earnest hope is that they are never overtaken by the darkness that tries to eat away at us all and did devour their mother.

After I was remarried for a couple years, it became clear we were not meant to continue the journey together. During a difficult time early on, she said that maybe we were just meant to be together for a season. To provide things for each other and each other's children at a critical time. I choose to believe in this assessment and hold onto the good.

The pain I experienced after this divorce became another dreadful "darkest before the dawn" experience, compelling me to look inward like never before. While in those depths, I finally discovered self-love and acceptance for *all* parts of me and my journey. Finally gaining independence from an old version of me who was in constant need of the validation, affection, and love of a woman in order to feel worthy and whole. I came to understand the dynamics involved in serious relationship loss when the other person is still alive. The chapter on this issue would have never been written if I had not gone through this experience. And because break-ups are one of the most common catalysts for suicide, that chapter is one of the most important of all.

For a time, my old conditioning had me thinking that "a future of rainbows" meant a woman, a love, a mother for my children, and a whole family again. But when that fell apart for a second time, I began to realize that just as there are really infinite colors in every rainbow. There wasn't one person or thing that could give me the love or life I was looking for. It made me see that my own life was the rainbow and is the most valuable gift I have. And that no matter what, I'm worthy, just as I am. Now, I don't forget my inner child and give myself the patience and kindness I've always needed.

As my awareness and wisdom have grown, so has my ability to better handle life's difficulties. Less and less do emotions and thoughts rule my life. Instead, I see them clearly. I no longer seek external validation by people pleasing while betraying myself. Social and material success are less important, as the intensity and beauty of my life experience is what matters more to me now. My daily intention is that presence and gratitude light my way. All has led me towards the relationship I now enjoy, and we have every intention of doing the rest of the journey together. We are excited to share every rainbow yet to come.

Now and again, in quiet moments, I think of Cindy and contemplate all the time that has passed since she died, and continues to grow with each passing year. I ponder on how she has been totally gone since that morning I found her. How she's missed every single moment of life she would have otherwise experienced since then. Just what she has missed with her children is incalculable. I can't help but feel sad for her that she is missing it all.

If somehow, she is aware in some afterlife realm, she'd have to feel profound regret for taking extreme actions during a difficult time, and losing her life as a result. There's no doubt, those couple of weeks were incredibly hard for her, and that morning was especially awful. It must have felt like the worst day of her life, given the heartbreaking choice she made. If she had somehow made it through and could look back now, I'm sure she would've seen it for what it was, a really terrible period of time. And like all really bad moments, they eventually pass, and life goes on. Unfortunately for Cindy and all others who end their own lives, this natural ebb and flow of ups and downs abruptly ends. The lessons and growth that were being offered by the painful experience never gained. That bright new dawn after the long dark night was never savored.

When in pain, try to remember that life is unpredictable and that wonderful things could be waiting, just on the other side. We can remember that we are designed to live in this world and specifically equipped with all the strength and resiliency needed to handle all that is inherent to life. We must remember how pain and suffering can deceive us into feeling worthless and hopeless. This trap must be recognized and overcome again and again.

You are here to experience darkness and light. So, even when you feel like you have learned enough, the trials will continue to come anyway. Because you deserve to keep growing and learning, life will continue to serve you by providing opportunities for you to progress into an even better version of yourself. Life and creation only happen within a continuous dance of chaos and order. This is existence. You can choose to embrace and play with this reality or resist it and remain in miserable frustration. This is the realization and the choice that can fundamentally change your life.

Whether things happen the way you would want them or not, you can always choose gratitude and love. You can accept and embrace life as it unfolds and be freed from frustration, anger, and bitterness. When darkness comes, you remain in control, saying, "There you are, hello again," and you keep moving forward. You never forget that you are living in a universe out of your control.

Learn from Cindy and all others who were deceived by pain and became lost in the darkness. Observe how a decision of total destruction was made in the midst of a hard period of time. She had many tough times before as well as lots of good ones. Why was this one so different? Why was this the reason to choose the "I'm taking my own life, I'm out of here forever" path? What a tragedy this mindset is, considering there are countless other ways to respond to a difficult time. There are so many other paths we can choose, ones that lead to healing and peace instead of more pain and loss.

For those of us who have had a part of us torn out forever by trauma, there is no magic pill to make the pain go away or restore what was lost. During the worst of my experience with Cindy's suicide, it felt like I was dying in slow motion. It was as if the grief was leaking the very life out of me. I did not want to accept this as my fate. I did not want the end of her life to be the end of my well-being. Seeking understanding about suicide, then prioritizing my own needs, was the most positively impactful thing I did. Later, when my soul hit rock bottom after the divorce, everything shared in this book is what brought me back to the light.

The darkest parts of my journey have taught me that chaos and order are the life process. Change, which we deem good or bad, never ends. Embracing this reality as both inevitable and acceptable is critical for a pleasant experience of life. Our response is the one thing we have control over. A life by intention means taking full responsibility for living in integrity with our highest selves. The result is a life of patience, compassion, gratitude, and love. Which not only saves us from the darkness, but it also brings the healing and peace we are all searching for.

In authoring this book, I was mentally confronted daily with the worst events of my life. Many times, I wanted to close the story and bury it, never to look at it again. But I knew there are those out there who are meant to find this book. Thinking about them and about you is what kept bringing me back, again and again. In doing it for you, I ended up helping myself too. It helped me work through my experiences more deeply. It gave me further purpose and meaning during the hardest years of my life, and became an integral part of my healing and personal growth. Though I don't think there is ever a place of total healing where all traces of the pain are gone.

Suicide is truly so terrible and dark that if we are willing to see the lessons, it can teach us all profound lessons about life. Even if it's just to understand the ultimate dangers of lacking well-being. Where we could descend if we aren't dedicated to healing our wounds, self-discovery, and loving ourselves.

My intention with this book is to provide support in the four areas most critical in dealing with suicide. The purpose of Section One is to help everyone gain a deeper understanding. A suicidal person being driven by their traumas and conditioning is like being blindfolded while walking a tightrope. Knowledge and wisdom about the trial they are facing can remove the blindfold and help get them on stable ground. For those who care about a person struggling with suicidal thoughts, understanding empowers more effective support. It is also critical in the healing journey after losing someone. Understanding accelerates the restoration of our hearts and our lives.

The purpose of Section Two is to help support sufferers and their loved ones during times of severe suicidal crisis. To prepare for and survive periods of greatest danger. A lot can be done, and there is much reason to hope.

Section Three supports those of us who have lost someone. The pain of losing someone is deep and lasting, but healing is possible. Having tasted some of life's worst suffering, those who have lost a loved one can rise above the pain and come to know the beauty of life as few others can. Learning about the impact of suicide on loss-survivors can also help those at risk consider what happens to those they would leave behind.

Section Four provides the most effective and long-term solution to suicide. As principles of well-being are practiced, the joyful self is realized, and our highest self becomes dominant. The lie that we are condemned to pain and hopelessness is overcome. Suicidality and all other undesirable states of being fade as light grows.

It has been my honor to journey with you through these words for a while. I am all for your life's success, just as so many others are. I wrote this book for *you*. Even without meeting you, I know how valuable you are. Because to know oneself is to know all.

For those of you who know someone who is struggling. Hear them, and support them the best you can. Show them, by word and deed, how much they are valued, wanted, and needed. Hold their hand on a path of intentional healing. Don't underestimate the positive impact you can have. And if all else fails, maybe you can simply love the darkness right out of them.

In a world where darkness comes for us all, we need all the love we can get.

The words of my heart for anyone who may find themselves on the edge of suicide are these:

Your pains, your sufferings, and your hopelessness are all conspiring to take your opportunity at life away from you. I am so sorry that you are going through this. The darkness must be truly terrible, and I can only try to imagine how awful it feels. I can't know fully what you are going through, though I have felt its shadow.

What I know all too well is the pain that comes after giving up. I was there as the story of Cindy's life, full of color and vibrancy, suddenly went dark. How one day, during her 34th year of life, it all just vanished, the remaining pages of her life left forever blank. Rare is the day I'm not conscious of how much Cindy is missing. Watching every smile and special moment of our two children pass as she misses it all.

I experienced how the darkness you are currently feeling goes nuclear upon the destruction of oneself, sending decimation racing in all directions. The suffering it spreads is merciless. I am all but sure that if she could have been conscious of the bigger picture, she would not have chosen to be dead.

Before you decide to take the last action of your existence. Before you lose every single second, minute, hour, and year of possibility ahead of you. I invite you to take the most vivid and realistic look at that future. Visualize your body, rotting underground in total darkness. Above you, standing on the grass, are the people who love you, their hearts and minds shredded into pieces. Your parents, siblings, spouse, friends, and children never to be the same again.

Have you ever wondered where you got the idea that death is a desirable option for dealing with life's difficulties?

Where did this belief system come from? What is the allure that death holds for you? Will it give you what you are looking for? Will it fulfill your highest priorities and achieve what matters to you most? What do you really know about death? Maybe things will actually be much worse for you. Or perhaps there will be nothing, who knows?

Many of us hope for an afterlife that fulfills our greatest desires and assuages our deepest fears. But maybe it's nothing like we imagine it to be. Maybe there won't be a joyful reunion with all the loved ones we've lost, or maybe there will. Personally, I choose not to rely on idealizations to find purpose, ease my sadness, or calm my fears. Death is coming sooner or later no matter what. Is going there any earlier than you must, really what you want? Existing means to struggle with existence. You are not alone. We all have our hard to deal with.

This, here, now, is what we know. It may very well be the one chance we will ever have. And since this life is all we can be sure about, it only makes sense to live it out to the fullest, to treasure and to savor it. Even with all the body's limitations and potential for pain, the opportunity it provides to access the world is a remarkable gift. Eyes that can witness beauty, wonder, and majesty. Able to see the face of a baby or watch a sunset transform from pink and yellow to orange, then fire. To witness lightning create cracks in the sky for a mesmerizing instant. Ears that receive a world of wonderful sounds, music, voices, and all of nature's songs. Touch, smell, and taste, gifting further access to endless layers of a world of breathtaking abundance.

While I don't know the intensities of severe suicidal pain, I do know the pain of standing on that grass, staring down at the ground because someone you loved chose to be in that coffin. Of having parts of me that can never fully heal because resolve can never be had. If death is chosen, you will be gone, but we, the survivors, will go on. With long lives left to live, accompanied by the horror and grief that would be your death by intention.

These words and my experience are not meant to shame you into staying alive. But to have you confront some realities that might be worth your consideration. You deserve to make the wisest decision possible. It is ultimately your choice of course. I, however, sincerely suggest that you hold on. Life is part pain; that much is clear to you and me at this point. But it's also very surprising, unknowable, and full of possibility. A future you'll love could be just up ahead, just beyond your most painful days and darkest season. Stay with us. Please. One more day, then one more week, and then another year. Stay for you.

Give yourself the invaluable gift of all the wonderful and happy times still to be yours. Continue loving those who love you and the many who truly need you now and in the future. Remember that you have had ups and downs before. This hard time, no matter how bad, is also one of those times you can eventually look back on and not only be glad you made it through, but you'll see how it helped you grow.

You *can* overcome depression and suicidal ideation. You are far from alone. This is a human experience. It is among countless possible challenges that could have been yours to confront. Suicide is a big one, there is no mistaking that. Nevertheless, it is, after all, one more opportunity to be courageous, patient, resilient, and victorious. To choose light over darkness.

You can change the direction of your life by prioritizing your well-being. Your life is a one-of-a-kind, irreplaceable, and priceless gift, no matter what may have happened or what you're afraid might happen. You can make it out of the darkness. Your mind and body are yours to control. When all else fails, slow down. Take long and deep breaths, remembering that you are not your thoughts and emotions. You are not your mistakes nor shortcomings. You are not the things, situations, or people that have hurt or are currently hurting you. These are all temporary comings and goings in life. Decisions made when we are feeling at our worst rarely serve to improve our lives.

Your life deserves to be experienced in the fullest and most wonderful way. There are so many people whose lives are and will be made so much better with you in it. Never forget that your truest essence is goodness. All things that have led you to think and feel otherwise are deceptions. The negative impacts on you are real, but the way they have diminished your peace and happiness, and how they have led you to lose your self-love and hope. This is the great Lie. Even on the cloudiest of days, the sun is still always right there behind it all. So it is with your highest self, no matter how much darkness has covered you. No matter how bad it feels, just hold on. Please don't go. The same intense energy pushing you towards death can be redirected and used to change everything for the better. Many people are ready and sincerely wanting to help and support you. Please stay.

Alexandre Dumas said, *"It's necessary to have wished for death in order to know how good it is to live."* Starting now, claim the power that is your highest self. Take the very pain which threatens to kill you and let it be converted into a love for life few others could ever know. The depths and darkness to which you have fallen have also presented a stairway to heights you will cherish as you take each step upwards. Let your wounds be the place where the light enters you, as the ancient poet Rumi expressed so vividly. Don't be deceived by pain and allow your suffering to oppress or destroy you. It is intensely trying to guide you towards something better. It is teaching you wisdom about love and goodness, impossible to learn any other way.

I am humbled to have been able to share our story with you. I sincerely hope this book has expanded your understanding of suicide and given you new insights and tools to support your well-being. May you continue to know your truest self and this life in a deeper way. An intentional death would mean that it all went wrong, and that you became lost. That is not your story. Yours is going to be amazing.

It's time now for you to take your own hand. The hand of that inner child who is in desperate need of your truest self. It's time to give yourself the kind of love and care that others never could. You can do it. The power to live a life you love is right inside of you. It's always been there.

You are *Love*, and your light can outshine any darkness.

Life Saving Contact Information

Emergency help: Dial 911.

Suicide & Crisis Lifeline: Dial 988.

Crisis Text Line: Text HOME to 741741.

The Veterans Crisis Line. For veterans, service members, and their loved ones: Dial 988 and then press 1 or text any message to 838255.

The Trevor Project crisis and suicide intervention support for LGBTQ young people ages 13-24: Call 1-866-488-7386 or chat with a counselor on their website at thetrevorproject.org.